ANGELA LANSBURY

A LIFE ON STAGE AND SCREEN

Rob Edelman and
Audrey E. Kupferberg

A BIRCH LANE PRESS BOOK
Published by Carol Publishing Group

A Birch Lane Press book
Published by Carol Publishing Group
Birch Lane Press is a registered trademark of
Carol Communications, Inc.
Editorial Offices: 600 Madison Avenue, New York, N.Y. 10022
Sales and Distribution Offices: 120 Enterprise Avenue, Secaucus,
N.J. 07094
In Canada: Canadian Manda Group, One Atlantic Avenue, Suite 105,
Toronto, Ontario M6K 3E7
Queries regarding rights and permissions should be addressed to Carol
Publishing Group, 600 Madison Avenue, New York, N.Y. 10022

Carol Publishing Books are available at special discounts for bulk
purchases, sales promotion, fund-raising, or educational purposes.
Special editions can be created to specifications. For details, contact:
Special Sales Department, Carol Publishing Group, 120 Enterprise Avenue,
Secaucus, NJ 07094.

Manufactured in the United States of America
10 9 8 7 6 5 4 3 2 1

Library of Congress Cataloging-in-Publication Data
Edelman, Rob.
Angela Lansbury : a life on stage and screen / Rob Edelman and
Audrey Kupferberg.
p.   cm.
"A Birch Lane Press book."
ISBN 1-55972-327-0 (hardcover)
1. Lansbury, Angela, 1925–   . 2. Actors—United States—
Biography.   I. Title.
PN2287.L2845E33   1996
792´.028´092—dc20
[B]   95-49371
                                                            CIP

ANGELA LANSBURY

For Rae and Anne

Contents

Acknowledgments

Many individuals and organizations deserve grateful thanks for their assistance during the preparation of this book. They are Sonia Long and the staff of the Amsterdam Free Library, Amsterdam, New York; Howard H. Prouty of the Margaret Herrick Library, Center for Motion Picture Study, Academy of Motion Picture Arts and Sciences; Patricia King Hanson of The American Film Institute Catalog of Feature Films; Monty Arnold; David Bartholomew; Spencer M. Berger; the Bohman-Fannings; Dr. Howard Gotlieb, Margaret Goostray, and Karen Mix of Special Collections, Mugar Memorial Library, Boston University; Marialana DeRossi of C&C Computer Solutions; Len Cariou; Ginny, Dick, and Kate Donnelly-Phillips; Steve Feltes; Mark Goodman; Linda Goodrich; Hurd Hatfield; Dan Jury; Leonard Maltin; Madeline Matz of the Motion Picture, Broadcasting and Recorded Sound Division, the Library of Congress; Alvin Marill; Ronald S. Magliozzi of the Film Study Center, the Museum of Modern Art; V. A. Musetto; Ron Simon and Gary Rutkowski of the Museum of Television and Radio; the New York Public Library at Lincoln Center; Sonya and Sam Seigal; Phil Serling; Maryann Chach of the Shubert Archive; Renata Somogyi; Christopher Creed of USA Network; Jeanine Basinger and Leith Johnson of the Wesleyan University Cinema Archives; Maggie Williams; Michael Kerbel and Sharon Della Camera of the Yale Film Study Center; Dr. Alex and Inge Zimmerman.

Special thanks go to John McCarty for his invaluable input; Karen O'Hara for service beyond the call of duty; Rick Scheckman for his kindness and video collection; and Allan J. Wilson for being a great editor.

Introduction

On the tenth anniversary of the premiere of *Murder, She Wrote*, Angela Lansbury's long-running television series, the actress appeared as a guest on *The Larry King Show*. During a viewer phone-in segment, King asked a twenty-four-year-old caller why she was so enamored of Angela. "Her charm, her motherliness," the woman quickly responded. "She's very respected. She's a love, and she reminds me very much of one of my family members."

In these few sentences, the caller put forth not only the reasons for the enduring popularity of Angela, who then was a year removed from her seventieth birthday, but also captured the essence of the actress off-camera. The fact is, Angela Lansbury is the real thing. Not only has she been a hardworking and thoroughly professional actress, but she remains a class act.

Fame often does odd and unfortunate things to people. Too many who have found it have responded by becoming insufferable fools.

Not Angela. Despite her success, she remains a person of integrity, who understands the meaning of friendship and loyalty. In the privacy of her home and family, she is as unaffected as your next-door neighbor with whom you might chat while gardening or shoveling snow.

In a career spanning over fifty years, Angela has had her triumphs and disappointments. Her motion-picture career, which began so promisingly with an MGM contract at age seventeen and two Best Supporting Actress Oscar nominations (for *Gaslight* and *The Picture of Dorian Gray*), has never reached fulfillment. However, beginning with *Mame* in 1966, she became one of Broadway's premier musical-comedy stars. With the success of *Murder, She Wrote*, she earned a fame and, eventually, a power afforded few women in television.

Before her public, Angela has been the consummate professional. While immersed in an energetic routine at a 1973 tribute to Stephen Sondheim, her oversize dangle earrings fell to the floor. As she retrieved them, she covered the gaffe by exclaiming to her audience, "Diamonds—what are they compared to a good performance?"

In an industry where marriages and relationships are as perishable as a carton of milk left out of the refrigerator overnight, Angela—after a brief and controversial first marriage—has been a partner in a loving union that began in 1949. She is a mother and grandmother, and she enjoys a close alliance, both personal and professional, with her family.

This has not always been the case. Back in the 1960s, when her children Anthony and Deirdre became enmeshed in the era's drug culture, Angela was slow to recognize the crisis within her home.

Despite that painful episode, Angela's life has not been a grab bag for the gossip columnists. "If you want scandal about my personal life, dear," she explained, after winning her fourth Tony Award on Broadway, playing Mrs. Lovett in *Sweeney Todd*, "you're going to have to do enough digging to get to China."

Angela may have earned adulation across the years for her performances in *The Manchurian Candidate* and *Mame* and *Murder, She Wrote*. But she has earned equal respect for her spirit. As her twenty-something fan concluded on *The Larry King Show*, "She just has that love and spark in her eyes, and she can do anything."

Photo Credits

Angela Lansbury

1

An Irish Beauty and a Mutton-Chopped Pacifist

Angela Brigid Lansbury was born in London on October 16, 1925. Her father was well-to-do lumber merchant Edgar Isaac Lansbury, chairman of the Board of Guardians of Poplar, an immigrant and industrial district in the city's East End. Her mother was Irish-born actress Moyna MacGill.

Baby Angela's life was blessed with abundant gifts, including two loving parents and social status in a nation where one's place in society depended upon the class into which one was born. Plus, Angela—who was called Bidsie (or Bidsy), a nickname that lasted into her adulthood—had a very special grandfather. He was the Honorable George Lansbury, a leader of the British Labour Party and a renowned pacifist, women's suffragist, and humanist.

Added to her blessings was a half sister, Isolde, four years older than herself, the offspring of her mother's first marriage to Reginald Denham, the actor, writer, and stage and film director. Young Angela and her sister (who was to become the first of actor-writer Peter Ustinov's three wives) would amuse their elders by creating and then performing skits and dances. The girls displayed a talent for the theatrical that could be traced back to their great-uncle, Scotland-born and Belfast, Ireland–bred Shakespearean actor Robert B. Mantell.

In 1878, twenty-four-year-old Mantell was playing the supporting role of Tybalt to Mme. Helena Modjeska's Juliet in an Albany, New York, production of *Romeo and Juliet*. The legendary Polish tragedienne informed him, "With your clear-cut features, well-shaped body, and wonderful voice, it is a pity you have to die so early in the play." Mantell was not fated to play secondary roles for long. He was to become especially well known for touring across the United States and bringing the Bard to cities from Hartford to Detroit to Norfolk. Within one week's time, he would play the leads in *The Merchant of Venice, Richelieu, As You Like It, Julius Caesar, Macbeth* and *Hamlet*. Between 1915 and 1917, he also appeared in a half dozen feature films.

"I'm eternally grateful for the Irish side of me," Angela, whose visage actually bears a resemblance to Mantell's, once recalled. "That's where I got my sense of comedy and whimsy. As for the English half—that's my reserved side. . . . But put me onstage, and the Irish comes out. The combination makes a good mix for acting."

The Lansbury family was completed upon the birth of twin boys, Bruce and Edgar, when Angela was four years old. Both would enjoy successful show business careers. Bruce became a writer, television executive and producer (of the hit series *The Wild Wild West* and *Mission: Impossible*, among others), and occasional Broadway producer. Edgar became a Broadway scenic designer and producer; his credits range from *The Subject Was Roses, Godspell,* and *American Buffalo* to revivals of *Long Day's Journey Into Night, Waiting for Godot,* and *Gypsy* (the latter starring his sister).

Upon the twins' birth, the Lansburys moved from a private flat to a more spacious house, located in the Mill Hill neighborhood of London, at No. 7 Weymouth Avenue. "The world of the thirties, when I was a child, was such a magical place," Angela remembered. "I miss the old sweetshops where you could get Knickerbocker Glories. You could have a great adventure with a spare sixpence in those days." Edgar Sr. also purchased a charming, three-hundred-year-old farm outside Oxford, which became the family's weekend retreat. On Fridays, when the school week ended, Angela, Isolde, and their friends would be transported to the farm. They would spend the next two days hiking, fishing, and riding horses and bicycles through the countryside.

Furthermore, what fun for a child to think of having Moyna MacGill as one's "mum"! Moyna was an attractive Irishwoman with piercing eyes and a gentle smile. "Her beauty absolutely dazzled me as a child," Angela observed.

Moyna was born on December 10, 1895, in Belfast, the daughter of William McIldowie, a high-profile lawyer who also was director of that city's opera house, and his wife, Cissie (Mageean). Two of Moyna's brothers, James and Dennis McIldowie, also acted on the stage, with the latter touring the United States under the name Dennis Mantell in a production of John Drinkwater's *Bird in Hand*. So it was no surprise then that she too wanted to be an actress. According to first husband Reginald, she was "an inspired interpreter of Celtic folklore; she gave recitals of poetry all over Ulster and was unrivaled in that field. . . . There was a special magic in her cadences. . . . She belonged in the castle of the Countess Kathleen and was pure Yeats."

She changed her name from Charlotte Lillian—nicknamed Chattie—McIldowie to Moyna MacGill upon being cast in a stage production of James M. Barrie's *Dear Brutus* in 1914. Although by no means one of England's great stage stars, she became a working actress in top London productions, who managed to be steadily employed in secondary parts and leading roles opposite Basil Rathbone, Gerald Du Maurier, John Gielgud, and Herbert Marshall.

Moyna made her London debut on January 26, 1918, at the Globe Theatre, playing Hortense in *Love in a Cottage*. She understudied various roles (Joanna in *Dear Brutus*, Daphne Grey in *The Law Divine*, Marjorie Caner in *The Cinderella Man*), delighting in the occasional opportunity to appear onstage. She was cast as Comfort Tuke in *Homespun*, which opened at the Gaiety Theatre in Manchester at the tail end of 1919.

Moyna's list of 1920s West End credits is lengthy, and occasionally prestigious. She earned her first salutary notices for *John Ferguson*, by St. John Ervine, which opened in February 1920 at the Lyric Theatre in Hammersmith. She played Hannah Ferguson, daughter of a farmer struggling to pay off a mortgage; in the oldest tradition of melodrama, the villain of the piece offers to settle the debt only if the Ferguson lass will wed him. The *London Times* critic called it "a most affecting little play," describing Moyna's performance as "excellent."

She next played Phoebe in *As You Like It* at the same theater. The *Times* critic grouped her with others in the cast whose work he labeled "a real delight." However, he paid Moyna a left-handed compliment when noting that, in depicting the "shrewishness" of the character, she "all but concealed her Irish accent."

In 1921—quite a busy year for her—Moyna was cast by actor-producer-director Basil Dean in *The Wonderful Visit*, adapted by H. G. Wells and St. John Ervine and based on a story by Wells. In his book *The Footlights Flickered*, W. MacQueen-Pope described her as "a lovely girl and sensitive actress then just emerging from the understudy stage and given a chance by Dean." Moyna next replaced Madge Titheradge as Desdemona to Basil Rathbone's Iago in *Othello*. She closed out the year by playing Anne Hathaway in the conjectural biographical drama *Will Shakespeare*, which depicted Shakespeare killing Christopher Marlowe in an outburst of envious fury. The critic of the *London Daily Chronicle* called her performance "altogether beautiful." And the following year, Moyna appeared in yet another production of *Dear Brutus*, this time in the role of Mrs. Purdie.

Moyna was charming onstage and regularly received positive notices, but her appeal did not cover the fact that she was no Mrs. Patrick Campbell. In 1924, she was cast in *A Magdalen's Husband* as Joan Potten, a woman whose jealous husband is murdered by the man she really loves. Critic James Agate called the play "in every way the best piece yet produced by the Playbox" and went on to praise Moyna's fellow cast members. But of her performance, he wrote, "The part simply did not lie within the scope of this actress, who brought to it an appealing voice and some dairy-maidish costumes *à la* Patience, and nothing else. . . . A teacup or a pillbox would have sufficed for the heroine's emotions. Joan should have been played by Miss Edith Evans—how Mr. Dean can be so blind in that direction amazes me—by Miss Laura Cowie, or, possibly best of all, by Miss Mary Clare, who is in the company."

A year after Angela was born, Moyna played Elizabeth Jane in John Drinkwater's adaptation of Thomas Hardy's 1886 novel *The Mayor of Casterbridge*. At one special performance, at the Weymouth Pavilion Theatre, the venerable Hardy himself was in attendance (along with his wife and Drinkwater).

In 1927, Moyna appeared with John Gielgud in Eugene O'Neill's self-described "mystical mystery play," *The Great God Brown*. Gielgud remembered it as an unsatisfactory experience, noting, "We held masks in which we covered our faces in certain scenes and speeches, which seemed to me rather a pretentious and unsatisfactory convention." In spite of the disappointment with the play, Gielgud and Moyna were to establish a friendship which spanned the next five decades.

That same year she appeared in a Roland Pertwee–Harold Dearden murder drama titled *Interference*. Also in the cast were Gerald Du Maurier (who also directed), Herbert Marshall, and Frank Lawton. *New York Times* critic Charles Morgan, writing from London, said that the play was presented "with so much freshness and vigor." He noted, "Moyna MacGill, as the wife, happens to be being blackmailed and to be carrying prussic acid in her handbag, but you have not the least difficulty in believing that, in happier circumstances, she would very pleasantly pour out tea for you or, when alone, very comfortably curl up by the fire." Added the *London Times* reviewer, "Miss Moyna MacGill has the hardest task, for there is an inherent improbability in these wives who rush to the extremes of prussic acid and leave indiscriminating handbags to mark their innocent tracks; but she performs it with admirable tact."

The show was to enjoy a yearlong run.

And very early on in her career, Moyna even appeared on-screen. The story goes that she was sitting in a subway (or "tube") train. Film director George Pearson happened to be seated opposite her. He introduced himself with a "you oughta be in pictures" line. Pearson, however, was no two-bit hustler on the cinema side-lines who was looking to pick up pretty young women. He was one of England's most famous silent-movie directors, and he signed Moyna to a deal with the Welsh-Pearson Film Company. In 1920, Moyna had the female leads in the Pearson-directed *Garryowen* and *Nothing Else Matters*. Appearing in the latter in a small role was Reginald Denham.

Denham and Moyna had met during World War I, while he was in the military stationed in Ulster. Denham remembered, "It was only natural that Moyna and I should get together; we were two highly artistic people with a similar love of poetry, music, and the arts generally." The pair married in 1919, after Moyna had come to London to break into the theater. Particularly after her success in *John Ferguson*, her career progressed at a faster pace; Denham recalled being introduced at parties as "Moyna MacGill's husband." By the time he began to find success, their marriage was doomed to failure.

In the year preceding their January 1924 divorce, conflicting work schedules kept them apart. "Practically the only time when we did meet was on the eleven-thirty train, at night to Hemel Hempstead," Denham recalled. "I'd be off to rehearsals in the morning long before Moyna had woken up. It was therefore pretty inevitable that we should drift apart, because companion-ship, the basis of all lasting marriages, had gone out of ours."

Denham went on to describe the circumstances surrounding his split from Moyna. "Somewhere around March 1923, Moyna asked me for a divorce: she had fallen in love with someone else. When the actual moment of the break came, it was a bitter shock: we had been through so many ups and downs together. But, nevertheless, I felt that it was only right for us to call it a day if she so wished it. One can't cling to something that doesn't exist just for the sake of clinging. Sometime in October, Moyna left and took Isolde with her."

In a caption under three photographs and the headline "Moyna MacGill in Divorce Suit," a Manchester, England, newspaper, dated December 28, 1923, reported, "The Divorce Court list for next term, opening on January 11, includes the suit brought by Mr. Reginald Denham (inset), the actor and play-producer, against his wife, Moyna MacGill (right), the actress. Mr. Edgar Lansbury (left) is named in the case." By the end of 1924, Denham also had remarried. His new bride was Lilian Oldland, an actress. Denham's third wife was Mary Orr, with whom he was to share writing credit as a prolific playwright. In fact, Ward Morehouse was to dub Denham "Man of 100 Plays."

As the years passed, whatever anger Denham felt over Moyna's infidelity had long been tempered. In the late 1950s, he reminisced that Moyna was "the best Desdemona I have ever seen." They would occasionally see each other socially, and he maintained an amicable relationship not only with Moyna but with her children by Edgar Lansbury. "Are we all friends?" Denham asked rhetorically during a 1975 interview. "Oh yes, oh yes."

Until the time the twins were born, Moyna maintained her busy stage career without neglecting her domestic duties. In the West End, she was Moyna MacGill, glamorous actress; a few miles away in the East End, she was Mrs. Edgar Lansbury, mistress of a prosperous household, mother of two young daughters, and hostess to her husband's colleagues in London business and politics and to their mutual friends in the arts.

With the dual responsibilities brought on by her busy career and a hectic family lifestyle, one might believe Moyna was a shoulder-to-the-grindstone kind of woman. She was not. The graceful lady who spoke with a lilting Irish intonation had a soft and whimsical nature. Future son-in-law Ustinov described her as "a delightfully vague and splendidly proportioned lady."

Imagine the nightly scene as Angela and Isolde entered their mum's room to play with her for a while before she left for the theater, or to be dazzled by mother's sleek new dinner dress or evening gown. The girls would help their mother get dressed. Angela recalled that Moyna would then "go out in a flurry of powder and perfume and get herself up to go to the theater. She'd say, 'I'm going to cut a bit of a dash.'"

And so the girls fell asleep with images of sequins and silk, humming the latest tunes their mother had taught them. But Angela was a self-described sensitive child, who would sometimes cry when Moyna left for the evening. By the following morning, though, the fun would continue as Moyna reported exciting tales of notables who had been in the audience. Perhaps she even surprised her daughters with floral bouquets presented at the stage door by ardent admirers.

For this was London between the world wars, and the lights of the city's West End theater district glistened. At posh nightclubs, wealthy Londoners danced to the rhythmic strains of their own composer Noël Coward and his American cohorts Cole Porter, Jerome Kern, Irving Berlin, and George Gershwin. Along with Coward, entertainers Gertrude Lawrence and Fred Astaire and his sister Adele were introducing new dance steps to an elite social circle who frequented the theaters and later danced and dined at the Savoy and Ritz or at such popular night spots as the Kit Kat Club, Ciro's, and Café de Paris.

So it certainly is no understatement when Angela observed, years later, "I can't say we had an ordinary childhood, because my mother was terribly artistic and knew all the artists and writers and musicians of her day. She had a salon, and I remember ladies coming to pose nude for artist friends of my mother. I was quite used to seeing glorious redheaded ladies with enormous bosoms lying on our couches being painted. And singers would come and sing and it was all quite marvelous." Moyna was also a member of the League of Health and Beauty, a women's club that assembled weekly in Regent's Park to exercise. Little Angela and other girls her age would be garbed in tunics and, along with their elders, would perform Isadora Duncan–style dances; it was here where Angela first became conscious of her body and learned to move rhythmically and walk with correct posture.

After the birth of her twins, on January 2, 1930, Moyna almost entirely gave up the stage to devote herself full-time to her children. When she did appear, she could still command leading roles and earn good reviews. In *The Bond*, a drama in which she starred eight months after her sons' birth—and her last stage role in London until 1948—she played Jacqueline Heron, loving wife of an alcoholic. The *London Times* critic noted, "Jacqueline is at once gentle and steadfast, and Miss Macgill [*sic*], blessed with an opportunity (now becoming rare) to represent a woman who faces her difficulties without self-pity, charmingly employs it."

This stage role was prophetic in the sense that Moyna herself would soon be facing the responsibilities of life without the support of her husband. Just a few months before Angela's tenth birthday, Edgar Lansbury died.

He would be remembered first as a humanist. Despite his position as a lumber merchant, Angela's father had exhibited a concern for those less fortunate than he in his position as chairman of the Poplar Board of Guardians. In a 1924 letter to the *London Times*, he took the British government (and specifically the Ministry of Health) to task for its complaints regarding the council's dispensation of relief to needy individuals. "May I conclude by a protest against the misuse of the word 'waste' in connection with Poplar," he wrote. "It is true that we pay about 100,000 [pounds] a year more in relief than would be paid under the [Sir Alfred] Mond scale. But surely it is an error in terminology to call this 'waste.' If you consult our scales you will find little room for waste on the part of any recipient of relief."

And Edgar Lansbury would be fondly recalled for his devotion to Moyna. "My father wasn't in the [entertainment] business at all," Angela remembered. "But he loved the theater—and adored my mother."

Now, as a widow with four children to raise, Moyna no longer pursued an interest in parties and other social activities, ending young Angela's encounters with bohemian glitter and elegant nightlife. In fact, Moyna's financial resources dwindled precariously, to the point where she was all but broke.

"Mother had a terrible time adjusting to our new circumstances," Angela noted. "But she was incredible. She got herself 'engaged' to a nice gentleman, and we all went to live with him [in Hampstead, then a London suburb]. He paid our school fees and for our music lessons. So I had piano lessons and dancing lessons and tap lessons and drama lessons, and I learned to sing 'My Heart Belongs to Daddy.' "

Peter Ustinov, upon beginning to court Isolde, described Moyna's beau as a "Scottish military gentleman." "The atmosphere in this house was somewhat strained," he remembered, perhaps with a touch of whimsy, "since the Scottish officer kept his tin hat from the Great War and a loaded revolver from the same conflict suspended from a hook on the bedroom door, threatening to use the gun on himself if ever his mistress should leave him. The expression in his bloodshot eyes when aroused tended to confirm his sincerity."

However, Angela's brother Edgar remembered him as a "nice man."

Her father's death was the first of several major shocks to hit Angela during her youth. For a child who had been born with so many gifts, so many blessings, she would have to learn to cope with deprivation at a time when another child's worst fear might be the loss of a favorite toy.

Among the many adjustments for Angela was a new school. The sister of Stephen Potter, who had been Edgar Lansbury Sr.'s best friend, was the headmistress of the South Hampstead High School for Girls. This connection resulted in Angela's enrollment there.

As with many children who lose a parent, Angela turned inward. She could have fooled some people; Ustinov, for one, described her while he was dating Isolde as "a gawky and very amusing child of twelve or thirteen." However, from the relatively carefree girl who loved to play the piano and perform skits for family members, Angela had become an often unhappy child who would escape the reality of her situation by retreating into a fantasy world and playing at being other people.

Young Angela had been "abandoned" by her father, and so, in her insecurity, she sometimes became upset when her mother left her side and became what she would later describe as "a skirt hider-behinder."

Angela often had to take charge of her twin brothers, who were four years her junior. On special occasions, there would still be time for childhood antics; during Christmas, 1935, Angela played Little Red Riding Hood in a family skit, with little Edgar appearing as the Big Bad Wolf. Also at Christmas, Edgar remembered, "my mother and sister did an impromptu sketch for family and friends. Angela was terrific with dialects. She and mother would dress up in weird clothes. It was all slapstick nonsense. Christmas will always be synonymous with laughter for me."

Unfortunately, every day could not be Christmas for Angela. "I was an old lady at ten," she recalled. "When my father died, I became the partner with my mother in bringing up my brothers. I had to grow up fast."

This unusual sibling relationship was to last throughout the Lansbury twins' childhood. Edgar described his association with Big Sister as being not without difficulty. "But she was terribly sweet," he noted. "When I was a most irritating nuisance, she'd sit me down and teach me how to knit. But the lesson was always preceded by a shut-up-and-go-away warning. You see, I was always hiding behind the couch and throwing paper balls at Angela and her boyfriends."

During this low period of her youth, Angela became fascinated with the movies. She would purchase all of the American movie magazines and go to see films whenever she could. Forty years later, she reminisced about the joy of visiting a movie theater: "To me, the greatest luxury is to go to the movies in the afternoon. I feel it's the wickedest thing, and I adore doing it. I come out and it's still light. It takes me back to when I was nine and could go to the pictures by myself. I'd pay eight-pence to see Ginger Rogers and Fred Astaire, sit through it all until I came out with a splitting headache, then go home and throw up from eating too many chocolates."

Angela, it seemed, had become a self-described "complete movie maniac." She created for herself a make-believe world, in which she became the characters that so entranced her on-screen. She recalled, "I had a whole secret life and used to sit on buses, staring out of the window and looking as though I had TB, always playing someone other than myself." Angela would let her imagination run free, fantasizing about going to America where she would "walk down those golden sidewalks, step into a club, and meet Boston Blackie on the corner." One day she would pretend to be a coughing Camille, à la Garbo, and the next day she would be a gangster's moll.

On another occasion she noted, "I never dreamed that I would ever end up in Hollywood myself. A childhood friend and I carried on a fantasy life about Hollywood and the movies, and we drank orange-juice cocktails. When I actually did go to Hollywood, it was a wonder of wonders. I did not relate one to the other, the real to the unreal—only years later I realized I was living what I had dreamed years earlier."

Angela believed her most important learning experiences came outside the schoolroom. She educated herself by reading a great deal and listening to the world around her. She recalled, "I learned from books, from old movies, from the theater, from knowing people . . ."

Theater too had become a satisfactory escape for this preadolescent girl. When she was ten, Angela saw her mother's friend John Gielgud play *Hamlet* at the Old Vic; two years later, she sat through three performances of George Bernard Shaw's *Pygmalion*, also at the Old Vic. But stardom and acclaim on the Broadway and London stages remained decades into her future. It would be five long and eventful years of further loss and upheaval before Angela would appear in her first Hollywood film. Then, instead of providing an escape from reality into imagination, the movies were to become an escape from financial embarrassment to economic security for her and her family.

Despite this early preoccupation with movies, Angela's initial instincts were not toward a career in show business. As a youngster, she was interested in politics as a profession. To this end, she was inspired not only by the political involvement of her father but also by the charisma of her grandfather, the Honorable George Lansbury. As a little girl, Angela would accompany Lansbury on his walks through London. Years later, she met a Londoner who remembered seeing the small girl and her grandfather walking along Bow Road. She was hanging on to his coattails with a large black cat—the elder Lansbury's mascot—in her free arm.

"I was taken to hear him, and then, at home, I'd get up and

give extemporanous speeches imitating him," Angela remembered. "He awed me. He was a pacifist and a great friend of Gandhi's, six feet tall with muttonchop whiskers. When he said, 'Friends,' the whole hall just roared with appreciation."

Angela has retained a store of memories about her grandfather: "I remember him as a huge man. Of course he wasn't that huge, but he seemed a huge, enveloping, ruddy-faced man, with an incredible beard. I always remember the feeling of that beard when he kissed me when I was a little girl, and I remember his hands. The smell of him I remember, because he was a teetotaler and a nonsmoker and he always smelt of soap, and linen—his suits. I remember going to the House of Commons, having lunch there and sitting on the terrace and having tea. . . . I remember going to his house and his wife preparing lovely teas and cakes with violets on them."

George Lansbury, the son of a railway worker, was born in 1859. In 1868, his family moved to London's East End, with which he was politically and emotionally associated for his entire life. In 1875, at age sixteen, he met his future wife, Elizabeth Jane Brine, daughter of sawmill and veneer-works owner Isaac Brine, at the St. Mary's School in the Whitechapel district. She was two years his junior. They were married on May 29, 1880, and their union lasted until Elizabeth Jane's death in 1933. "I am sure our marriage was the most blessed and fortunate thing that ever happened to me," he noted.

At the time of his marriage, Lansbury and his brother toiled at unloading coal trucks onto barges. After a brief stint managing a coffee bar in 1883, he, Elizabeth Jane, their three children, and his brother emigrated to faraway Queensland, Australia, where he worked for a year as a manual laborer. Upon his return to England, he worked in his father-in-law's sawmill (which he eventually took over).

Lansbury's influences were many, varied, and at times seemingly incongruous. He was at once a convert to ethical rationalist Christianity and a devotee of the socialist Social Democratic Federation. He was an employer who did not forget his experiences as a laborer; his sympathies remained with workers and, even more so, with the unemployed. He even relished his time as a working man. "Our house in Bow was a four-roomed cottage," he recalled. "Our family ran up to six [George and Elizabeth Jane eventually had four sons and eight daughters], so we were a bit crowded. My wages were thirty shillings a week. How my wife managed to feed and clothe us all I don't know, except that she worked early and late at her job. Somehow our hearts kept young and the world seemed cheerful. Those early years of propaganda and hard manual labor were among the very happiest of our married life." He went on to succeed in the lumber business before entering the labor movement and British politics; by that time he had left the Social Democratic Foundation and had become affiliated with the British Labour Party.

From 1892 on, Lansbury was entrusted with the position of guardian of the poor for Poplar, London's East End wharf and warehouse district, which was heavily populated by immigrants, including Chinese, lascars, Indians, and Malays. With the passage of the Aliens Immigration Bill in 1905, he oversaw the first controls over the immigrant population. He helped reform the grim workhouses and established work-relief programs. He served on Poplar's Borough Council for thirty-two years, was the section's initial Labour Party mayor, and in 1922 took over Poplar's seat in the House of Commons (a position he had briefly held in 1910).

Lansbury described himself in *Who's Who* as a "Member of the Church of England; teetotaler; non-smoker; twice in prison." He was first jailed in 1913, for counseling women suffragists to "burn and destroy" to get the vote; he was imprisoned under a fourteenth-century statute of Edward III as "a wanderer, a beggar, and a piller from across the seas" and was freed after participating in a hunger strike. His second prison term came six years later after imploring London's East Enders to resist paying excessive property taxes.

Between 1929 and 1931, while in Prime Minister Ramsay MacDonald's cabinet in a minor position as first commissioner of public works, Lansbury upended London custom by having an artificial beach constructed in royally owned Hyde Park where female as well as male bathers were permitted; the beach came to be known as "Lansbury's Lido." He also caused a minor scandal by wearing a hat outdoors in the company of Queen Mary.

Newsweek (then known as *News-Week*) magazine characterized the seventy-six-year-old Lansbury in 1935 as "a mutton-chop-whiskered old gentleman with many friends and few enemies," adding that "he is not likely to be jailed for his ideas. But he has lost none of his old fire in expressing them." The London *New Statesman and Nation* described him as "immensely shrewd in practical affairs, and a most astute political fighter," as well as "the only name that is known in every town and village in Great Britain." But Lansbury's unwillingness to compromise his ideals stood above all else. In 1935, in an act of conscience, he resigned his leadership of the Labour Party (a position he had held since 1931), exiting His Majesty's Opposition in the House of Commons. Previously, the party had been squarely against England's involvement in a war of any kind. But its policies had shifted drastically, and Lansbury could not continue leading a party whose majority had become staunch supporters of the national government's backing of the League of Nations to halt the Italian conquest of Ethiopia.

Lansbury was the author of *My Quest for Peace*, published in 1938, several months after he made personal goodwill visits to Adolf Hitler, Benito Mussolini, and the heads of other European governments. As war clouds were inexorably building over Europe, the politician discussed the state of Europe and succinctly and movingly displayed his philosophies and hopes for the immediate future. His foreword began:

This book is being published during a most serious crisis in the history of the world. . . . Although the world is arming at an ever-increasing rate and civilisation is apparently rushing to destruction, I refuse to despair. Even yet I have faith that the principles I have endeavoured to express in this book and before statesmen will find support and avert the catastrophe of universal war. Pacifism is not on trial. The Spanish, Chinese and Abyssinian wars are not the outcome of the policy which pacifists advocate. The crime and outrage committed against the people of Austria are not the result of an effort to apply collective justice to the affairs of mankind. Therefore I send this book out with an appeal to all workers for peace. . . . Power politics is only apparently triumphant. . . . Hard and difficult though our path may be, we pacifists must preserve our faith that love alone will save the world—a love which in no way condones, excuses or palliates evil, but on the contrary recognizes and condemns evil of every kind by whomever it is committed.

In a chapter called "The Jews," Lansbury wrote:

There cannot be peace in the world until there is in all nations the willingness to acknowledge equal rights for all people irrespective of race, colour or creed. No nation possesses such superior knowledge and wisdom as to give it the right to claim special privileges at the expense of the moral and material rights of others. Here in East London where I live, the relatively big Jewish population lives side by side with the rest of us, sharing social, political, and industrial life. Occasionally we disagree, not because we are Jews or Gentiles but simply because we are equal citizens and find ourselves differing in our view on social and political questions.

It is no wonder that Grandfather Lansbury was such a figure of admiration and emulation for young Angela. George Lansbury died on May 7, 1940, in London, at age eighty-one, two years after the publication of *My Quest for Peace* and just over eight months after Hitler ordered German troops into Poland, and Great Britain and France declared war on Germany. Upon his passing, Oswald Garrison Villard wrote in *The Nation:*

A saint on earth died the other day, a man really too good for this kind of world. Of course I refer to George Lansbury, perhaps next to Gandhi the most outstanding pacifist in public life anywhere. I suppose that death was not unwelcome to him. At least he may not have wanted to carry on now in enfeebled health in a world which is so deliberately bent on self-destruction and will not read the simple and plain lesson of its war folly. . . . He was so simple, straightforward, and lovable, so completely uninterested in what happened to George Lansbury, so unwilling to conceal his lack of boyhood education, his humble origin, and his years of working as an ordinary laborer that one naturally thought of him as the "purest Christian in all England."

In his will, Lansbury directed that his body be cremated and his ashes tossed into the wind and sea. He wrote, "I desire this because although I love England very dearly and consider this lovely island the best spot in the world, I'm a convinced internationalist. I like to feel I'm just a tiny part of universal life which will one day break down all divisions of creed or speech and economic barriers and make mankind one great eternal unit both in life and death."

In 1973, upon Angela's triumphant return to London as the star of a revival of *Gypsy,* she recalled, "He was a giant in my youth because he was in our house all the time, and even now my name is not known for Angela Lansbury, but because I'm George Lansbury's granddaughter. A woman came to see me last night in the theater, and she had three medals with her he had given her as a little girl. Little tiny bronze medals she had won for net ball. She was so proud and she had them all wrapped up in little pieces of tissue paper. Luckily, by some curious stroke of fate, I had a photograph of him in my pocket a cousin sent me, and it was a very tender moment when I showed it to her."

My Quest for Peace—along with an address Lansbury delivered on December 17, 1937, to the Kulturbund in Vienna—was reprinted in 1972 under the title *My Pilgrimage for Peace and Peace Through Economic Cooperation.* In retrospect, wrote David Martin of the Department of Sociology, the London School of Economics and Political Science, in the book's introduction, Lansbury had gone to meet Hitler with a combination of "courage and naïveté

. . . only Augustinian rather than Tolstoyan or Marxist categories could have comprehended the magnitude of the moral disaster represented by the Hitler regime. Lansbury's method of personal appeal was doomed to failure." But at the same time, Martin noted, "Lansbury was a man of principle. . . . [He] was special in that he combined an economic analysis allied to the left-wing position with a religiously motivated pacifism and a commitment to the democratic process."

2

A Fledgling Actress

etween 1934 and 1939, Angela continued her studies at the
South Hampstead High School for Girls. However, her
young life was destined for further disruption. Adolf Hitler
and the Nazis were invading country after country on the conti-
nent, and the war officially came to Europe in September 1939.

Because of the constant bombing of London by Nazi warplanes, British schoolchildren were being evacuated to the countryside. As a single parent, Moyna—who for a time served as a
volunteer ambulance driver—was hesitant to have her children far
from her reach, she had to place their safety first.

Finally, she decided to send Angela to the relative safety of a
country boarding school, but the fourteen-year-old did not wish
to leave her mother. "Look, are you interested in studying acting?" Moyna asked Angela. "By all means, anything," she responded, "but don't make me go to boarding school." Angela set
about convincing her mother that her interest in acting was gen-
uine. She knew the theater training schools in London were—and
are—among the best in the world and knew that attending one
would enable her to remain in the city with her mother.

Moyna wanted to ensure that her daughter developed a solid
foundation in the profession. She allowed Angela to continue living at home while pursuing her academic studies with a tutor and
attending classes in singing, dancing, and diction at "a proper dramatic school." "It's very hard to describe how one goes about act-

ing," Angela explained. "But the English approach is that you learn the tools of the trade. The vocal equipment, for instance. You can have all sorts of dramatic passion, but if you can't use your instrument to convey it to an audience, you're only halfway there, aren't you? Laurence Olivier once said that the one thing an actor must have is tremendous physical strength, great stamina. I'm fortunate that I have that."

So that Angela could develop these skills, her mother enrolled her on scholarship in the Webber-Douglas School of Singing and Dramatic Art in Kensington, a wealthy borough in London's West End. It's unclear whether the scholarship was given due to the family's financial need or the unique talent of young Angela, or whether it was a prestigious honor bestowed upon the youngest generation of an old Irish theater family.

The year was 1940. Angela had not yet turned fifteen. She was a tall girl with the start of a woman's body, but with a child's round and pouty face.

Her initial stage role at Webber-Douglas was a brief appearance as a lady-in-waiting in a production of Maxwell Anderson's *Mary of Scotland*, a prize-winning play whose New York production had starred one of her mother's former leading men, Philip Merivale. How exciting it must have been for the young acting student to be thrust into the world of theater, to be playing a role onstage, however small, rather than sitting on buses and fantasizing herself as characters in Hollywood movies.

As a drama student, Angela began to see that acting might be her life's calling. A stage career was no longer a childish enthusiasm. She was no longer concerned only with sequined costumes and floral tributes, but with interpretation and performance.

As actresses, mother and daughter displayed different attitudes toward the profession. Years later, Angela described Moyna as "a far more ambitious actress than I am. She wanted me to become an actress, but she could never by any stretch of the imagination be called a stage mother. . . . My mother has always had a wonderful spiritual quality—sensitivity, an understanding of people. When she is working, she has a sense of well-being and accomplishment. Acting is a thing that she feels she needs to do, and she can't understand my attitude. She works on scenes from Shake-speare all by herself, for herself, whereas I am strictly practical and won't lift a finger unless I get paid for it." On another occasion, Angela explained, "I've never worked at being an actress. I'm the lettuce type. Between parts I just sit."

Those differences did little to affect Angela and Moyna's strong feelings for each other. But when Angela was starting to become serious about acting, they certainly provided the basis for a good many motherly lectures about homework assignments.

Ironically, then, it was the more cavalier Angela who was to reach the summit of the American entertainment industry. From the mid-1940s through early 1950s, Moyna was to play only oc-casional, mainly minor roles in Hollywood features. She was cast as Lady Godolphin in *Frenchman's Creek*, a seventeenth-century romance with Joan Fontaine, Arturo de Cordova, and her acting colleague from the London stage Basil Rathbone; Mrs. Blake in *Black Beauty*, an adaptation of the Anna Sewell novel about a young girl's love for a horse; and Mrs. Metivier in *Green Dolphin Street*, a nineteenth-century costume epic.

One of Moyna's more prominent parts was as Hettie, a spin-ster sister of the title character in *Uncle Harry*, a melodrama star-ring George Sanders, Geraldine Fitzgerald, and Ella Raines. Her performance was noted by the *Variety* critic, who wrote that the actress "neatly portrays the older sister." However, her surname was misspelled "Maggill." In *Three Daring Daughters*, a Jeanette MacDonald–Jane Powell–Jose Iturbi musical vehicle, *Variety* com-mented that "Moyna MacGill is okay as a flighty old gal who pitches for Iturbi herself." Moyna was also cast in two of her daughter's films: *The Picture of Dorian Gray*, in which she played a duchess; and as Mrs. Harkley in *Kind Lady*. Film historian Gary Carey observed of her minor role as an air cadet's mother in *Winged Victory*, "Also good is Moyna MacGill as a scatterbrained mother. She brings the one note of true humor to a film which is overrun with frat-hazing humor and camaraderie."

Moyna also returned to the stage, appearing first in London in 1948 in *Wonders Never Cease*, a comedy that lasted a mere fif-teen performances. Her next project was more successful: the

London and Broadway productions of Sandy Wilson's musical comedy *The Boy Friend*. The show is a nostalgic, affectionate pastiche of musical comedies of the jazz age, an era that Moyna as a young woman had been so much a part. Here, thirty years later, she played the supporting role of Lady Brockhurst, who turns out to be the mother of the messenger-boy hero.

The show played to standing-room-only crowds in London and opened to raves in New York in October 1954. If a nineteen-year-old star-to-be named Julie Andrews garnered the majority of the critical attention—*The Boy Friend* was to be her breakthrough vehicle—Moyna did not go unnoticed. Critic Robert Coleman, for one, cited her as "a really fine actress."

Moyna's credits extend into the 1960s, when she had small but regal roles in a pair of blockbuster movie musicals released in 1964: *The Unsinkable Molly Brown* (as Lady Primdale) and *My Fair Lady* (as Lady Boxington).

One other interesting theater credit came the previous year: a role as Nurse Guiness in *Heartbreak House*, George Bernard Shaw's spoof of upper-class society. The show was presented in Los Angeles by the Theater Group, a joint venture between professional actors and the UCLA Extension. Among those in the cast: a little-known forty-one-year-old actor, then beginning to play supporting roles in movies, by the name of Carroll O'Connor.

Back in 1940, however, ambitions and acting careers were fated to be placed aside, for bigger events had taken hold of the Lansbury family. That year, Angela suffered the loss of her beloved grandfather. By August, the Nazi bombardments on London had heated up and Moyna more than ever feared for the safety of her children. Taking a bold action, she obtained a job helping to supervise six hundred British youngsters who were being evacuated to the United States on board the ship *Duchess of Athol*. This was to be the final boatload of children to depart the British Isles before German submarines made Atlantic crossings impossible. Moyna was indeed fortunate to have obtained this position, which included passage for fourteen-year-old Angela and the ten-year-old twins.

Assistance in the evacuation was arranged by a Mr. Ascoli, an international businessman in the rubber trade whom Moyna had met at the wedding reception of Isolde and Peter Ustinov. Ascoli arranged for the four Lansburys to travel under the sponsorship of the family of Charles T. Wilson, a Wall Street businessman. As expected of a newlywed, Isolde chose to remain in England with Ustinov.

In mid-August, the *Duchess of Athol* arrived in Montreal. From there, Moyna MacGill and her three young children boarded a train to New York City.

Manhattan was a wonderful surprise for Angela and her young brothers. Evenings in the metropolis were quite different from the endless nights of the London blitz with its blackouts and noises of bombs and air-raid sirens. For many months, the children had had no respite from the war. Even aboard the *Duchess of Athol* there were nightly air-raid drills. Here in Manhattan they basked under the warm lights of the theaters along Broadway and in the West Forties. They heard the sounds of jazz artists and saloon singers when they walked along West Fifty-second Street, where wailing trumpets replaced the screaming sirens to which they had become accustomed. Craning their necks, they could see the brightly illuminated offices of the Chrysler Building and the Empire State Building instead of the dreaded glow of the air war over London.

From an optimist's view, the Lansburys were lucky to be together as a family in a peaceful country where benevolent sponsors resided. But then there was their homeless, relatively penniless state. As refugees, they had been forced to leave behind all their assets, however meager. In the United States, most privileges that arose from being the family of the late Edgar Lansbury and the late Honorable George Lansbury went unrecognized.

Furthermore, few people outside the British Isles had ever heard of Irish actress Moyna MacGill. As so many war refugees, the Lansbury clan temporarily pocketed its familial pride to accept the charity offered them, while dreaming of the day when they would once again provide for themselves.

Moyna and the children avoided what remained of the hot New York City summer by living rent-free as guests in Wilson's summer home on fashionable Lake Mahopac in New York's Putnam County. In the fall, they settled into a town house on East Ninety-fourth Street, with a kindly family of sponsors headed by George W. Perkins. Wilson, who remained Moyna's sponsor, provided her with $150 per month for expenses. To earn additional money, she and Angela began giving recitations at the Brearley School, Miss Hewett's, and other private schools. Angela remembered, "We'd do scenes from Shakespeare—mother would do the nurse and I'd be Juliet—things like that, and we'd get twenty-five dollars, which was a lot of money in those days."

Angela enrolled in the Feagin School of Drama and Radio, located in Rockefeller Center, on a scholarship Moyna arranged via the American Theatre Wing. The school's motto was a practical one: Learn to Act by Acting. Among its alumni were Susan Hayward, Jimmy Savo, Jeff Corey, Priscilla Lane, Dick (then known as Dickie) Van Patten, and Alex (then Alexander) Nicol. For her audition, Angela performed the balcony scene from *Romeo and Juliet*. Meanwhile, Moyna was able to place the twins at the exclusive Choate School, which had a policy of assisting the children of more prominent war evacuees. "Mother was *very* resourceful," Angela recalled.

Each day, Angela would walk from Ninety-fourth Street down to Fiftieth Street and Rockefeller Center. She was quickly becoming a young woman; these daily jaunts enabled her to lose some of her youthful chubbiness. At Feagin, Angela studied movement and fencing. And it was here where she really developed into a character player. She was beginning to learn to animate her face, to make her doe eyes sparkle wide in amazement or crinkle into narrow, defiant slits. She could rouge her round "baby" cheeks to show exaggerated innocence, accentuate her full lips to express the sensual, or purse them to play haughty spinsters. She could use her entire body to communicate a feeling or a state of being. As her comedic skills were refined, she was given small roles in classic comedies; a typical part was as sixty-year-old Lady Wishfort in William Congreve's Restoration-era comedy *The Way of the World*. Eventually, she was awarded the title role in *Lady Windermere's Fan*, Oscar Wilde's comedy of manners.

"I had a sort of comedienne thing about me. I was never the ingenue type," she recalled, "luckily, since there were too many girls who looked like ingenues. But I would have been a character actress in any case. It was my bent from the beginning."

Angela also was invited to the afternoon salon of Fritzi Scheff, famed star of early-twentieth-century musical revues. Scheff demonstrated the importance of emphasizing lyrics by singing the Victor Herbert waltz "Kiss Me Again," from *Mademoiselle Modiste*, her 1905 hit. This experience gave Angela a sense of how to interpret a song.

Angela graduated from the Feagin School in March 1942. By that time, the family had gained a certain measure of independence in their adopted country. They had moved from the Perkins residence to a one-room flat on Morton Street in Greenwich Village. But the accommodations were barely big enough to house them all, even with the boys boarded at school most of the time. On weekends, Moyna and Angela were still allowed access to the Lake Mahopac home.

Their apartment was outfitted with cast-off end tables, lamps, and other odd pieces from the Algonquin Hotel. Moyna had become friends with hotel manager John Martin, who provided her these furnishings.

As any young and aspiring actress, Angela was filled with dreams of a future amid the bright lights of Broadway. By the time she did attain Broadway stardom in 1966, the Great White Way had changed from what it was when Angela first came to New York. And by the 1970s, the blight of pornography was as much a fixture of the landscape as any legitimate theater marquee. Plus, many of the old-time theaters were falling to the wrecker's ball.

But Broadway was still very much in its heyday during World War II. In 1942 alone, dozens of legendary actors—actors whom Angela hoped to emulate—graced its stages. Katharine Cornell, along with Judith Anderson, Ruth Gordon, Dennis King, Edmund Gwenn, and a young star-to-be named Kirk Douglas, appeared in *The Three Sisters*. Cornell also revived *Candida*, with Burgess Meredith, Raymond Massey, and Mildred Natwick (who decades later would appear with Angela on *Murder, She Wrote*). Lynn Fontanne, along with Alfred Lunt and Estelle Winwood, was in *The Pirate*. The year's Pulitzer Prize was awarded to Thornton Wilder, for *The Skin of Our Teeth*, which starred Tallulah Bankhead, Fredric March, Florence Eldridge, Florence Reed, and a future star named Montgomery Clift. *Uncle Harry*, in the screen version of which Moyna would soon be cast, featured Joseph Schildkraut and Eva Le Gallienne.

Alec Guinness, Dorothy Gish, Lillian Gish, Jessica Tandy, Gladys George, Alfred Drake, Walter Hampden, Luise Rainer, Katina Paxinou, Sam Jaffe, Flora Robson, Gregory Peck, Jack Haley, Victor Moore, Gracie Fields, Ed Wynn, Mary Boland, Eddie Dowling, and Louis Calhern all appeared on the New York stage in 1942, as did actors with whom Angela would be sharing stages or movie screens over the decades: Katharine Hepburn, William Prince, Sam Wanamaker, Ray Bolger. Gypsy Rose Lee, who was destined to play a role in Angela's career as a character in (and author of the source material of) *Gypsy*, made a hit with comic Bobby Clark in *Star and Garter*.

Of course, Angela knew nothing of this as she walked down West Forty-fourth Street from the American Theater Wing's Stage Door Canteen, where she joined other young women as volunteers who danced and socialized with GIs. Here, though still a schoolgirl, she was in the company of professional entertainers, including actors and actresses who frequented the popular theater cafes and supper clubs. They spoke of Sardi's, the fabled theater-district restaurant and opening-night hangout. Angela remembered, years later, that her "head would buzz with excitement at the very thought of what could happen, what one could do. And standing outside Sardi's, it was even more exciting than getting in."

Later in 1942, Moyna found a job touring Royal Canadian Air Force bases in *Celebrity Parade*, a variety show featuring Anna Neagle, one of Britain's top stage and screen stars, and a group of other actors. It felt good to be again recognized for her stage talents, particularly by a star of Neagle's caliber, and it was fulfilling to rejoin the war effort with British compatriots.

Angela was eager to break into show business as a fledgling entertainer—and to collect a salary check or two to help her mother pay their expenses. One of her mates at the Feagin School, Arthur Bourbon—who was to become a professional dancer, and later a priest!—suggested she get up an act and audition at various New York nightclubs. With Bourbon, she developed a routine in which she sang songs and did a takeoff of Beatrice Lillie singing Noël Coward's naughty, sophisticated "teddibly" British number "I've Been to a Marvelous Party." She also impersonated Bea Lillie parodying opera singers and French chanteuses.

The teenaged Angela must have been a sight as she performed Coward's lyrics, going on about the season at Cap Ferrat and decadent party life on the Riviera. Using her collection of comedic expressions and gestures, and elongating her chin to resemble the horse-faced Bea Lillie, the sixteen-year-old auditioned for all who would listen. She lied about her age, claiming to be nineteen. Finally, she was signed for a six-week engagement in Montreal at a nightclub called the Samovar, where, as she later explained, "I sang and did takeoffs of Bea Lillie and Wagnerian contraltos." Her salary was sixty dollars a week.

For the first time in her life, Angela was out on her own. "When I first arrived, I stayed alone at a place called the Ford Hotel, where strange men knocked on my door at night," she remembered. "Arthur Bourbon had told me to stay there, because it was the cheapest place. I was very innocent, very green indeed. When older men made advances, I didn't know what they were doing. I moved into a rooming house. The nightclub was always filled with RCAF [Royal Canadian Air Force] men. It was a bit of home to them, to see an English girl making a fool of herself."

Angela's career benefited from her work at the Samovar. Any professional appearance certainly helped her test her ability to spark feelings in an audience. And from her roommate, a Yugoslavian singer named Blanka Peric, she learned how to do up her hair and apply makeup.

Upon completing her stint at the Samovar, Angela returned to New York. It was August 1942; she took charge of the twins, who had returned from a summer vacation with friends on Long Island, and packed them off to Choate. As she folded their mono-grammed blazers and checked their school ties for ice-cream stains, what were Angela's feelings toward the disparate lifestyles she and her brothers were leading?

Had she become so accustomed to playing surrogate mother that she accepted this role? Did it bother her that she was strug-gling to earn a living while the boys studied mathematics, history, and languages with the finest teachers and played sports with the sons of America's captains of industry? Even in the dark old days before sisters saw equal opportunity with their brothers, Angela may have had moments of bitterness.

Meanwhile, upon finishing her Canadian tour, Moyna contin-ued traveling westward to Los Angeles. She had reportedly been advised that apartments were cheaper in L.A. where you could live adequately in a $28-per-month rental, while the cramped Green-wich Village flat was costing them $42.

What's more, in Los Angeles there was Hollywood ... Ac-cording to a Universal Studios press release about Moyna in con-junction with the release of *Uncle Harry*, she headed west because she had "heard from her agent that she was being considered for a role in the Hollywood film *Commandos Strike at Dawn*. She came to Hollywood on her own, but didn't get the role."

Though she had not appeared in a film in more than twenty years, Moyna did assume that all sorts of opportunities awaited both mother and daughter in the movies. She wired Angela, telling her to "close up the apartment and come out to Los An-geles."

3

Angela Goes
to Hollywood

Hollywood, 1942. The major motion picture studios—Metro-Goldwyn-Mayer and Paramount, Warner Bros. and Twentieth Century–Fox—were the predominant industry powers. Clark Gable was the King; Orson Welles had just made *Citizen Kane*; James Cagney would win the Best Actor Oscar for *Yankee Doodle Dandy*; the year's Best Song would be Irving Berlin's "White Christmas," introduced by Bing Crosby in *Holiday Inn*.

The top ten box-office attractions were Abbott & Costello, Gable, Gary Cooper, Mickey Rooney, Bob Hope, Cagney, Gene Autry, Betty Grable, Greer Garson, and Spencer Tracy. Bright new faces on the Tinseltown horizon included Susan Hayward, Van Johnson, Alan Ladd, and Kathryn Grayson. Before the year was out, John Barrymore, Buck Jones, Carole Lombard, and Edna May Oliver would pass on to the Great Movie Set in the Sky.

According to the *Film Daily Yearbook*, 533 feature films were released in the United States; 488 were American-made, and 45 were imported.

The average price of a movie ticket was 27.3 cents. An average of 85 million people visited movie theaters each week.

Most telling of all, the United States had entered World War II, and Americans were preparing for a lengthy, laborious fight. Movie stars were trekking across the nation, making personal appearances to sell war bonds, and even entering the military and facing combat. To keep the nation focused on the objectives of the fighting, the studios were producing films that told stories of the war's great battles and life on the home front.

Additionally, due to the troubles in their homelands, hundreds of European actors, writers, and directors had taken up residence in Hollywood. Most of the top British names, however, had arrived before their country was imperiled. They included Charlie Chaplin, Ronald Colman, Victor McLaglen, C. Aubrey Smith, Cary Grant, Ray Milland, Stan Laurel, Boris Karloff, Herbert Marshall, Basil Rathbone, Cedric Hardwicke, Charles Laughton, and Elsa Lanchester.

Some, like Colman, remained indifferent to hobnobbing in any Hollywood social circle. Others became active in a "British colony," whose members, according to Hardwicke, "kept the flag flying and poured tea each afternoon at four." Smith, a distinguished character actor, was the colony's senior member; Hardwicke noted that his "craggy manner suggested that he had just completed a ceremonial tour of all four corners of Queen Victoria's empire." Upon the outbreak of the war, members of the British colony staged theatrical presentations and supervised teas, with the proceeds going to such wartime charities as Bundles for Britain.

Into these surroundings, seventeen-year-old Angela Lansbury, two years removed from playing a lady-in-waiting at the Webber-Douglas School of Singing and Dramatic Art, came to find her destiny as an actress. Upon arriving at her mother's doorstep, she had twenty dollars left in her pocket—and a tremendous sense of excitement that something extraordinary was about to happen to her.

Angela joined Moyna, who had been living (courtesy of her old friend Flora Robson, with whom she had acted on the London stage) in one of two small Alpine cottages perched on a hill in Laurel Canyon. Each bungalow had two rooms and a tiny kitchen.

"We went around to all the studios looking for jobs," Angela recalled, "but we didn't get anything." Her explanation for her inability to immediately crack into the movies: "I was always too something or other. Either I was too tall or too young." By that time, Angela had just about reached her full-grown height of five feet seven inches.

At Christmastime, Angela and Moyna obtained jobs in Bullock's Wilshire, the department store. "Mother was in the toy department," Angela recalled, "and I was a wrapper."

The pair, who knew what it was like to have afternoon cream teas, were now taking ten-minute coffee breaks. They merged their salary checks and, as Angela recalled years later, "bought a small Ford for one hundred and twenty-five dollars. It was a light creamy beige two-seater with a jump seat—and it was a dream! To be able to drive along Sunset Boulevard and not have to take the Red trolley car, which went on a track from Los Angeles to the beach, really represented freedom. Our Ford took us to the desert, to the mountains. It was our link to being able to discover and enjoy places which otherwise we would have never seen."

As a newcomer to any sort of regular work, it was easier for Angela to adjust to the rigors of retail. However, for Moyna, the comedown was devastating. She donned her plain black dress with a white collar each morning with more hesitation than the last and, within a short time, lost focus of her duties.

"Mother soon got fired," Angela explained, "because she spent too much time playing with the toys."

Coincidentally, this situation was loosely replayed some years later by Angela in her role as Mame Dennis in the Broadway musical *Mame:* A genteel woman is forced to take a nine-to-five job to pay the bills and is humiliated at being dismissed because of incompetence. Mame, rendered penniless by the 1929 stock market crash, tries one job after another with catastrophic results until she meets and marries the wealthy Beauregard Jackson Picket Burnside. In the nonmusical version starring Rosalind Russell, she meets Burnside while toiling ineptly in the toy department of Macy's; however, in the musical version, Mame meets "Beau" during a brief stint as a bumbling manicurist.

But there was no Beau to rescue Angela from the wrapping-paper desk. She remained at Bullock's to support herself and her unemployed mother and was eventually promoted to salesperson in the cosmetics department. Even though she has noted that she "was no good at mathematics, I could never figure the retail and wholesale prices," the powers-that-be at the department store determined she had the potential to become a buyer.

Angela, as thousands of other Hollywood hopefuls, might have gone on to work as a movie extra or perhaps obtained bit roles and felt fortunate to be earning a living in the industry. Or she might never have appeared on-screen at all. She might have married a rising young Bullock's employee, then awaited his return from the war and, eventually, raised a family. She might have lived her life in anonymity, with her artistic aspirations taking her no higher than stardom in amateur community theater.

"I was very much in awe of Hollywood and the movie stars," Angela recalled years later. "Seeing Mickey Rooney driving [down] Sunset Boulevard in a Buick convertible would make me gasp and say something like, 'There goes Andy Hardy!' " Little did Angela dare to imagine that she would soon be appearing with "Andy Hardy" in *National Velvet*.

How might Angela become one of the chosen few given a shot at celluloid stardom? Today, if your surname is Fonda, Bridges, or Carradine, you are guaranteed that opportunity. Countless second (and, lately, even third) generation movie stars have declared that, while they may have had a famous parent to open a door for them, their careers would not have flourished had they lacked talent. What they fail to recognize is that 99 percent of the game is getting inside the door. Thousands of actors who possess just the right looks and ability to make it on-screen never do, simply because they lack the appropriate contacts (or are unwilling to compromise themselves to win the favor of a producer or casting director).

While it did not hurt that Angela was the daughter of an actress, that fact alone did not give her entrée into the studios. The reality, of course, was that Moyna herself had been struggling to find work in the movies. Perhaps Angela might have been able to capitalize on being the granddaughter of a beloved, nationally known politician. Only trouble was, that politician was pacifist George Lansbury, a name virtually forgotten in wartime Hollywood.

Still, Moyna's professional history did allow her and Angela admission into circles not open to the average, anonymous Hollywood wanna-be. At this time, actors who were between projects would occasionally form small theater companies, enabling them to perform in front of live audiences. One such group appeared in a quartet of one-act plays at Los Angeles' Belasco Theater for a two-week run. Each play featured a psychological/horror theme. Included in the cast were Moyna, Flora Robson, Henry Hull, June Havoc, George Coulouris, Lester Matthews, and Barbara Everest. Angela was drafted into the company, but not as an actress onstage. She impersonated a nurse who would appear in the theater aisles offering smelling salts to any audience member made ill by the goings-on onstage.

Moyna's family (as well as professional) history allowed the two entrée into other inner circles. Almost every weekend, various top British and Irish stage and film people in Hollywood were invited for tea, soda bread, and cucumber sandwiches at the home of a prominent woman with the lyrical name of Mrs. May Flo Roden-Ryan, sister of Irish writer Oliver St. John Gogarty. Writer DeWitt Bodeen, then a screenwriter under contract at RKO, chanced to meet Moyna and Angela on one such occasion.

"I was very impressed with Miss MacGill," he recalled, "but I was absolutely enchanted with teenaged Angela Lansbury. She was entirely unaffected, and peaches-and-cream pretty, with wonderfully large, expressive eyes, and her every move was made with becoming grace. I noted that she listened well, smiled a lot, and although she was one of the tallest girls present, she was attractively shy." Angela told Bodeen that she was working in the Bullock's cosmetics department, and hoping to break into the movies.

At this point fate intervened. "It was just one of those lucky breaks in life," Angela remembered almost forty years later, "where I happened to come along to a studio like MGM at a time when they were looking for a young English girl. I was aided also by my mother Moyna's reputation."

In June 1943, Michael Dyne, an actor-writer acquaintance of Angela's, was up for the lead in the screen version of Oscar Wilde's *The Picture of Dorian Gray*, to be produced by Metro-

Goldwyn-Mayer. Dyne informed Angela that the studio was searching for said young English girl, to be cast in a key supporting role: that of Sibyl Vane, an ill-fated music-hall performer who is seduced and abandoned by the title character.

On a day off from work, Angela went to see the *Dorian Gray* casting director. While she eventually was to play the part of Sibyl Vane, *The Picture of Dorian Gray* was not to be her screen debut. As she walked on the lot, a man approached and ushered her into the office of George Cukor, one of Hollywood's top directors, whose credits included *Dinner at Eight*, *Camille*, and *The Philadelphia Story*. The filmmaker was in preproduction on a Victorian chiller, *Gaslight*, the story of a greedy man's attempt to drive his wife mad. Cukor was searching for the right actress to play the supporting role of Nancy, a sulky, sluttish cockney housemaid, a character Angela years later would describe as "a fancy, naughty little piece of stuff."

Back in 1943, *Gaslight* was a hot property. Based on a London stage melodrama, it had been brought to several summer theaters in the United States without attaining much success. Then, a major production was mounted on Broadway, where it ran for three years under the title *Angel Street;* its original cast included Vincent Price, Judith Evelyn, and Leo G. Carroll. (*Angel Street* premiered on the Great White Way two days before Pearl Harbor.) It had been filmed in England in 1939 by Thorold Dickinson under its original title, with Anton Walbrook and Diana Wynyard, and Cathleen Cordell in the role of Nancy. Allegedly, as part of MGM's plan for a remake, the studio attempted to destroy the negative of the British version, so that it would not compete commercially with the Cukor film. The plot was foiled, and today both movies survive.

"We'd looked for a girl for some time [to play Nancy]," noted George Cukor. "John Van Druten had done the script with Walter Reisch, and they were a very happy couple. In those days there were, somehow, happy collaborations. . . . Anyway, Van Druten said, 'Moyna MacGill is out here, she's a refugee with three children, and one of them is a girl about fourteen years old.' Then we discovered that Moyna MacGill's daughter was in fact sixteen or seventeen."

Cukor added, "This is a Cinderella story. We sent for her and she appeared, rather nervous. She'd never acted before, but I made a test of her and thought she was awfully good."

Both Moyna and Flora Robson coached her for the test. "I do believe that Flora recognized the fact that, as a youngster, I did have the potential, so she helped me with that reading and with the test," Angela recalled. "Not as a coach or a teacher but as a very warm friend. And as someone who knew, so I was certainly listening. Of course, I also had Moyna, my mother. But Moyna was Irish. This was a cockney girl and so I thought it was more up Flora's alley."

Of the test, Angela remembered, "First, I was given a costume from Character Wardrobe, and then they took a lot of trouble with my hair and makeup. They padded me out to make me look bigger. I did a scene with an actor named Hugh Marlowe, in which Nancy, the maid, sort of seduces the character later played by Charles Boyer. It was a scene from the play that wasn't in the movie. I can't say I was frightened. I was terribly interested in how it was all done."

Certainly, Cukor—who had propelled the screen career of Katharine Hepburn—knew talent when he saw it. But according to Angela, the various decision-makers at MGM were reluctant to cast her because of her tender age, while Cukor recalled they felt she lacked sufficient sex appeal. Added the director, "While they were still arguing, I telephoned [Angela] and said, 'Miss Lansbury, I don't know whether you're going to get the job, but you're a very talented actress.' And then everyone was suddenly happy and she was cast." Most assuredly, the deciding factor had to be that studio boss Louis B. Mayer was impressed with the tryout.

With Moyna's approval as Angela was still under legal age, she was signed to a standard seven-year studio contract with a beginning salary of $500 per week—$472 more than her weekly wage at Bullock's. For the two refugees who had been struggling to make their way in the United States, the contract was a godsend.

Angela also obtained her first Hollywood agent, Earl Kramer, pro-
ducer-director Stanley's uncle.

When Angela gave notice to Bullock's Wilshire that she was
leaving her $28-a-week job for a better one, her boss reportedly
responded, "Tell me how much they offered you. Maybe we can
give you the same—or even more."

"Well," she said, "they're going to pay me five hundred dollars a week."

And so it happened that Angela's budding career in the department store business was permanently sidetracked.

If not for the outbreak of war, the young actress might still
have been attending school in Kensington; instead, she was making her screen debut in a meaty role in a major Hollywood motion picture. "On the first day of shooting," recalled Cukor, "even
though she was only seventeen and had no experience, she was
immediately professional. Suddenly I was watching real movie acting. She *became* this rather disagreeable little housemaid—even her
face seemed to change, it became somehow lopsided, and mean
and impertinent. I was delighted with her from the start."

The facial expressions that Angela had rehearsed in mirrors
for months while at the Feagin School had born fruit just one year
and three thousand miles from the classroom.

Gaslight, mainly set in Victorian London, is the story of Paula
Alquist (Ingrid Bergman), an innocent and vulnerable young
woman who falls in love with a man she has known for just two
weeks, Gregory Anton (Charles Boyer). However, amid her
bliss—"I've found peace in loving you," Paula says to Gregory—
she also prophetically observes, "I don't know you. I don't know
anything about you." Paula is eventually driven to the point of in-
sanity by her ruthless, murderous husband. As the story pro-
gresses, Anton browbeats Paula, pounding into her brain that she
is ill, that she has been forgetting things, that she is going mad.
Eventually, Brian Cameron (Joseph Cotten), a detective, unmasks
Anton and comes to Paula's rescue.

Twenty-five minutes into *Gaslight*, Angela makes her initial
appearance as her character is hired by Anton. Clearly, Nancy is

no ordinary servant. A cheap, mean-spirited tart, she looks at once tawdry, bored, and self-absorbed as she is hired. Yet Anton notes to Paula, "She looks like a nice girl." However, a nosy next-door neighbor (Dame May Whitty) observes, "The way she carries on with that policeman on the beat. It's scandalous."

Nancy thoughtlessly and impertinently asks questions that are out of place for a servant. At one point, she queries Anton, "Seems to be getting worse, doesn't she, sir?" She and her employer begin flirting. When Gregory warns her about gentlemen who might want to take liberties with her, she responds knowingly, "I can take care of myself . . . when I want to." There is also tension between Nancy and Paula, as if the wife and servant are competing for the husband, who eagerly encourages this rivalry.

The character of Nancy might easily have been perceived and played as a caricature, but as interpreted by Angela, she is a complex person. Under Cukor's expert tutelage, Angela makes her three-dimensional and intriguing.

Intuitively, Nancy senses that Anton's roots are not in the upper class; he is as unscrupulous as she would be if she were in his situation. This is made apparent in Angela's quick, knowing looks and wry smiles as she converses with the various inhabitants of the Anton household and observes their activity. Angela more than holds her own in *Gaslight*, most notably in her scenes with Boyer.

As Cukor described the filming of the sequence in which Nancy is interviewed for her job by Anton, the prospective maid also had to meet the house cook. This encounter had not been written into the script; Van Druten, who was on the set, penned the dialogue on the spot. In the scenario, the cook is less than impressed with Nancy's character. Cukor reported that Angela cleverly improvised a bit of dialogue upon the cook's exit: Nancy tells Anton, "She's a real Tartar, isn't she? I won't share a room with her!"

In one sequence in *Gaslight*, Nancy smokes a cigarette. But its filming had to be put off because the studio's schoolteacher and social workers, in charge of looking after the welfare of underage contract players, refused to allow Angela to light up until she turned eighteen.

Indeed, it was during the shooting of *Gaslight* that Angela reached her eighteenth birthday. "They had a lovely cake, and the stars were wonderfully sweet to me," she remembered. "I thought, well, this is making movies. . . . I happened to see *Gaslight* not long ago on television. I was amazed. I thought, 'My God, how did I have all that assurance?' I have much less assurance now. In those days, I suppose, I went ahead on trust."

Years later, critic Pauline Kael noted that Angela may have been "only in her teens [when she played Nancy], but you couldn't guess it." Angela would describe the role as "a wonderful way to start [my career]. It really was. It embodied everything I would know, coming from England. Cockney accent, easy. Victorian England, I understood that. It all existed around London when I was a child. . . . It was a good thing to start off with, I was very fortunate."

On the *Gaslight* set, seventeen-year-old Angela had displayed a professionalism well beyond her experience. "I was so astonished with this young girl who just came in to make her first film and was so calm," Ingrid Bergman once told Hurd Hatfield. He had first met Angela when the pair tested together for *The Picture of Dorian Gray*. Perhaps it was this aura of maturity that, for better or worse, led to Angela's being cast as characters well beyond her years.

"She's always had her feet on the ground," added Hatfield. "Even though she was pretty much unknown [when we met], she was a settled person. She's very imaginative, but she's really ideal as an actress because she never is thrown by anything. She's so self-possessed. She doesn't have runaway nerves, the way some actors do. And she's never lost her way, despite the discouraging times. We all have our ups and downs, but she's kept at it. She went on with her career."

Maggie Williams met Angela in 1944 after she and her husband, actor Scott McKay, had come to Hollywood. Williams's first impression of Angela was that "she was a lady, she had the great charm of a real lady. She knew how to make you feel at ease. She was considerate, and caring about other people. I think that came from the fact that, as an adolescent, she had to take care of her brothers."

On one occasion, Williams expressed to Angela awe over her ability to step into her role in *Gaslight*, despite her limited professional experience. Angela's response: "Well, you know, I went to drama school and people said, 'Go and do that.' And I thought, 'I can do this.' I've always been like that. I'd say, 'I'm a trained actress. I can do it.' "

In recalling how she was able to handle all of this "instant success," Angela reflected, decades later, "I guess something in me, a sort of inner 'age' or maturity, shall we say, seemed to hold me on an even keel. Maybe it was my Englishness that allowed me to accept the enormous responsibility of a prime role in a huge movie with those great stars, George Cukor, and the whole idea of suddenly being under contract to MGM, you know."

Just as likely, as Maggie Williams observed, the maturity came from the years of accepting more responsibility than a child should have been expected to shoulder.

For after her father's death, Angela had had to delve deep into her inner resources to combat a child's fear of being left alone. Add to this her trying experiences as a war refugee, and the aging process is completed. Angela may have been only seventeen when she began filming *Gaslight*, but she had the worldview of a woman.

Because of her age, the law required that a social worker be on the set with Angela. Her elders were allowed neither to smoke nor swear in her presence. But her age did not deter Cukor from using ripe language in front of Angela, at which point he would mischievously cover her ears.

Certainly, being placed under the wing of a director as talented as Cukor also was a boon to the young actress. She recalled, "There is no question that he was the most understanding, humorous, delightful man you could possibly imagine. He had the patience of a saint. He was in no hurry and his only interest was in getting the scene right." During a 1978 Lincoln Center tribute to Cukor, Angela declared that, when she was signed for *Gaslight*, "I didn't know my ass from a hole in the ground. He introduced me to style."

Interestingly, upon its release, *Gaslight* received mixed reviews. *New York Times* critic Bosley Crowther observed that the film omitted "much of the fearful immediacy of the play." But the performances—including Angela's—were praised. *Variety* noted that the property "has been given an exciting screen treatment," and that it "can't miss at the box office." The film proved to be a popular success and earned a respectable $3 million in its original release.

Influential gossip columnist Louella Parsons wrote, "In many a day I haven't seen a young actress who impressed me as much as Angela Lansbury in *Gaslight*. Although barely eighteen, she stood her ground with such experienced actors as Ingrid Bergman and Charles Boyer. She gave a performance worthy of a trouper twice her age." Parsons described Angela as "a tall English girl with skin like alabaster and dark eyes offset by a frame of blonde hair," and "a self-contained, self-assured, poised young lady."

In addition, Angela quickly learned how to play the Hollywood game of lavishing praise on one's "betters"—especially in the presence of a gossip columnist. Parsons quoted Angela as saying, "I was fortunate to have [Cukor] for a director and to play with Miss Bergman and Mr. Boyer, both of whom were extremely kind."

Gaslight earned six Academy Award nominations, including newcomer Angela's for Best Supporting Actress. She was at once awed by—and proud of—the honor. Her competition included Ethel Barrymore *(None But the Lonely Heart)*, Jennifer Jones *(Since You Went Away)*, Aline MacMahon *(Dragon Seed)*, and Agnes Moorehead *(Mrs. Parkington)*. Barrymore prevailed.

This was the first of Angela's three Best Supporting Actress nominations. She never won. "You get so excited," she later told gossip columnist Cindy Adams. "People say you're going to win, and you go through this shocking experience of highs and lows. Anyone with his head screwed on right shouldn't be exposed to that horror."

After *Gaslight*, MGM did not know what to do with the British teenager. She did not fit the various categories for standard Hollywood starlets of the early 1940s. She was neither the statuesque sex goddess nor the classically pretty girl-next-door. Oftentimes actors who were hits in their screen debuts were recast by their studio in roles that were carbon copies of the characters that had so entranced audiences. With Angela, MGM executives sought another route.

Her success in *Gaslight* led to her being assigned two roles that were markedly different from that of Nancy. She was cast as twelve-year-old Elizabeth Taylor's boy-crazy teenaged sister in her first Technicolor feature, *National Velvet*, based on the novel for children by Enid Bagnold. After that romp, she took on the more complex adult role of the sweetly naive music-hall singer in Oscar Wilde's *The Picture of Dorian Gray*.

Today, *National Velvet* is best remembered as an Elizabeth Taylor vehicle, and the film did in fact solidify her motion picture stardom. But Taylor (who was to go on to become Angela's lifelong friend) is actually billed third in the opening credits. Mickey Rooney, then a reigning MGM star, gets top—and solo—billing; his credit is followed by "with Donald Crisp, Elizabeth Taylor, [and, in smaller letters] Anne Revere, Angela Lansbury, Jackie Jenkins, Arthur Treacher." The film is set "in England, in the late nineteen twenties—a long time ago in a spinning world," and opens with singing children in a classroom in a small, seaside village. Among them are the Brown sisters: Velvet (Taylor), Malvolia (Juanita Quigley), and the eldest, Edwina (Lansbury).

Angela has her most prominent scenes early on, as her character is contrasted to Taylor's: Velvet cannot understand what Edwina sees in boys, while Edwina cannot understand what Velvet sees in horses. When the teacher notices Edwina is wearing nail polish, Edwina offers as an excuse, "I only put it on this morning." Velvet, the kid sister, tells the teacher that, later in the afternoon, Edwina will be meeting a boy.

Ever the big sister, Edwina, almost a head taller than Malvolia and Velvet, bosses her siblings. "Velvet," she declares, "you're too young to understand some things. Have you ever really felt keen about anything?" Velvet answers that she loves horses. "What does it feel like to be in love with a horse?" Edwina wants to know. "I lose my lunch" is Velvet's response. Edwina tells her, "You're a child," adding that when you are truly in love, your heart skips a beat.

This sequence establishes that Velvet is a dreamy young girl who lives and dies for horses. Meager as it is, it is Angela's key scene in the film; from hereon, she is mainly a bystander.

Mickey Rooney, who at age twenty-four still exhibited the boyish charm that made him the original Michael J. Fox of motion pictures, stars as an ex-jockey and drifter. Half a century later, Angela as mystery writer Jessica Fletcher and Rooney as an ex-jockey and horse trainer, appeared together before the cameras in a sweep of nostalgia for an episode about horse racing on *Murder, She Wrote*.

National Velvet, for all of its special MGM warmth and entertainment value, did nothing to further establish Angela. Although she played the part of Edwina with ability, the MGM powers never again called upon her to play that type of role.

In the 1940s, the Hollywood studio system merchandised its starlets through fan magazine photos and articles, and through product endorsements and live publicity appearances. So that they could identify with the stars of motion pictures, the public was deluged with stories and photos that created a "personality." Whether a star was shown breakfasting in a cozy nook with a favorite pet or dancing the rumba at a trendy Hollywood night spot, the studio provided a carefully designed set of images that sold the star to the public.

But MGM did little to build up Angela. If the audience was beginning to think of her as the tawdry little tart from *Gaslight*, then her appearance in *National Velvet* must have been disconcerting. The one way the studio could have reconciled the disparity of roles was to choose a personality for their new starlet and then plaster her picture, along with descriptions of her "private life," all over the fan magazines.

Perhaps Louis B. Mayer was losing interest in his new starlet, or perhaps she did not fit the usual categories. The result was MGM's failure to adequately merchandise Angela to the public. This negligence hindered her attempts to succeed as a motion picture star.

Nevertheless, the quality of Angela's performances could not be faulted, and in *The Picture of Dorian Gray*, she displayed the full range of her acting talent. "Miss Lansbury bounced into my office like a young heifer," recalled the film's director, Albert Lewin. "To my mind, she was the farthest from what I wanted for the role." Still, Lewin was intrigued by the young actress, and he altered the role to fit Angela.

Angela is fourth-billed in the film (after George Sanders, Hurd Hatfield, and Donna Reed). As was *Gaslight*, this film is a thriller about strange goings-on in Victorian London. Based on Oscar Wilde's 1891 novel, the plot focuses on the title character (Hatfield), a handsome but evil upper-class gentleman. Gray has "the most marvelous youth," which by man's nature cannot last, as aging is inevitable for mortals. Yet Gray's youthful beauty does last because artist Basil Hallward has painted his portrait, which ages and decays in the attic while Gray maintains his radiance. For he has made a pact with the devil: "If only the picture would change and I would remain the same as I am now. I'd give up my soul for that."

Enter Sibyl Vane (Angela), a young singer at the Two Turtles, a lower-class music hall to which Gray goes slumming. He watches as she performs "Goodbye, Little Yellow Bird" (a number that is reprised throughout the film), first onstage and then as she walks among the patrons, with paper snow tossed lightly over her head.

Gray is clearly enamored of Sibyl's combination of attractiveness and innocence. He stares at her, and she looks away shyly. "She's taken with you, sir," Gray is told. Night after night, he returns to watch her perform. As she postures and sings, she is an idealized icon of womanhood. She may lack education: when Gray plays a Chopin prelude on the piano, she asks him who wrote it; to her, music is not intellectual, but strictly emotional. Still, she is a virginal young lady who despite her lower station in life would make a fine, upstanding wife for Gray. Eventually, he kisses her— and she does not resist. To Sibyl, Gray is like a knight in shining armor who has come to whisk her away into a new and wonderful life. In fact, she begins to call him Sir Tristan.

The Picture of Dorian Gray is also a story of the inequities of the British class system. This theme becomes apparent when Gray, on the counsel of Lord Henry Wotton (George Sanders), "tests" Sibyl by suggesting she stay the night after she views his portrait late one evening. Sibyl is saddened because she senses that Gray's "intentions" have been less than honorable. She heads for the door, but returns when Gray begins playing his piano, a look of resignation on her face. She is of a lower class, so how could he ever view her as respectable? If she wants him, she will have to have him on these terms.

After that, Gray rejects Sibyl. He sends her a "Dear Sibyl" letter, informing her that she "cannot possibly have any part" in his life. But his experience with Sibyl has changed him in another way. Physically, he is the same, but his portrait is different. It now has a "touch of cruelty in the mouth." He soon experiences guilt over Sibyl and writes her a follow-up note imploring her forgiveness and expressing his desire to marry her after all. But before Gray sends the second letter, Wotton arrives to tell him the sad news. Sibyl is dead. She "swallowed something by mistake" and died instantaneously. "Haven't you read the morning papers?" Wotton asks. "There'll be an inquest, and you mustn't be involved in it. . . . If you married this girl, you would have been wretched."

Angela is on-screen only in the film's first section. Her performance is subtle. In her initial scenes, she effectively captures Sibyl's innocence and vulnerability. But what makes her performance memorable is the scene in which Gray tests her, which is one of the film's key sequences. Here, in an instant and with a maturity beyond her years, Angela shows how Sibyl's romantic expectations are irrevocably and tragically transformed into heartbreak and resignation.

James Agee, the esteemed critic, gave *The Picture of Dorian Gray* a less than enthusiastic notice in *The Nation:* "A good movie might have been made from Wilde's story. [Director] Albert Lewin's version is respectful, earnest, and, I am afraid, dead." But he quickly went on to praise Angela: "I very much like Angela Lansbury as Sibyl Vane. Some people are liable to laugh at her and to think of her as insipid, but I think she is touching and exact in her defenseless romanticism and in a special kind of short-lipped English beauty, appropriate to the period and to Sibyl's class, and evocative of milkmaids in eigthteenth-century pornographic prints."

The *Variety* reviewer noted that Angela "registers strongly and very sympathetically. Miss Lansbury sings 'Goodbye, Little Yellow Bird,' a haunting old English music hall number." Years before she debuted on Broadway and earned great acclaim as a musical performer, this song came to be associated with Angela. More than forty years later, Angela delighted her fans by performing it one more time on an episode of *Murder, She Wrote*.

Angela earned a Golden Globe Award for her performance in *The Picture of Dorian Gray*, as well as her second Best Supporting Actress Oscar nomination. Her competitors were Anne Revere, her costar in *National Velvet*; Eve Arden and Ann Blyth for *Mildred Pierce*; and Joan Lorring for *The Corn Is Green*. Revere was the winner.

Over the decades, *The Picture of Dorian Gray* has come to be regarded as a minor cult classic. "We showed it in Germany two years ago," noted Hurd Hatfield in 1995. "Hundreds had to be turned away. I was amazed."

"Oscar Wilde left so much unsaid," Angela commented years later. "He implied the murkiest, the most god-awful depths in this man's life, and yet I didn't know what they were. I've not even thought about it since particularly. But we were stuck for weeks on those East End sequences around the docks, and the place where I sang 'Little Yellow Bird,' and I remember sensing the most incredible evil. It was as if Albert Lewin, the director, and Gordon Wiles, his assistant and production designer, had created more than just sets. I felt they knew what it was all about, but I wasn't about to ask—and they weren't about to tell me. It really comes across in the film, I think."

4

Mrs. Roy Radabaugh

T*he Picture of Dorian Gray* was released in March 1945. Around that time, Angela began to be courted by a boyishly handsome but aging juvenile leading man who was fifteen years her senior.

"There was an actor named Richard Cromwell," remembered Maggie Williams. "He was crazy about Moyna MacGill and was determined to meet her. He had seen Moyna in *The Clock* in a scene with Keenan Wynn, in which she had to do all this eating of spaghetti or something. I think she gets her pearls all mixed up with the spaghetti. It was very funny. He was crazy about this [routine] and was determined to meet her.

"I don't know if he knew that she was Angela's mother. But we went to his house one day and there they both were, the mother and Angela. They were drinking tea in his kitchen.

"Angela is a big tea drinker, and I am too. She kept drinking this tea that looked like brackish water. She said to me, 'You can't possibly drink this very strong tea.' I said, 'Oh, no, I'm on your side.' So we all got to know one another."

Williams described Cromwell as "a charming person, just as he came across in the movies. He had that same sweetness, very much like Michael J. Fox. He looked like such a kid. He was one of those eternally young men."

Cromwell pursued Angela in a polite and friendly manner, building on their relationship with gentlemanly concern, taking care not to overpower the teenaged actress. They were married on September 27. Angela moved into her new husband's home above Sunset Strip, leaving behind Moyna, her twin brothers (who had by this time come to live in Los Angeles and entered Hollywood High School), and a pair of beloved pets, a dog named Fellah and a cat called Ingrid (named, as one might expect, for Ingrid Bergman).

Despite her splashy Hollywood debut, something was missing from Angela's life. You might call it personal intimacy, someone with whom to share her triumphs and frustrations. Angela was a young woman now, so her mother would no longer suffice in this role. At the same time, Angela felt overshadowed by all of the beautiful women on the MGM lot. "I was a young woman looking for glamour and attention, and I didn't really get it," she observed years later. "So what did I do? I got married at nineteen."

"I think she loved that life," said Maggie Williams, recollecting of the time she and Scott McKay spent with Angela and Cromwell. "She's said to me, 'I knew very few people back then. You and Scott, and Zachary and Elaine Scott, who also lived very near the Strip." Of Cromwell, Williams added, "He did a lot of ceramics, and that sort of thing. She loved that. We all did. He was very amusing, and very loyal. He kept going off to the Valley to visit the old-time movie stars.

"He was a poor boy. He remembered being a charity case when he was a child. One Christmas he and his brothers and sisters were given lots of toys, and the charity people had come to look at the children through a window. He was very unhappy about that. He said, 'Can you imagine! These young kids didn't know they were being peered at as examples of charity.' He never got over that. It was a very deep wound. His charming house and pool were very important to him. They were like a monument to his success, to his no longer being a charity case."

Williams's memories aside, the Lansbury-Cromwell union was to be at best a learning experience for Angela, and, at worst, an aberration. She and Cromwell lived under one roof for just nine months. They were divorced the following year.

"Richard knew absolutely everybody in Hollywood," Angela remembered in 1979. "He had a marvelous house, and he was one of the most charming individuals I'd ever met. He was handsome, blond, suntanned, funny, witty, and he adored me—he thought I was the prettiest thing on two feet. Well, it was the most ridiculous marriage ever."

She added, "Things just disintegrated and fell apart and I came out of it terribly hurt and monstrously unhappy. Actually, I never quite got over it, because those are the rocks that become you in the end."

Upon hearing of the Lansbury-Cromwell separation, Maggie Williams was astounded. "They seemed to have had a wonderful life. Never did I see any friction. But naturally, one didn't ask, 'Why did you break up?' One didn't do that."

Forty-seven years after the divorce, a notorious supermarket tabloid announced in a front-page headline, "Angela Lansbury's Gay Husband Revealed: Tragic secret of *Murder, She Wrote* star's 1st marriage." According to the story, Lansbury divorced Cromwell after discovering him "in the arms of another man." Prior to his marriage, Cromwell was said to have had a sexual relationship with Howard Hughes, as well as with many other men. When Angela married him, she was "young and naive." However, years later she claimed, "I didn't know until after we were separated that he was gay."

Considering the young actress's life to that date, it is easy to believe that Angela was too caught up in caring for her family and fashioning a career as an actress to have made time for romance. At age nineteen, she had experienced life in ways other teenaged girls had not, but she was a babe in the woods when it came to love affairs.

Born Roy Radabaugh in Los Angeles in 1910, Richard Cromwell was trained as an artist and decorator. In fact, his friends continued to call him Roy years after he found celluloid stardom.

He first attempted to establish a career as a painter, and as a creator of mask likenesses of celebrities. But he soon became interested in screen acting. After a brief stint as an extra, the sandy-haired, green-eyed actor won the lead in John Blystone's 1930 remake of *Tol'able David*, which had been successfully filmed nine years earlier by Henry King, starring Richard Barthelmess. Cromwell was then all of twenty years old. Throughout the decade, his youthful good looks allowed him to be cast in leads and supporting roles in such high-profile features as *Tom Brown of Culver*, *The Lives of a Bengal Lancer*, *Poppy*, *Jezebel*, and *Young Mr. Lincoln*.

In 1943, the thirty-three-year-old actor's screen career was declining. He already had made most of the films—and all of the major ones—in which he was to appear. After serving in the Coast Guard during World War II, he was to play in only one other feature: *Bungalow 13*, a forgettable 1948 private-eye melodrama in which he is miscast as a crook.

According to the tabloid article, rumors of the actor's sexual preference were preventing him from maintaining his career. Indeed, an examination of fan magazine articles written about Cromwell at the onset of his career reveal more than subtle hints about his masculinity and sexuality. A profile in the February 1931 *Photoplay*, which focuses on his *Tol'able David* stardom, begins:

> He always knew it was to happen. He isn't surprised. But he is thrilled! Blushes mount to his pink cheeks. Tears flood his eyes. He is bewildered with the wonder of it. He is a really, truly, honest-to-goodness movie star. . . . When the casting director looked them [actors testing for the role in the film] over and sent them away, Roy Radabaugh hid on a dark stage and cried. A kindly office girl found him there. He became Richard Cromwell, the "find" who was to play David. Richard continued to cry through the filming of the picture. He cried when he thought he'd done something clumsy. He cried when the studio people were kind to him. He cried during the big emotional scene of *Tol'able David*. And lo, and behold, he is a great "emotional actor."

Furthermore, according to writer Paul Jarvis, a radio speech was written for Cromwell to deliver while on a personal appearance tour for the film, and "Richard almost cried from fright when he delivered it." In an article in the March 1931 *Picture Play* that also highlights *Tol'able David*, he is quoted as observing, "Look at the pretty flowers," while breakfasting with writer James Roy Fuller. One cannot imagine Gable or Cagney or Robinson making such an observation, or crying his way through the making of a movie.

Another fan magazine article, written by Maude Lathem, headlined "The Most Unusual of Hollywood's Untold Romances," and subheaded "Dick Cromwell's Love for Clare DuBrey, Told for the First Time," promises a saga of male-female romance. While Cromwell does describe DuBrey as being "as exotic as Barbara Lamarr, as glamorous as Garbo," the piece reveals more of a friendship between Cromwell and DuBrey, described as a "film actress, possibly twice his age," who over several decades had mainly supporting and bit roles in such films as *What Every Woman Wants, Madame Spy, A Man and His Money, Only a Shop Girl, The Girl of Gold, Infatuation, The Exquisite Sinner,* and *The Devil Dancer*.

The Cromwell-DuBrey relationship is depicted in the story as a Svengali-Trilby alliance, but with a twist. There is a change of gender, with the mentor being the older woman and the younger man being the innocent she shapes and guides. Cromwell is quoted as observing:

> Clare insisted that I could be an actor if I really wanted to be. Because of her faith in me, I really allowed the idea to take root more firmly. It was Clare who brought Anna Q. Nilsson to my shop to order book plates. It was she who interested Marie Dressler and Joan Crawford in my paintings. . . . There's nothing I haven't talked over with [Clare] in the intervening six or seven years I have known her. She has always had time to hear my plans, my mistakes, my ambitions, my doubts or my disappointments. . . . Possibly the greatest thing in the world that Clare ever did for me was to make me respect myself . . . I mean respect myself impersonally and know I owe something to myself. You see, she knows so much more than I can ever hope to know.

Cromwell's offscreen interest in women is more accurately reflected in the headline and subhead of yet another piece targeted at movie fans, written by Madeline Glass. The headline is "Tol'ably Different." The subhead is "Richard Cromwell's indifference to the heavy-lidded sirens has got them on his trail." In a letter to the editor, published in the April 1934 *Silver Screen*, Virginia Downs of Fairmont, West Virginia, asks, "Pal Dick Cromwell: Just what kind of a fellow are you anyhow? The more interviews I read, the more puzzling the situation becomes. . . . Are you a shy guy with a too-tender heart and a bawling tendency? . . . Please, straighten me out, Mr. Cromwell. You've been a favorite for several years and I'd really like to know about your character! Once again . . . are you a shrinking violet or a caveman?" The actor's response is ambiguous: "A great deal depends on the time, the person and the place. I act as I feel except for social functions, which leave me completely 'jittery' and consequently am likely to act almost any way."

Finally, in the October 16, 1932, edition of the *Los Angeles Times*, there is a photo of Cromwell and one of his latest artistic creations. The caption reads, "Before embarking upon a screen career, Richard Cromwell was an artist. This mural in oil is a recent painting." The work shows a muscular, erotically posed nude male, his private parts discreetly hidden.

During the short-lived Cromwell-Lansbury marriage, a fan magazine picture essay portrayed the pair as a happy couple awash in domestic bliss. "When *Screen Guide* last reported on Angela," it was noted, "she was single and was completing work on *The Picture of Dorian Gray*. Now, a year later, she's the bride of former actor Richard Cromwell."

This was a cruel description of Cromwell, a man still actively pursuing his career. What these words may be revealing is Cromwell's motivation for marrying a woman to whom he could give only a friend's love, instead of husbandly devotion. His acting career was on the downslide, while Angela appeared to him to be a rising comet in the Hollywood skies. He may have believed he could resurrect his failing career by making a profitable marriage.

The article continued by describing Angela as newly "established as one of Hollywood's finest young actresses. In a town famous for its glittering ostentation, Angela has done all this quietly, modestly. Angela tells us, 'I was afraid if the story got out something might happen to spoil our romance.' "

What did Angela mean by that last line? Was she simply indicating that she did not want the glare of publicity to intrude upon their intimacy? Or was she only too aware of the limitations of her marriage by that time? Did she realize that she must keep Richard's "secret" in order to avoid embarrassment and scandal?

"In the Cromwell menage, the coffeepot is never off the stove," the article revealed. "Friends drop in constantly, leaving Angela and Dick little time for Hollywood's social whirl. Placid as this may sound, for Angela it is the most exciting, important time of her life." Photos accompanying the piece included one of Angela showing off her wedding band, resting on a sofa in their "simple and artistic" living room, pouring grape juice into a crystal goblet that was a wedding present, and playing with her pet cockatoo, Dorian (whose name "derives from the film that won her an Academy Award nomination"). She posed in their bedroom and walked alongside their "small but lovely" swimming pool. In one of the studio publicity unit's trumped-up domestic scenes, Angela and Richard are shown "washing windows while humming their favorite tune." One of the captions noted, "Angela's talented husband designed her wedding band. 'It's the most beautiful I've ever seen,' says Angela."

Angela has acknowledged her marriage to Cromwell at various times throughout her career. In 1961, one year after his death from cancer, she declared, "I was married for the first time in 1945, to the late Richard Cromwell, the actor. The marriage lasted nine months, and, thank goodness, did a great deal for me. I learned the meaning of marriage and a lot of other things, and I had a better idea of what it was all about when I married again."

In a 1966 profile, she observed that her marriage was "a mistake, but a very good lesson. . . . I wouldn't have *not* done it." Even as recently as 1993, she described Cromwell as "my first great, great romance. It was a terrible tragedy. The desperate part was that I was so in love with him." But she has never spoken publicly about the specifics of their breakup.

Angela filed for divorce on the grounds of extreme cruelty. The decree was granted on September 11, 1946—sixteen days short of what was to have been their first anniversary. In 1949, Angela wed Peter Pullen Shaw—a union that was to be loving, and long-lasting. But she did eventually absolve Cromwell, and the pair remained friendly until his death.

Certainly, her experience with Cromwell soured Angela on relationships with actors. In 1961, she was asked if she would want her children (son Anthony and daughter Deirdre, her offspring with her second husband, and stepson David) to be in show business. She felt that it would "be all right for Deirdre. I certainly wouldn't encourage it for my boys unless they were writers or directors, which is a far better life for a man than being an actor. Unless men are big stars and real money-makers, it's a difficult existence. In many cases they're sort of pathetic people."

5

Disappointment
at Metro

"I would like to do Bessie Watty in *The Corn Is Green*, but the studio said no," Angela told Louella Parsons after filming *The Picture of Dorian Gray*. "I guess they know what they want me to do."

"I would like very much to play in a modern version of *Trilby* and also in *Nana* by Emile Zola," she told a fan magazine interviewer.

These are the hopeful words of a young and ambitious actress, new to the ways of Hollywood, who innocently exudes blind trust toward those who control her future, and her fate. Indeed, this is as close to public complaining as a contract player could get without jeopardizing her association with her studio.

On these occasions, Angela politely voiced her career aspirations, and frustrations. But she was not without anger over the situation, which would sometimes simmer over into print. Not long after her divorce from Richard Cromwell, Angela proclaimed to journalist Erskine Johnson, "I want to play a scene with Clark Gable or Jimmy Stewart, or some other he-man in which he breaks down the door and I'm behind it. I want to be the reason he broke down the door." Of being cast in nonromantic roles, she added, "It's getting monotonous."

In retrospect, MGM did not know what to do with their 129-pound, ash-blond property. It is no exaggeration to say that, until her contract expired in 1951, she was both misused and underused by the studio. During her seven MGM years, Angela appeared in only thirteen features, whereas other contract players were cast in four, five, or six roles per year. "She didn't fit in with those nymphs and nymphets they had out there in those naive pictures," recalled Hurd Hatfield. "Angela said to me at the time, 'They have to keep me because I'm under contract, and that's the way it is.' " Decades after leaving MGM, Angela astutely observed, "I went through a period almost of being an imitation of what [the studio bosses] wanted—which wasn't the actress that I really was."

Despite her display of acting range in *Gaslight* and *The Picture of Dorian Gray*, and her two Oscar nominations, Angela was to appear in pitifully few prestige projects during her remaining years under contract. One was *State of the Union*, in which she played Kay Thorndyke, a millionaire newspaper publisher who becomes embroiled in a presidential campaign. Even that film was not really an MGM production, but an independent picture produced by Liberty Films, in conjunction with MGM. The film's producer/director, Frank Capra, was appreciative of Angela's talent when he remembered her as "that amazing British gal that could play anything and everything well."

Her faithful mentor George Cukor summed up Angela's dilemma in retrospect: "After [*The Picture of Dorian Gray*] she was consistently miscast."

It was not until the early 1960s, with *The Dark at the Top of the Stairs, All Fall Down*, and especially *The Manchurian Candidate*, that other filmmakers would tap Angela's reserves as a brilliant character actress.

In more recent years, Angela came to understand why the powers-that-were at MGM pigeonholed her. "I wanted to be like all the other girls at MGM at that time. I thought they were terribly successful and glamorous: June Allyson, Gloria DeHaven, Janet Leigh. But I didn't look like they did. I was much bigger than they were, I was taller, and I didn't look like the girl next door. At least MGM didn't see me that way."

She also added, "They felt I had a sexy quality, but only as a bad girl. The psychology of sex was different then."

Countering that claim, an unnamed MGM publicist who claimed to have known her when she broke into movies recalled in an interview, "Angela couldn't play ladies, and that was the era of the ladies. She was very young, but looked mature. That was because she was so chubby. She ate all the time, chocolate bars, Fig Newtons, cookies. She wasn't a compulsive eater—she was a hungry eater."

Absolute drivel! Even though Angela was to admit, "I was chubby because I ate all the time, Fig Newtons, chocolate bars, fudge," photographs of her from the mid and late 1940s prove she controlled her weight beautifully. Columnist Earl Wilson noted in 1947 that she was "a fascinating English glamour-puss" and "as pretty as an apartment lease." Accompanying his *New York Post* column is a photo of Angela in which she looks as lithe and sexy as any pinup. Today, all one must do is view Angela in *Samson and Delilah*, in which her slim, bared midriff tells the story more plainly than an unnamed publicist's complaint.

Certainly, Angela could have played a number of roles in late-1940s MGM features. Even that early in her career, she had become a consummate professional. Reported columnist Sidney Skolsky in 1947, "She comes on the set knowing her job and her lines. She has a conception of how she wants to play the character but is eager to listen to direction. She enjoys her work. She would like to appear in a picture opposite Clark Gable."

One only can imagine Angela tangling romantically with Gable in either of two MGM features he made in the immediate postwar years: *The Hucksters* (in Deborah Kerr's role as high-minded—and British—war widow) and *Homecoming* (in Lana Turner's role as a combat nurse). Further, one can imagine her as the title character in *Madame Bovary* in Vincente Minnelli's version of the Flaubert novel of a romantic adultress who brings tragedy upon herself. She came to the studio too late to be cast with Greer Garson in the British wartime story *Mrs. Miniver*, but a role could have been written for her in the sequel, *The Miniver Story*. Unfortunately, the studio was not noted for film noir; Angela would have made an excellent heroine or villainess in any number of dark crime dramas of city life.

Early on in Angela's career, word was out that she was being considered to star in a remake of Greta Garbo's first talkie, *Anna Christie*, based on the Eugene O'Neill play about a waterfront prostitute. Nothing ever came of it.

Angela especially coveted the title role in the costume drama *Forever Amber*, the lusty, sexy heroine of Kathleen Windsor's popular novel, filmed by Twentieth Century–Fox in 1947. She fervently believed that her being cast as Amber would allow her entry into the front ranks of movie stars. She approached Fox through her agent. Various actresses were being considered for the role. In the end, Linda Darnell played Amber.

MGM also failed to utilize Angela's musical talent, which was to become so evident two decades later on Broadway. During her tenure at the studio, MGM produced a number of musical extravaganzas, including *The Pirate, Summer Holiday, Easter Parade, Good News, Take Me Out to the Ball Game, On the Town, Words and Music, The Barkleys of Broadway*, and *Annie Get Your Gun*.

Room could have been made for her in at least half these films, yet she appeared in only two MGM musicals: *The Harvey Girls*, cast as Em, a dance hall singer who plays villainess to Judy Garland's heroine; and *Till the Clouds Roll By*, a musical biography of Jerome Kern, in which she appears in a specialty number singing "How'd You Like to Spoon With Me?"

The Harvey Girls, Angela's follow-up to *The Picture of Dorian Gray*, is of importance to her career mostly because she got to play her first "American" character. It is set in Sandrock, a wild-West town about to be tamed by the arrival of the title damsels. They are girl-next-door types, "winsome waitresses" and "unsung pioneers" who went west to work for a restaurant chain forming along the new Santa Fe Railroad. "Wherever a Harvey House appears," the waitresses are told as they are set to arrive in Sandrock, "civilization is not far behind."

Em is a brassy, hard-hearted honky-tonk singer at the Alhambra, a Sandrock saloon owned by Ned Trent (John Hodiak). Her role in the story is that of the "other woman." Beneath her surface toughness, Em has a secret love for Trent, and her instincts tell her to beware of Susan Bradley (Judy Garland), newly arrived from "a little town in Ohio," whose sweetness, sincerity, and spunk are sure to attract the saloonkeeper.

Em is a bad girl. She is constantly confronting, threatening, or sneering at Susan. In several scenes she is garbed in a black gown, which symbolizes her loose morals. Unlike Susan and the virginal Harvey girls, Em and her saloon gals are thinly disguised whores. "She was a madam, is what she really was, but we never discussed that in those days," Angela recalled years later. "She had a very high-class house."

The "immorality" of the *Harvey Girls* script is cloaked in euphemisms. Em and her girls offer the cowboys "a little recreation" and a "wild time." "Our profession is entertainment, see," she says, with *entertainment* being an ambiguous term. Em even butchers the English language. "The men started marrying them waitresses faster than the company could replace them," she declares at one point. On all levels, she is a character who is not fit to be in the company of the likes of Susan and the other Harvey girls.

While he is against the Harvey House, Ned clearly is a decent sort, and you know that he is destined to win Susan. Em is fated to ride out of town at the finale, in search of another Western burg to corrupt (but not before sanctioning Susan and Ned's true love, a state that a woman like Em can never achieve).

Angela reported that she was once hissed in public by a Judy Garland fan because of the manner in which Em treated Susan in *The Harvey Girls*. This is no surprise as Em is essentially a one-dimensional character whose sole purpose in the story is to counterpoint Susan's goodness. Angela goes through the film with a perpetual pout on her face; she is not allowed to bust loose and act, sing, or dance. The film's premier musical number, the Oscar-winning "On the Atchison, Topeka, and the Santa Fe," is performed by Garland along with the actors playing the Harvey girls and Sandrock townsfolk. Angela is nowhere in sight.

In fact, all the musical performers in *The Harvey Girls*—Garland, Ray Bolger, Virginia O'Brien, Marjorie Main, Cyd Charisse, Kenny Baker—are given ample screen time in which to shine. But

Angela appears only briefly in a couple of dance hall routines, rather than in any of the full production numbers.

The final indignity: Angela, who would become a Tony Award–winning musical-comedy star, had her singing voice dubbed by Virginia Rees! Thirty-three years after the release of *The Harvey Girls*, Angela noted, "I never forgave Kay Thompson and Roger Edens and Arthur Freed [who headed the musical unit at MGM]. They didn't think my voice was heavy enough and it probably wasn't in those days. I didn't have that deep throaty voice that they wanted." On another occasion, Angela admitted, "I always fancied I had a sexy singing voice, but no one would ever let me use it." And yet again, Angela noted, "In Hollywood, they thought I had a reedy little voice." Until her breakthrough on Broadway in *Mame*, Angela would occasionally sing on-screen and her assessment was that "half the time they dubbed in another voice."

Angela noted, "At MGM, I came in at the end of a very lush period. L. B. Mayer was always terribly nice to me. He always seemed interested in how the family was getting along." In fact, Mayer wanted to place Angela's teenaged brothers under contract, reportedly to star in a remake of *The Prince and the Pauper*. However, she and her mother objected because they did not want to put undue pressure on the boys, who were continuing their studies in high school to be followed by stints at UCLA. "The last thing the Lansbury ladies wanted for us to be is stagestruck," remembered Edgar.

But in 1972, Angela was more cynical when she recalled of Mayer, "I think he looked on me as a rather interesting piece of horseflesh; that's the only way I can describe it. He was interested in breeding blood strains, and he applied the same sort of terminology to actors as to fillies. His talent lay in picking winners from both. And [with regard to Mayer's attempt to sign the Lansbury twins] he liked the idea of having the whole stable under his wing." Added Edgar, "Mayer loved to control his stars. If he got us, it would be a juicy family operation."

From 1946 through the end of her contract, the majority of Angela's films either were mediocre or did not offer her the opportunity to display her talent. As a result, none of them did anything for her career.

First came *The Hoodlum Saint*, in which her role was strictly a throwaway. She played Dusty Millard, saloon singer with a crush on a cynical World War I veteran (William Powell). Angela is a mere diversion, wedged in between Powell's more serious romancing of Esther Williams.

The Hoodlum Saint is a confusing, unfocused film, and Dusty Millard is strictly a second-rate character. "I was a torch singer who was the other woman in William Powell's life" was how Angela described the role. "I should have seen the pattern MGM was setting for me." What's more, a good portion of Angela's screen time is spent singing—and her voice is again dubbed!

At the time of her appearance in 1947 in *The Private Affairs of Bel Ami* (done on loan to United Artists), in which she was reunited with *Dorian Gray* director Albert Lewin and star George Sanders, Angela told the press, "I have a straight, leading-lady part, not a cockney servant, like Nancy, nor a silly ingenue, like Sibyl." Indeed, *The Private Affairs of Bel Ami*, based on a novel by Guy de Maupassant, was one of Angela's better early credits. "It's a highly literate film," Angela noted later on, "which probably doomed it at the box office."

The setting is Paris during the 1880s. Sanders plays Georges Duroy, a penniless former member of the Sixth Hussars. The scheming, manipulative Duroy rises within the Parisian social and political order; to further his ambitions, he uses (and breaks the hearts of) various women. Angela plays one of Duroy's "private affairs," Clotilde de Marelle, whom she described as "the girl to whom [Duroy] always returns." Her performance is fine, but is overshadowed by Sanders at his caddish best.

Of *If Winter Comes*, released in 1948, Angela explained, "I was twenty-two years old, playing Walter Pidgeon's nasty shrew of a wife with a drab makeup and hairdo to make me middle-aged so I would be convincing when I told Deborah Kerr where to get off." It is no wonder that Pidgeon (playing Mark Sabre) no longer cares for wife Mabel. Kerr has the more appealing role of Nona Tybar, Mark's true love.

Angela was to describe this role as the "break" in her "resolution to admit that that studio knew what was good for me." She added, "It was wonderful to play opposite Walter Pidgeon, but as the wife I had to be small-souled, bitter. . . . Director Victor Saville talked me into it." Indeed, the results were dreary, an overripe literary property that had been filmed more successfully in 1923, with Percy Marmont.

Tenth Avenue Angel is strictly a sentimental (and, at its worst, hokey and syrupy) Margaret O'Brien vehicle, with the child star cast in this Depression-era melodrama as a tenement girl. Angela is her aunt Sue, the sweetheart of an ex-con (George Murphy) trying to go straight. "This movie was filmed in 1946, then held up for two years before it was released," Angela said, "which probably tells you everything you need to know about it. I do, however, have fond memories of Margaret. When I started at MGM, there was still gas rationing due to World War II. So I rode to work every day on the bus with Margaret and her mother."

Ever increasingly, Angela was to have little or nothing good to say about her roles. Of *The Red Danube*, a 1949 drama in which she was recast opposite Walter Pidgeon (playing a British colonel repatriating Russian refugees in Vienna after World War II), Angela pronounced, "I was a woman soldier. I made some real stinkers." *The Red Danube* is of historical note as one of the virulently anti-Soviet films Hollywood made during the postwar House Un-American Activities Committee inquisition. But as drama, it was mostly dull. Angela's character, Audrey Quayle, might have been a "General Staff officer third grade, rank junior commander—that's equivalent to captain," but in reality she is the colonel's glorified secretary. Angela has little to do beyond the film's first few minutes, except be turned down politely by the film's second leading man, Peter Lawford.

Angela did acquire a bit of glamour when she was loaned to Paramount for Cecil B. deMille's 1949 sword-and-sandal epic, *Samson and Delilah*. Five costume designers worked on the film; the most renowned, Edith Head, was assigned to dress Angela and Hedy Lamarr (playing Delilah). In Angela's first appearance on-screen, she is tossing a javelin. This proved prophetic: partway through the story, her character (Semadar, Delilah's older sister, who is the love object of Samson and Ahtur) is skewered with a javelin—and on her wedding night, no less! "To this day, people ask me if that spear hurt," she remarked.

On one level, Angela suffered the indignities experienced by studio contract players, from major stars to minor supporting performers. If you will, they were akin to trained monkeys with the studio heads as the organ-grinders.

In Angela's case, this manipulation became most obvious when she was working with DeMille. "DeMille loved all the color and the trappings and the characters who took attitudes," she recalled. "They were vessels to be filled. In a sense, it was all mechanical. He cast you by your feet, not your profile; if you had good feet, you were in. He insisted that everyone wore sandals. You weren't told in so many words, but Edith Head, the costume designer, explained that I'd have to walk around barefoot in his office one day. I wasn't to feel badly about it; he'd just like to be sure. He'd take a quick look as you walked by and give her a nod if all went well."

Such demeaning experiences may have allowed Angela to win roles, but at the same time she was never able to transcend the B list of MGM contract players. Her situation did not improve when, in 1948, Dore Schary was named executive vice president in charge of production. (In 1951, Schary would oust Mayer in a power struggle.)

This changeover was the result of the industry's falling fortunes in the years immediately following World War II. In 1946, an average of 82.4 million movie tickets were sold across America each week, taking in $1.7 billion. After the war ended, America's moviegoing habits rapidly changed as returning soldiers started families and built houses in the many suburbs sprouting up across the country. These communities were miles away from the movie theaters in the cities; furthermore, young marrieds were kept home with their infant children, where they could also be entertained for free by television. By 1953, movie ticket sales were sliced practically in half.

Metro-Goldwyn-Mayer, once the jewel of all movie studios, was losing its luster. *The Yearling*, which featured the MGM lion roaring before its opening credits, was among the Best Picture Academy Award nominees in 1946, but the studio went without nominees in that category in 1947 and 1948. Many of its films— including *The Harvey Girls, Till the Clouds Roll By, Cass Timberlane, Green Dolphin Street*, and *A Date With Judy*—were profitable, but were far from classics.

On February 19, 1948, an article published in the *Wall Street Journal* was headlined, "Hollywood's Wallet: Film Economy Splurge Is Succeeding; More Movies for Less Money . . . $2 Million Picture Made for $850,000; Shooting Time Is Cut; Sets, Scripts Cheaper—Unemployment Is Increasing." Indeed, during the first three years of Schary's MGM stewardship, there was a 27 percent across-the-board cost cut at the studio. Thirteen producers were on salary, where there had once been thirty; thirteen directors, instead of thirty-five; thirty-five scriptwriters, not one hundred and ten. Among the first wave of stars to have their studio affiliations severed were Mickey Rooney, Judy Garland, Marjorie Main, Mary Astor, Keenan Wynn, Margaret O'Brien, and Frank Sinatra. They were followed by Clark Gable, Spencer Tracy, Katharine Hepburn, Fred Astaire, Kathryn Grayson, Red Skelton, Van Johnson, Greer Garson, Peter Lawford, June Allyson . . .

While the quality of the studio's output increased beginning in 1949, when *Battleground* put MGM back into the Oscar race, the firings were not to be replaced by hirings. From then on, stars were signed for single-picture deals. The era of the seven-year contract was ended.

Amid this turbulence, Angela found herself increasingly at odds with studio brass. Typical of her growing frustration was her disappointing experience in *If Winter Comes*. "I wanted to play the role Janet Leigh did"—a young, unwed girl in an English village who becomes pregnant—"and I thought that's what I was going to play. Then, suddenly, I had the [less juicy role of the hero's] wife thrown at me."

She politicked to be cast as the fiery, evil Milady de Winter, "the most notorious woman in France," in the 1948 remake of *The Three Musketeers*, but the part went to a more buxom blonde, Lana Turner. Angela even pleaded with Louis B. Mayer for the role: "I told him, 'This could be a wonderful opportunity for me.' I remember he came to see the tests. He sat beside me in the projection room. I kept saying, 'Won't you let me play it?' He said, 'We need to use Lana in this role. You'll be wonderful as the queen.' "

The "queen" was Queen Anne, a smaller and less exciting part. The other female lead, that of the sweet, forgiving Constance, described by Gene Kelly's D'Artagnan as "my angel of goodness," was given to June Allyson. Angela recalled that she "hated every minute" of the film. "I refused at first," she continued, "and almost went on suspension for it. Some of the films I did at MGM—between the good ones, if you know what I mean— were made quickly by directors whose interest was story, action, and visuals. They weren't interested in character."

Years later, husband Peter Shaw explained, "When she was at Metro there was [sic] Ava Gardner and Lana Turner and all these beautiful women, and she'd play the Other Woman always."

Angela would have given anything for a meaty comedy part, "like the kind Jean Arthur does." There were to be no such roles in her future at the studio. In fact, almost four decades after leaving MGM, Angela remembered, "I kept wanting to play the Jean Arthur roles, and Mr. Mayer kept casting me as a series of venal bitches."

It is commonly assumed that Angela was typecast at MGM in the role of the villainess. While she played more heavies than heroines, she did not replay the same personality in film after film—witness her roles in *National Velvet* and *The Picture of Dorian Gray*. But to an extent she was typecast in another way, playing women who were years older than her actual age.

In 1948, Angela appeared in *State of the Union* as Kay Thorndyke, publisher of a newspaper chain and a hardened veteran of the Washington political wars. Kay is supposed to be forty-five years old; at one point, she describes herself to her editors as "a woman and still under sixty." Yet, incredibly, Angela was *twenty-three* when she made *State of the Union*. While she does project the sense of power and cynicism required for the role, critic Bosley Crowther was not off-base when he noted, "It is slightly incredible that a lady of such obvious youth and immaturity as Angela Lansbury could make a wised-up Spencer Tracy jump through hoops, which is what she does in this story."

In *If Winter Comes*, she played a woman who was supposed to be thirty-five years old. Her character in *The Harvey Girls* is far older and wiser than twenty-one, which was Angela's age when she played the role. In fact, it was originally to be played by Ann Sothern, who is sixteen years Angela's senior.

Casting her in *Samson and Delilah* as the only blond Philistine in biblical history was fatuous, even by Hollywood standards, but the part was yet another that played havoc with Angela's age. While Semadar is twenty-four years old in the script—just a year older than Angela's real age—she is supposed to be the older sister of Delilah. That role went to Hedy Lamarr, who was actually twelve years Angela's senior.

"I just sort of did it," forty-six-year-old Angela recalled in 1972, just as she was set to open on the London stage in Edward Albee's *All Over*, playing a character who was sixty-one. "No great fuss was made of it, no great makeup, no graying of the hair. I had an air of maturity that I seemed to be able to infuse into my own youthful talent. It was a peculiar talent: I don't think I was even aware of how peculiar it was. Now when I look back, I'm quite sort of boggled by it."

Upon watching Angela in her early roles, she in fact looks her true age. Her comportment is what covers her youthful appearance. She was twenty-one when she made *The Hoodlum Saint*. In it, she is pretty, but she nonetheless has the face of a pouty child. She carries herself beyond her years, which is what enables her to play a less-than-virginal saloon singer.

By the time she was cast in *All Fall Down* and *The Manchurian Candidate* in 1962, Angela's features had taken on a certain maturity. Her neck in particular belied the approach of middle age. Both films were made when Angela was thirty-six. Yet in *The Manchurian Candidate*, she played the mother of Laurence Harvey—who then was thirty-three! In *All Fall Down*, she was the mother of Warren Beatty, a mere babe next to Harvey: he was all of twelve years her junior.

Beatty's Berry-Berry Willart appears to be in his mid to late twenties; he becomes involved with thirty-one-year-old Echo O'Brien (Eva Marie Saint). After Berry-Berry and Echo spend a night on the town, Angela's Annabel Willart observes, "Lord, I wish I was young and could go dancing again."

In 1984, near the beginning of her long run as Jessica Fletcher on *Murder, She Wrote*, Angela (who was then fifty-nine years old) exclaimed, "I'm surprised a lot of people don't think I'm eighty-five." And several months into the show's run, when she had not yet turned sixty, she discussed her early typecasting by noting, "There was something mature about my face and my demeanor. I always felt twenty-nine. I felt twenty-nine for years and years. Now I feel forty."

Industry insiders were aware of Angela's typecasting. Noted Phil Koury, in a *New York Times* article published in the late 1940s:

> Fans who have been caught up by Miss Lansbury's special brand of radiation may be more than mildly surprised to learn that she is only twenty-three, an age that doesn't fit in at all with the glacial composure, the delicate and ruthless reality she has managed to get into certain of her characterizations. . . . Much of her mail, Miss Lansbury says, is from fans who think she is in her forties. . . . In the meantime, Hollywood's love of repetition being what it is, Angela will have to put up with the spate of oldish, adderish portrayals until some astute producer discovers what most observers already concede, that here indeed is a versatile and exciting screen personality.

When Angela was thirty-one, journalist Kevin Delany wrote, "Because she played a series of older women, to this day, many of her fans consider her eligible for old age pension."

"I started playing mothers at twenty," she noted. "I fought like crazy against it. But I soon figured I'd get better parts if I played mothers." This certainly was the case with *The Manchurian Candidate*. But three years after that film's release, she observed, "As things worked out, I missed my entire adolescence. I was married

. . . before I was out of my teens. I was in my twenties when I was actually a teen."

Certainly, Angela's time at MGM was not completely squandered. At least she was a working actress, while thousands of other Hollywood hopefuls had not—and never would—progress beyond jobs as waitresses or in department stores. And also, Angela was able to observe and work with some legendary screen talent. Of her experience with Tracy and Hepburn on *State of the Union*, she remembered, "They helped me enormously, and especially Mr. Tracy, because most of my scenes were with him. He was patient, and very earnest, and quite comforting. What was exciting about Spencer Tracy and Katharine Hepburn was their presence. Each, of course, has fantastic individual presence, but I mean collectively. Their personalities as well as their talents were orchestrated so marvelously. I began to think of them as one person, really; I suppose most people did."

Angela had heard that Hepburn requested her for the film. "I was terribly flattered by this," she said. "I found that out, and it made me very pleased." However, when Angela was cast by Capra, Hepburn herself was not officially in *State of the Union*; Claudette Colbert had been signed to appear opposite Tracy.

Newspaper reports of the day suggested that Capra was having difficulty casting Angela's part. Ava Gardner, Alexis Smith, Audrey Totter, Margaret Lindsay, Frances Gifford, and Florida Friebus were either considered or tested for the role. However, according to gossip columnist Hedda Hopper, Capra saw Angela in *If Winter Comes*—ironically, a film Angela despised—and declared, "That's our gal." *Daily Variety* reported a similar response from the director after seeing her in a test she had made with Tracy for *Cass Timberlane*.

In any case, Angela and Peter Shaw, her husband-to-be who was then her boyfriend of several months, had departed Hollywood several days before Capra's casting decision. She was so upset after attending a preview screening of *If Winter Comes* that she had requested and was granted a month-long vacation. "Anything, to get away and try to forget that role," Angela noted.

She left no itinerary with the studio, and she and Peter began driving cross-country to New York. They were a week into their trip when she was located in Cleveland, placed on board an airplane, and returned to Hollywood where she began preparations for the role. Peter continued heading east.

State of the Union, based on a play by Howard Lindsay and Russel Crouse, was to be Angela's last substantial part in a first-class film for quite some time. While not the leading character, her Kay Thorndyke is present throughout and is a major player in the story. As the film opens, Kay's ancient newspaper publisher father is on his deathbed. It is observed that Kay is "tougher than her old man." Her father tells her, "Kay, I used to hate you for being a girl. I always wanted a son like me. But you're bigger than any son. A woman's body with a man's brain. My brains. Use them. You'll make the White House, Kay, one way or another."

The crafty, icy-cold Kay cannot run for president because she is a woman. She is unmarried, so she cannot push forward her husband (as her character does in *The Manchurian Candidate*). Enter Grant Matthews (Tracy), an up-by-his-bootstraps airplane manufacturer and bonafide man-of-the-people. Matthews may have a wife (Hepburn) and two kids, but he has been enticed into an affair with Kay. She and political kingpin Jim Conover (Adolphe Menjou) back Matthews as a dark-horse prospect for the Republican Party presidential nomination. Kay knows that if Matthews gets to the White House, so will she.

"The 'Kay' character is becoming a much more vital person," Capra observed in a memo to Lindsay and Crouse as the play was being adapted to the screen. "She wants something now—she wants power. She has been at outs with the Republican National Committee in the past because they ignored her. We have in mind a scene between Kay and Conover in which they both have a showdown as to what each is to get out of this if Grant is elected. She intimates she will settle for a Cabinet position."

State of the Union is a witty, knowing look at politics American style, with a script loaded with asides about politicians: "You're not nominated by the people. You're nominated by the politicians"; "Politicians seem to think there's a law against paying hotel bills";

"You politicians have stayed professionals only because the voters have remained amateurs"; "A good president is one who gets elected." At one point it is noted that a certain governor is prone to snoring, and "that's an occupational disease of governors."

Prior to its release, an elaborate publicity campaign was laid out to trumpet Angela's appearance in the film. One aspect of its strategy was called "Lansbury Landslide," an appropriate moniker given the nature of the film. It was described as follows:

> Still photographer on *State of the Union* to keep track of the "Lansbury Landslide"—everyone is interested in interviewing—photographing—and talking to Angela. Layout to show: 1. Fan magazine photographers taking pictures of Angela on the set. 2. Angela being interviewed by newspaper reporters. 3. Tracy and Capra congratulating her. 4. Visitors having their picture taken with the actress. 5. Being photographed at home—with her brothers—mother. 6. In the still gallery posing for glamour art. 7. Reading a newspaper which features her picture in an interview (can do this with Sunday *Times* interview which shows Angela with Capra).

State of the Union was to be a fine credit on Angela's résumé. "I was especially glad to see Angela Lansbury get such a meaty part for a change," movie fan Frederick Spragg wrote Capra after seeing the film in London (where it was known as *The World and His Wife*). "She has qualities which definitely make her a star of the first water [*sic*]."

The only trouble was, Angela was unable to sustain her career with equally strong roles in comparable films. Angela's problem with the movies, both when she was at MGM and afterward, was aptly summed up in 1974 by Gene Siskel: "In her early films for MGM, Lansbury's essential problem was foretold—she was too damn intelligent for the parts being written. . . . As for the last dozen years . . . Lansbury has been ignored by the movies like any other actress who exudes intelligence."

In Angela's own words, "I was the only seventeen-year-old character actress in the business."

And she must have been especially incensed whenever her ire over the course of her career was whitewashed by the Hollywood PR machine. Another part of the *State of the Union* publicity campaign was titled "Polly-Angela." In it, she was to be marketed as "Hollywood's Glad Girl": a Pollyannaish creature who "can be MAD and GLAD at the same time!" Angela would be sold as having had "the sense to be happy and thankful" about every aspect of her career, beginning with the fact that she is "GLAD she isn't pretty or beautiful in a stereotyped way," "GLAD she made her screen debut in a 'character' role," and "GLAD she has had to work for a living."

But the fact remains that Angela did not work as often as scores of established character performers. To paraphrase the studio's slogan, she never became one of the shining stars in the MGM heavens.

6

A Self-Described Homebody

Yet one more segment of the promotional campaign designed to sell Angela to the public after her *State of the Union* casting centered around her being a single, eligible, attractive young woman. As was expected of any such woman in the prefeminist, post–World War II years, she had supposedly developed her skills at manipulating men. The campaign was to include:

Fan magazine interview with Angela on "how to charm the opposite sex." What constitutes a woman's charm—what are the little things she can do to attract a new beau—keep an old one—conversation tricks—how to make a man feel that he is all-important and at the same time keep away from coyness—be both intelligent and feminine—tricks about dressing—how to entertain.

Angela is a popular young lady in Hollywood, is beaued to the famous night spots by some of Hollywood's most eligible young men. She is just twenty-one and is the same age as most girls who are dating and interested in being "the most popular girl in the crowd." Let Angela help them gain their goal—she is one of them and not some oldster giving "advice" which is usually resented.

Angela then was described as being "as modern as tomorrow."

The truth was that she was wholly disinterested in developing such feminine wiles. Industry hype aside, Angela, even as a young, recently divorced actress—a fact discreetly omitted from the PR—had no urge to be photographed at movie premieres on the arm of some powerful studio executive or hunky actor, or to party the night away at Ciro's, the Cocoanut Grove, or the Mocambo.

Rather, she was a self-described homebody. "I don't think I've ever actually believed it's all real," she once observed of the Tinseltown glamour whirl. Even though Angela had won Academy Award nominations at an age when most girls were planning senior proms and high school graduations, she was more apt to describe herself as "a rather conventional person."

Angela fancied quiet evenings with friends, playing bridge or gin rummy. "She loved staying at home and spending time by the pool," Maggie Williams recalled, of Angela's time with Richard Cromwell. "We talked a lot about what was going on in our world. We all went to Palm Springs for a weekend and enjoyed ourselves. Or we'd listen to Noël Coward and Bea Lillie records."

Angela had become a fine cook. Among her specialties was a dish she had brought over from her native country: beefsteak kidney pie, which she served with artichoke salad and lemon-French dressing. Decades later, Williams visited with Angela at her Ireland home. "She asked us all to tea, and she had made with her own hands a marvelous orange cake. I said, 'Good God, how did you get the time to do this?' And she said, 'You know, I'm so used to doing this kind of thing that it's just second nature.' "

Angela also enjoyed tennis and horseback riding, the latter an avocation from her childhood. She read profusely. Among her favorite authors were F. Scott Fitzgerald, James M. Barrie, George Bernard Shaw, Philip Barry, Tennessee Williams, and Thornton Wilder. Second husband Peter Shaw noted in 1950, "Because of her extreme youth, I think it's most unusual that she loves deep discussions. Angie's a thinker and I warn anyone against getting her started on the evolution of man!"

He continued:

She is great at mimicking people and yet I have seen her taking herself pretty seriously; but the next minute she'll be doing a takeoff of herself *being* serious. She spends hours at the piano mastering a passage from Bach, then suddenly breaks into a mad boogie-woogie. Besides acting and playing the piano, she paints. She also applies the same amount of ambition when she fishes. I remember once at Lake Tahoe she sat miles out on the edge of a rock. It was pitch-dark, she was still sitting there, still believing she'd catch a fish. She caught a fish.

Peter also reported that Angela "dislikes washing dishes; people who talk incessantly and presume everything they say is interesting; cake, which means she never eats her own birthday cake; radios half-on when no one is listening; the moaning of the electric organ during those soap operas; and insincerity in any form, at any time." She also relished a good cry while watching a class-A celluloid weeper—a fact that Peter would sometimes forget. "Invariably, in the middle of a heartrending scene," he noted, "I nudge her and ask what's upsetting her. At that moment my loved one could easily strangle me."

Angela rarely drank. Perhaps her biggest vice was that she continuously smoked.

Most significant of all, as did her great-uncle Robert B. Mantell, Angela enjoyed gardening, a pastime that would remain a special favorite throughout her life.

Anyone who assumed that Angela was in any way like the characters she played on-screen would be sorely mistaken. Frank Capra supposedly wanted her to play Kay Thorndyke in *State of the Union* based in part on her appearance as Mabel Sabre in *If Winter Comes*. The director and actress had never met. As the story goes, Capra was astonished upon first greeting the youthful Angela, who had a pink ribbon in her hair. Still, Capra had enough sense to allow Angela to play the role. Despite Bosley Crowther's observation of her youthful presence, the fact remains that she turned in a polished, believable performance.

Reported the *New York Times'* Phil Koury:

A visit to the *Samson and Delilah* set the other day revealed how thoroughly Miss Lansbury's particular type of incandescence has taken over. It was easy to see she had captivated the entire crew—from 'props' to [director Cecil B.] DeMille. Even electricians, who owe much of their eminence on the set to an adamantine uncommunicability, had warmed up like Kleig lights to the youthful actress. As one of the traditionally uncommunicative electricians put it, "Angela is really lighting up the joint." Even "C.B.," usually as solid as the Himalayas, freely admitted the effects of the powerful Lansbury wattage. "Some folks use raw alcohol to get warmth and Dutch courage," he smiled. "We have Angela."

Prior to her 1949 marriage to Peter Shaw, Angela purchased a house in the affluent oceanside community of Malibu. A fan magazine described it as being "a dream of a house" and "a beautifully modern honeymoon house with an 'out of this world' view." Its location was "way up in the clouds, overlooking the Pacific Ocean." The sitting-room part of the bedroom featured traditional wallpaper and a fake fireplace that Angela had purchased for ten dollars and Peter had refurbished. The living room walls were painted in beige tones, "but Peter has great plans for redoing it in bright colors." The view from each side of the room "is different, breathtaking."

That same magazine described her as being an excellent cook, specializing in enormous Sunday-morning brunches, and a competent pianist who often accompanied her twin brothers, who played the cello and violin. As if that weren't enough, she even "designs and makes many of her gowns and hats."

As the years passed, Angela's likes and tastes changed little. She would still prefer a good home-cooked meal and a quiet night with friends or with her nose in a book, to a fancy dinner at a glitzy Hollywood night spot.

During a 1961 interview, gossip columnist Cindy Adams observed that Angela wore no jewelry or nail polish, just "a skinny wedding band." "I'm a country girl, y'know," she said. "I like doing things with my hands like needlepoint cushions, crocheted bedspreads. [I just] finished a huge afghan. . . . No, I don't dress like a glamour star. It's the bane of my existence. I always feel so underdressed. If I'm not dressed and I have to go down to the store for something, why I just go ahead and go anyway.

"I spend less time than the average woman on glamour. Most women go to the beauty parlor once a week. I don't. I do my own nails, wash and set my own hair, even color it a lot of the time."

Twenty-five years later, Angela declared, "I'm not a big jewelry person. Peter bought me a beautiful diamond sea gull recently. Haven't even worn it yet."

In 1966, when she was appearing on Broadway as *Mame*—a character who was a noted clotheshorse—Angela explained, "The trouble with me is that I prefer shopping for housewares to shopping for clothes." The forty-one-year-old actress then enjoyed tennis, swimming, waterskiing, sewing, cooking, fishing, and raising Tropicana roses.

However, Angela is not averse to clothes selection. This especially is the case on *Murder, She Wrote*, where she has been deeply involved with choosing Jessica Fletcher's attire. "She loves those wonderful, dashing Irish shawls that you can drape around you," explained Maggie Williams. "She told me she got one to wear on *Murder, She Wrote*. She loves that kind of thing, but when she's at home, she's inclined to wear slacks, like everyone else."

Angela also has had a special fondness for Ireland. For her, the Emerald Isle is akin to a garden of unspoiled beauty, into which she can make brief but well-earned escapes from the rigors of Broadway and Hollywood. And it served as a refuge in the early 1970s, when Angela and Peter's son, Anthony, was desperately ill and in need of rest and relaxation after becoming immersed in the 1960s drug scene.

Angela and Peter purchased a former Georgian rectory, built in 1825 near Cork. Its address: Knockmurne Glebe, Conna, Mallow, County Cork. She described it as being "totally without any star trappings." At first, Angela considered this new home a "strategic retreat," rather than an escape. But it ended up being the Shaws' salvation for the seven years in which they owned it. "I used to love that place," explained Hurd Hatfield. "It was called the Uplifters Ranch. It was a marvelous, comfy house."

The rectory was set on twenty wooded acres filled with three-hundred-year-old elm trees. A river ran down in back, and it was surrounded by vibrant Victorian gardens.

While in Ireland, Angela and Anthony would go antiquing and purchase old furniture, which they would restore themselves, piece by piece. Angela took an active part in redoing the 145-year-old house. She helped to strip off the eight coats of paint on its doors, then sand the original wood. She purchased an old sewing machine in Cork, on which she made all of the house's drapes.

In 1973, Angela told Rex Reed that she and Peter

> tore out the entire cellar and put in a dream kitchen. Everybody hangs around while I do the cooking, and they dip into the soup or help or play chess or knit or read. We have an incredible hi-fi setup, which works like a great recording-studio sound-reproduction unit, piped into the kitchen through a two-story stone stairway. Everybody has a fireplace in their bedrooms and breakfast in bed and it's a complete indulgence. We lease our fields to a neighbor who breeds steeplechase horses, beef cattle, and lambs in the spring, so we're surrounded by animals. I have a garden. I've got a bag of spinach in the icebox now that a friend brought from Ireland yesterday. Last year we had forty pounds of raspberries. This year strawberries are going to be very good, and we grow lettuce and asparagus and I planted three dozen rose beds last spring.

"The raspberry netting needed mending and I mended it," Angela matter-of-factly told a reporter in 1975 as she described a recent sojourn to Ireland. "The netting is to keep the birds from eating the berries. Well, there I was under all this netting, and the biggest bumblebees were buzzing around my head. I hate bees but these were very busy with their pollinating and didn't bother me at all. They were quite polite, really." That same year she observed, "I have a lot of other interests besides acting, and I always have a continuous tussle whether I'm going to be acting or whether I'm going to be home."

Here, indeed, Angela could be just another person. She could take pleasure in her cooking and gardening, and in looking after the property. Remembered Fritz Holt, who was to be one of the producers of her *Gypsy* revival in London and New York, "One morning I'm fast asleep in the guest room and there's this knock on the door. This lady sets down a tray with juice and coffee, stokes the coals of the little fireplace, then exits without a word. I come out of my grogginess and realize, 'Gee, that was Angela!' She's like the mother of us all."

Even during the second half of the 1980s, when Angela's success on *Murder, She Wrote*—it was then television's highest-rated drama series—could have allowed her and Peter all the trappings of the affluent, their lifestyle remained relatively simple. As a way of alleviating the daily tensions of starring on the show, Angela might spend her free time cleaning the dining room windows of her Brentwood home. She and Peter purchased the property in 1984. It featured three bedrooms, four fireplaces, tiled floors, a swimming pool, and skylights. The rooms were decorated in natural tones and pastels. The rugs were designed in a flower motif. The rooms were filled with antiques, bric-a-brac, and family photos and memorabilia.

"The most exciting part of my day is to come home and find out what my favorite visitor, United Parcel Service, has brought," Angela told an interviewer in 1987. "The other day was a real banner day. UPS brought an ironing-board cover."

She added, "I love the world of housekeeping. Saturday and Sunday, when I don't have a housekeeper, I love making beds. There's a whole art in that. I have magnificent pure linen sheets from Ireland that I absolutely adore, but they're enormous. If I send them to the laundry, they'd get torn. So I wash them in the machine and iron them on the dining-room table, which I cover with a blanket. I love ironing. The only problem with linen is that it's impossible to keep unrumpled. You have to change sheets every day. I don't, of course. I just lie flat, perfectly still, in a little section of bed. I don't move."

A reporter visiting their house for an interview would more than likely be greeted by Angela or Peter, rather than a secretary or servant. Peter might offer some fresh-brewed coffee. Angela might offer English muffins. The talk between star and journalist might take place over a mound of interior-decorating magazines, with Angela and the writer seated on comfortable couches.

Of all Angela's pastimes, gardening remained her prized activity. Moyna had a green thumb, which Angela inherited. From the time she and Peter married, all of their homes had gardens. Angela would experience her greatest sense of tranquillity as she devoted many hours to her various gardens. Her all-time favorite was in their house in Ireland: two and a half acres total, including a wooded area filled with beech trees. Each spring, the garden would be covered with bluebells and primroses.

As she settled into the Brentwood property, she dug up the soil on a slope behind the house, weeded it, and turned it into four terraces that would be ideal for the planting and growing of vegetables and flowers. Gardening was a ritual being passed down through the generations; on weekends, Angela would plant and harvest peas, tomatoes, and beans (as well as bike, swim, or walk) with her grandchildren. Gardening remained a part of Angela's life even when her home base was New York City. During her run in *Sweeney Todd*, she grew tomatoes on the windowsills of her New York apartment.

Yet Angela never allowed herself to become a woman of leisure. After all, she craved a career as an actress. Once she achieved her first successes, she learned that she would have to try to keep repeating those successes. Otherwise, she might quickly become a working actress struggling to win roles (if not a has-been only to be recalled by film buffs). Frankly, before her superstardom in *Mame*, Angela's career was headed in this very direction.

Even when her starring status and lasting fame were assured, Angela did not allow herself to slow down.

As she explained in 1981, "That's the malaise that accompanies any person who has a very active career in any walk of life. I've subjugated myself as an individual because I've had to do first things first. I suppose I find myself very much caught in the trap where, yes, I do lead a glamorous existence by all normal standards, and yet yearn to be able to participate in a more normal life with certain continuities, a beginning, middle, and end to the day."

7

Lovely, Lovely Peter

In December 1946, Hurd Hatfield, Angela's costar in *The Picture of Dorian Gray*—who forty-nine years later was to describe her as "my old chum"—invited her to a party in the Ojai Valley. Angela had been separated from Richard Cromwell for six months.

"It was for my birthday," recalled Hatfield. "Since she'd never been there, she said that Moyna would come with her, would drive her. And then she said Moyna didn't feel quite up to it.

"Of course, she'd stay overnight because it was about eighty miles [from Los Angeles]. Well, I said, 'I'll find you a blind date'—someone who was attractive and who would be her escort. I thought of Peter, who was English and just out of the army and back in Hollywood and terribly impressive. She said, 'He sounds awful to me. He's in the paper one moment with Joan Crawford . . .' I said, 'He's very nice.' I had to talk her into it."

Peter was a six-foot-two, dashingly handsome Englishman, Peter Pullen Shaw. He was seven years Angela's senior. Thirty years into their marriage, Angela would refer him as "lovely, lovely Peter."

Further ironies played their way into the scenario surrounding Angela and Peter's meeting. Had it not been for a missing telephone, that momentous blind date might never have occurred. "I was subletting an apartment at the time and using the original tenant's phone," Peter wrote in a 1950 fan magazine article titled "I Married an Angel." "With five million daily dialers to worry about, the telephone company made this interesting discovery on the day I was to call for Angie. Bright and early that memorable morn, a cheery gentleman arrived and proceeded to yank this instrument out by the roots! Now in the meantime, my bride of the future had been trying desperately to call me and cancel the trip." Hatfield, it seemed, had been unable to convince Angela of Peter's being anything less than a cad. As Peter noted, "It seemed the lovely lady had suddenly developed qualms" about the date.

But Angela, much to her eventual delight, was unable to cancel it.

Peter Shaw had started out as an acting hopeful and was signed to an MGM contract. The studio attempted to market him as a potential celluloid heartthrob. Read the caption of a photograph of Peter and a starlet, which appeared in a period fan magazine, "May Mann gets all the breaks . . . here she's dancing forehead-to-cheek with MGM's new British-born swoon boy, palpitating Peter Shaw, at the Beverly Tropics."

"He played very good tennis," remembered Hurd Hatfield. "He was part of a set, you know, of attractive people. He was full of fun." And Peter was considered one of Hollywood's Eligible Bachelors. On the same fan magazine page was a shot of Peter with Joan Crawford, who had divorced Philip Terry in 1946. "Joan Crawford (at this writing) has the Number One priority on Peter Shaw's heart—and vice versa," began the caption. Crawford biographer Fred Lawrence Guiles noted that Crawford dated Shaw during an on-again, off-again relationship with movieland lawyer Greg Bautzer. "Shaw, however, was too strong a personality to remain long as a prince consort to the queen of Hollywood," according to Guiles, "and they soon parted."

Peter's on-screen career failed to materialize; he constantly found himself compared to Tyrone Power and especially Errol Flynn, which did not augur well for an original presence on-screen. At Hatfield's birthday party, Angela had told Peter that Flynn had been one of her favorite childhood movie stars. After the weekend, Peter sent her flowers with a note signed, "With apologies for being the poor man's Errol Flynn." And years later,

Rex Reed was to write that Peter "looks like a Mississippi riverboat gambler in an old Tyrone Power movie."

In the fall of 1947, upon Angela's heartbreak over seeing herself on-screen in *If Winter Comes*, she and Peter headed via automobile from Los Angeles to New York. Angela's intention was to enjoy a much-needed respite from the disappointments of her career; Peter's goal was to attempt to crash Broadway and earn the stardom that had eluded him in Hollywood. While his temporary address was a prestigious one—the Algonquin Hotel, where he joined Moyna—he was unsuccessful in securing a stage role.

Peter eventually was to take a healthy-minded attitude toward his failure as an actor. Although he did not dwell on this lack of success, years later he frankly admitted, "I was an actor who couldn't act." He credited Angela for helping him come to this realization. The two of them had made a screen test together. Later on, as Peter recalled, "Angie said, 'Peter, you can do anything you want in the world, but not act.' She was the only one with enough guts to tell the truth. Bless her heart."

Indeed, Peter was once asked why he did not continue with his career. "Did you ever see an actor called Richard Greene?" was his response, referring to the British-born leading man best known in the United States for playing Robin Hood on television during the 1950s—and who had won the role as the second male lead in *Forever Amber*, a part that Peter had coveted. "Well, I was as bad as that."

Peter was perceptive enough to acknowledge acting was leading him nowhere and to switch professional paths. He became a behind-the-scenes industry professional; however, at the time of his 1949 marriage to Angela, he still was very much an unknown quantity. In an Associated Press announcement of the Shaw-Lansbury nuptials, he was described as a "scene designer"; the *New York Times* item noted that he was an "Irish-born actor." In "I Married an Angel," his profession was listed as "interior decorator."

Peter eventually was to be a film executive and agent; he became assistant head of production at MGM and was in charge of the worldwide offices of the William Morris Agency. In 1973, Angela and Peter's union became professional as well as personal when husband began managing wife's career. Peter later became a special adviser to Angela on *Murder, She Wrote*.

When Peter met Angela, he too was separated. His soon-to-be-former wife was Mercia Lydia Squires, who had remained in England. Plus, he was the father of a young boy, David.

In the year after Angela and Peter met, columnist Sidney Skolsky reported, "[Angela's] current beau is Peter Shaw. He is just a dining and dancing friend, but she does intend to get married again." *Daily Variety* added that the pair were "so-o-o in love! As far as marriage plans, however, all rumors are slightly premature."

"We had a very slow sort of courtship," Angela recalled. "Peter had a little boy, David. And I'd been burnt. We didn't get married until two years later."

Angela also noted, "We became friends, and then we became lovers." Added Peter, "We'd have become lovers much quicker, but she kept saying things like, 'Oh, don't be silly.' It's hard to be romantic when someone's laughing at you."

However, Hurd Hatfield offered a slightly different (and slightly more risqué) version of the very early Angela-Peter relationship. In "I Married an Angel," Peter reported on his and Angela's blind date: "As I look back on that ride up to Ojai, I remember Angie was guarded and very much on the defensive." But apparently, that defensiveness soon melted away. Hatfield's reminiscence dates to the morning after his party. "I was a terrible clown," he declared. "And so I pretended to be a French maid and came into [Angela's] room in the morning. [Peter] had gotten into her room. Angela was being very proper. She wasn't parting the sheets, and I was dusting as if I didn't know they were in bed."

Afterward, Peter told Hatfield, "I think she's *wonderful*." Hatfield responded, " 'She is,' " adding, " 'I hope she thinks you are.' And they haven't separated since. They've made a wonderful marriage."

Peter certainly sounded like a man in love when he wrote, in "I Married an Angel":

In Hollywood, glamour is practically a drug on the market. But I personally feel that Angie has *real* glamour, as opposed to the rather superficial quality possessed by some of the girls I used to date. To me, a glamorous woman never disappoints you and Angie never does. She is a person who improves every time you see her—from one day to the next. She is completely different from the usual Hollywood woman, about whom you learn all there is to know in a few hours. There's a definite reason for this. Angie has a great love of music, art, literature, people. She is *not* in love with—herself.

It is clear from Peter's comments that his amorous feelings for Angela were compounded by a respect for her as a person, resulting in a solid base upon which to build a successful marriage.

Angela and Peter did live together before their 1949 nuptials. Of course, this fact—along with Peter's having accompanied her on her cross-country vacation—was not publicized, as it would have meant professional suicide for Angela. And it was Angela, not Peter, who proposed. "I just asked him if he were of the mind, and he was," she recalled. "It's always up to the woman to decide these things."

Angela and Peter's wedding plans and ceremony were not without incident. "They wanted to be married in England," reported Hurd Hatfield. "Anytime Angela started to leave, the studio wouldn't let her go. She was in tears finally. I remember staying with her through all of that upset, trying to get her off with Peter."

Once they finally were able to get away, another problem developed. An Associated Press item from London, dated August 3, 1949, informed the world that

Angela Lansbury, cockney-born Hollywood actress, and Peter Shaw, scene designer, will be married Aug. 12 by the Rev. R.F.V. Scott in the chapel of the St. Columba's Church, of the Church of Scotland, Miss Lansbury announced today. Miss Lansbury originally wanted to be married in the historic Bow Church, of the Church of England, where her father and grandfather worshipped. She was refused permission because she is a divorcée. She formerly was married to Richard

Cromwell, the actor. . . . Miss Lansbury and Mr. Shaw received offers from ministers of the Congregational and Methodist faiths after the Bow Church rector refused them. The Rev. Dr. Scott said that when he agreed to marry the pair he did not know of their search for a church. "I went to Norway for a holiday on July 14 and did not return until last Saturday," he explained, "and I did not see an English paper during that time." Asked how he felt about the marriage now, he replied, "I cannot go back on my word to them."

Angela and Peter did not passively accept their disappointment over the Bow Church turndown. Noted Peter, "Wasn't there ever an exception to the rule? we pleaded. Yes, said the vicar, there was *once*—for Henry the Eighth!"

No less a personage than Lord Beaverbrook denounced the Reverend G. F. J. Ansell, the Bow Church vicar, in a *London Daily Express* editorial, for his refusal to perform the ceremony. Beaverbrook dubbed the decision "callous and cruel," adding, "As years roll on the Church of England makes no change, no alteration, no variation at all in rules which belong to the dark ages. Thereby it forfeits leadership among the young people it should love and cherish." At the end of July, upon their arrival in England, Peter had noted in frustration, "We've been hunting hard for two days and one thing is certain—we can't be married in any Church of England church because we were both married before."

Nevertheless, the ceremony did take place on schedule at St. Columba's. Angela was wed in a dress made of rose taffeta and Chantilly lace, and a headdress of orange blossoms and roses. Another Associated Press item, dated August 12, concluded with the following bit of information: "Miss Lansbury did not promise to obey."

Angela was escorted by nineteen-year-old Edgar Lansbury, who gave the bride away; he and brother Bruce had flipped a coin for the honor. Her matron of honor was half sister Isolde. Standing up for them were Moyna and Peter's father, Walter Pullen. Peter's brother Patrick was best man. A picture taken on their wedding day shows a radiant, beaming Angela and Peter, surrounded by their proud relatives. After the ceremony, a reception was held for two hundred friends and relations. Then the newlyweds boarded a plane for Paris. They returned to Hollywood after heading to the south of France for a honeymoon in Nice, Marseilles, and Cannes.

Hollywood marriages are notoriously fragile; witness Angela's first union, to Richard Cromwell. When two performers of equal or near-equal fame become involved, the result might be clashing egos under the constant glare of the media; this has been the case over the decades, from Douglas Fairbanks and Mary Pickford to Liz and Dick to Sean and Madonna. If one-half of the union is a star and the other half is an unknown actor or a behind-the-scenes professional who is neither a famous director, producer, nor agent, the latter might wilt under the pressure of being viewed solely as a reflection of the celebrity spouse. This can be especially problematic when the lesser-known partner is male, given the fragility of many a male ego.

In her brief years in Hollywood, Angela had learned this lesson well. "The Hollywood men," she told Earl Wilson in 1947, "are so darned keen on themselves. They don't take a minute out to talk about you. They adore themselves so much, they make love to themselves constantly. When I get married again, I expect to marry somebody who isn't an actor at all."

Angela and Peter's successful marriage might be attributed to the fact that Angela has never flaunted her fame, and Peter is secure enough in his masculinity to be supportive of her career. Each partner in the union has respect for (and confidence in) the other. "Ofttimes after marriage, you hear of one person trying to change the other," Peter wrote in "I Married an Angel." "Angie has never tried to change me in any way and as a result I believe I *am* quite a changed person. By knowing her and loving her, by her believing in me, which she does, I have come to believe in myself."

Over the years, Angela's dependence upon Peter to keep order in her hectic life has increased. "Peter's wonderfully clever at getting her life organized, so she can think about her acting," explained Maggie Williams. "For instance, I went to see her in *The King and I* on Broadway. There were a lot of people milling around her dressing room afterwards. It was a matinee, and Angela had to prepare for the evening performance. I saw how cleverly Peter was able to clear the dressing room. Suddenly you somehow found yourself out on the street. He did things like that with such grace. He just knew how to make things go."

Recalled Len Cariou, Angela's costar onstage in *Sweeney Todd*, "Every once in a while we'd go out and have dinner after the show. Peter usually would be the one to make the reservation. I'm sure he just said to the maître d', 'Listen, I'm bringing Angela Lansbury and Len Cariou to dinner, and we don't want to be disturbed.' I'm sure he laid the law down pretty good, to protect her very carefully."

"Neither of us has ego problems," Angela observed thirty-six years into the marriage. "My greater public recognition as an actress is no problem for him. Although he's self-effacing, he's a very warm and outgoing, attractive man. He gets a tremendous amount of attention on his own terms."

Perhaps if Peter had been a successful actor, the marriage might have been troubled. "I'm glad he's not an actor," Angela once observed. "I'm sure we'd get into fights if he were. I can't bear fights. Some people fight to make up. When anyone picks on me, I say, 'Don't goad me into a fight.' I don't want that as a basis for a relationship. If husband and wife get into the habit of fighting, that's the beginning of the end."

But at the same time, Peter's professional connection to show business allows him to understand Angela's professional lifestyle. "Having my husband on the Coast has been a great readjustment, however," Angela explained in 1961, while appearing on Broadway in *A Taste of Honey*. "'Tisn't satisfactory a-tall. He was here Christmas and we ring each other on the phones midweek and on Sundays, but . . . if it weren't that he's involved in this business and totally understanding, I don't think it could be worked out."

Angela's frustration over her mishandlng at MGM perhaps was a blessing for her on a personal level. "I never had those chocolate-box looks they wanted for romantic leads in those days," she recalled. "But as a character actor I achieved . . . a healthy sense of my offscreen self and my private life, which I learned to keep separate from my screen characters." This attitude has proved to be another component of Angela's ability to be a loving partner in marriage. "I never let Hollywood interfere with my home life," she explained a quarter century into her marriage. "As an individual, a human being, I need to have a very strong line between my personal life and my work, and Peter happens to be of the same mind. We were married in 1949. People in Hollywood in those days discussed their personal lives down to the minutest detail with any columnist who asked them a question. They were delighted to pull out all the stops and make their private lives public. Peter and I never did.

"We were talking the other day about Elizabeth Taylor—the way her breakup with Richard Burton was conducted. We felt she was appealing to the world, 'Pray for us'—but how can you ask John Public to have a part in your anguish, your personal life and happiness with a man you intimately love?"

Angela added, "Peter and I sort of grew together. We started off poor. He didn't have a job, and my career wasn't in very good shape at the time. But we always had an absolutely burning mutual interest in our marriage and in our children, and we never did things separately, except when our jobs intervened. I think that by keeping our marriage a very private world, Peter and I consciously managed to steer it through what could have been difficult years, when we were separated a tremendous amount. Remaining happily married so long is more of an achievement than almost anything I've ever done."

Upon meeting Peter, another woman—one who was more steeped in society's conventional roles for men and woman— might have pushed aside her romantic inclinations. Despite his good looks and charm, Peter was not much of a marriage prospect. At age thirty-plus, he had not succeeded at his chosen profession. He had little money, and his prospects as a breadwinner were questionable. He was divorced, and the father of a young son whom Angela would have a major role in raising. Marrying Peter meant—and for the time being would prove to mean—a certain amount of financial insecurity.

However, none of this would deter Angela. She was independent and free-spirited enough to accept and love Peter, sensing within him the character traits that would make for a truly happy marriage.

Still, no relationship is entirely tension-free. According to Peter, some of their biggest quarrels occur when he attempts to assist her in memorizing a script. "If you just read lines flat, they don't sound like anything, so I give them a little help, and that's when she says, 'Oh, for God's sake, don't act out the bloody thing. You can't act. It sounds awful.' That starts a row, so then I must be careful to just read without any inflection. It's very difficult."

Such situations are the exception, rather than the rule, for Angela and Peter. One time she told an interviewer, "Peter is one of the nicest men you've ever met. Do you want to see a picture of him?" She promptly produced a framed portrait. "Here he is. Isn't he a lovely man?"

She also explained, in 1966, "We have a marvelous relationship. So comfortable with one another, and so in love with one another. Which is wonderful after all these years."

In 1951, Angela became a naturalized American citizen; she had taken out citizenship papers around the time she appeared in *The Harvey Girls*. She and Peter were to have two children: Anthony Peter, born in 1952; and Deirdre Angela, who came a year later.

Explained Maggie Williams, "My child, Peter McKay, was born in 1945. Angela was wonderful about that. She was very interested that I was going to have a baby. When he was six weeks old, we took him to Roy's and Angela's [she still was married to Richard Cromwell] for his first day at the pool. This was a big deal. She was very pleased about the baby and loved him. So it was wonderful when she had kids of her own."

During the summer of 1952, when Anthony was only six months old, Angela completed a grueling six-week season on the summer theater circuit in the East, starring in two recent Broadway hits: Howard Lindsay and Russel Crouse's *Remains to Be Seen*—a year later, Angela would have a featured role in its screen adaptation—and Louis Verneuil's *Affairs of State*. "Anthony slept all over the place," Angela recalled. "We trouped around together.

I did it because Peter and I were sort of struggling along, and one could make a thousand dollars a week in summer stock."

On August 11, Angela appeared in *Affairs of State* at the Sacandaga Summer Theater in Sacandaga Park, New York, then a popular resort in the Adirondack Mountains. After the performance, she came out onstage with infant Anthony in her arms. She held the baby out toward the audience and exclaimed, with great pride, "Here's my baby." The audience was delighted for her and applauded. It was a sweet family moment.

8

A Decade of Struggle

Having a young family did not prevent Angela from maintaining her career throughout the 1950s. After leaving MGM, she freelanced and obtained work at various studios. But precious few of her films, or the roles she secured, were worthy of her talents.

Granted, not all of her screen work was forgettable. But of her movie career during the 1950s and 1960s, Angela was to recall with a touch of bitter humor, "I was always in makeup to play beastly women in their forties or fifties. My movies usually were stinkers."

She began the decade by appearing in *Kind Lady*, released in 1951 and based on a play by Edward Chodorov (from a Hugh Walpole story). The property had originally been filmed in 1936, with Basil Rathbone and Aline MacMahon. Now, Ethel Barrymore had the title role, an elderly woman whose wealthy home is adorned with El Grecos, Rembrandts, and Whistlers, and who is tricked into taking a miscreant (Maurice Evans) into her abode. Angela played one of Evans's band, who poses as a maidservant. The character could have been an older version of *Gaslight's* Nancy; at the same time, any competent actress could have played the part. "I spent the film terrorizing Ethel Barrymore," was Angela's less-than-enthusiastic description of the role.

During the filming of *Kind Lady*, Ethel Barrymore took ill. The cast was laid off, with pay, for several weeks. This extra money was put toward construction of a swimming pool at Angela and Peter's house, which they fondly dubbed the "Ethel Barrymore Pool."

The following year came *Mutiny*, a boring potboiler set during the War of 1812. In this low-budget affair, shot in a little over two weeks, Angela played a French adventuress. "Don't wait up for it on the late show" was her commentary on the film.

Remains to Be Seen, released in 1953, was another celluloid nadir (and, not without irony, the final film Angela made under her MGM contract). Angela played a villainess.

"Dreadful movie" was how she described it. "I don't think I ever saw it. The only thing I can remember was coming through a bookcase [actually a primitive African sculpture] that swung open. I was wearing a black dress. Mercifully, I have forgotten everything else." This is not surprising, as she had dialogue only in one scene. Otherwise, she is meant to be a disturbing dragon-lady-like presence in her role as the head of an organization promoting a universal language, who expects to be awarded a murder victim's fortune. For her trouble, her corpse ends up in a closet.

What is especially depressing about *Remains to Be Seen* is that it was released just five years after *State of the Union*. Both films were based on Lindsay-Crouse plays. Both featured Van Johnson. Yet in such a short time, Angela's screen career had sunk so low. The fact that she had starred in the play in summer stock just a year earlier made her quick disappearing act in the film version seem even more of a comedown.

From that point on, Angela, along with the hundreds of other actors being released from their studio contracts, began to freelance. In the 1955 melodrama *A Life at Stake*, she played another villainess. "I was nastier than ever" was Angela's assessment of her character. The film is so obscure that it was never even reviewed in *Variety* and has been confused with the 1957 British thriller *The Key Man* (which also is known as *A Life at Stake*) and a 1956 Czech film whose English title is *Life Was the Stake*.

With so many bombs to choose from, Angela was to designate *The Purple Mask*, another 1955 feature, as "the worst movie I ever made" and her career's "all-time low point." In this a leaden swashbuckler set in 1803 France, Angela appears in a nondescript supporting role: a seamstress who is one of a number of Royalists rebelling against Napoleon.

The star was Tony Curtis, then a pretty-boy leading player with an unmistakable Bronx accent who would utter such immortalized on-screen lines as "Yonda lies the castle of my faddah" in period action-adventures. "All I remember about that picture," Angela said of *The Purple Mask*, "was lunch at the Universal commissary."

Most actors who have worked with Angela have only kind things to say about her. Curtis (with whom she was to appear again in 1980 in *The Mirror Crack'd*) is an exception. "I was disturbed by Angela Lansbury, who had a small part in that film," Curtis wrote in his autobiography. He claimed that she "wrote a book in which she said, 'I needed the money so badly that I played a seamstress in a Tony Curtis film.' I thought that was unkind and unnecessary, and fuck her if she can't take a joke. I found her to be most disagreeable and arrogant."

Curtis's facts are slightly askew. The book to which he refers is a 1987 biography of Angela, in which she makes no such claim. Rather, the author, Margaret Wander Bonanno, at one point writes, "Angela may have done [the film] because she needed the money." Back in 1966, upon her success in *Mame*, Rex Reed (writing in the *New York Times*) quoted Angela as declaring, "The all-time low point for me was when Peter and I needed money so badly that I played a seamstress in a Tony Curtis film."

Her next feature, *A Lawless Street*, also came in 1955. Angela described it as "a B western. I rode off into the sunset on a buckboard with Randolph Scott. Fortunately, no one remembers it." Angela plays Tally Dickinson, a "star of great renown" who is touring the wild West. She is the estranged wife of fearless roving sheriff Calem Ware (Scott) and arrives in Medicine Bend, his current residence. The two had parted for several years because of her desire to have him hang up his gunbelt. Predictably—after Angela gets to perform one unmemorable musical number—her character comes to see the need for men like Calem in the West. Without them, there would be complete lawlessness. One might consider *A Lawless Street* a thinly veiled 1950s-style pro–Joe McCarthy allegory; however, the result is so bland and boring that any analysis of hidden meanings seems an indulgence.

"One of the ironies of my career," Angela once observed, "is that throughout my youth, when I was being cast as all those heavy harpies, I considered myself a comedienne." Even though her first professional job was doing a comic impersonation of Bea Lillie, she lamented that she "never got to play comedy on film." This changed in 1956 with her role as Princess Gwendolyn in the Danny Kaye farce *The Court Jester,* produced, scripted, and directed by Norman Panama and Melvin Frank.

Kaye was the focus of the film, playing a bogus jester who becomes immersed in romance and intrigue (and gets to recite his classic poem about the pellet with the poison and the vessel with the pestle, along with other specialty material by Sylvia Fine). Angela, Basil Rathbone, Glynis Johns, Cecil Parker, and Mildred Natwick lent Kaye solid support. But it must be noted that Angela was the second female lead, after Johns. Both their characters become romantically involved with Kaye, with Johns winning out in the end. Angela's princess rejects her father the king's demands that she enter into an arranged marriage with the oversize and unappealing Sir Griswold. But at the finale, with no character as a romantic alternative to Kaye, Princess Gwendolyn is left at the side of Sir Griswold.

Still, Angela described the film as "a delightful change of pace. Everyone involved in it, on both sides of the camera, was enormously talented. As a result, I think the film still holds up as a classic comedy." Indeed, film historian Leonard Maltin calls it "one of the best comedies ever made."

The Court Jester was nothing more than a pleasant sojourn for Angela. Her follow-up film, also released in 1956, was *Please Murder Me*, in which she played a duplicitous blonde who murders her husband (and later claims she did so in self-defense). *Variety* aptly called it a "program meller [melodrama] for general lowercase bookings." "Back to the drearies" was how Angela described the film. "Hollywood simply defeated me."

Angela admitted, "I thought that perhaps my Hollywood

career was over, but in New York I got a call from Jerry Wald, [asking if I] would play a small character part in *The Long Hot Summer* with Joanne Woodward and Paul Newman. To be the girlfriend of Orson Welles."

She added, "It was a character part, a girl somewhat older than I was." In spite of this by now tiresome toying with her age, Angela enjoyed working with the film's director, Martin Ritt. "He has a marvelous kind of vocabulary for actors," she said. And she was to describe her work as "a satisfying experience, indeed."

Even though Angela is billed before the title in the opening credits, along with Paul Newman, Joanne Woodward, Anthony Franciosa, Orson Welles, and Lee Remick, her on-screen presence is almost nonexistent. The film is based on William Faulkner's novel *The Hamlet*. Newman stars as Ben Quick, a young drifter-stud with a reputation for being a barn-burner and hothead. He comes to the small town of Frenchman's Bend, "the most nowhere place in the whole state of Mississippi," where he influences the lives of the members of the Varner family. Angela plays Minnie Littlejohn, and she appears on-screen just four times, in brief scenes with Welles (playing the family and town patriarch). Her character pressures Welles's to marry her; at the happy-ending finale, he offers her a wedding ring. Minnie is on the periphery of the story, and Angela is not afforded the opportunity to create a performance or render a character.

Perhaps her best screen role of the 1950s is one of her last of the decade: *The Reluctant Debutante*. This film, directed by Vincente Minnelli and based on William Douglas Home's stage play, is a lightly likable farce, and the stars are Rex Harrison and Kay Kendall (who had just been married). Their characters, Lord Jimmy and Lady Sheila Broadbent, were also newlyweds. The setting is posh London, and Jimmy invites his American daughter by a previous marriage, seventeen-year-old Jane (Sandra Dee), to England during the "coming out" party season. The well-born British boys bore Jane; she particularly is not attracted to tiresome David Fenner, a lieutenant in Her Majesty's Royal Horse Guards. For reasons unimaginable, Sheila would like to arrange a match between Fenner and her stepdaughter. Instead, Jane falls for a fellow American (John Saxon), a handsome drummer with a notorious (though predictably unwarranted) reputation as a womanizer.

Angela played motormouth Mabel Claremont, friend and scheming social rival of Sheila Broadbent, whose daughter Clarissa favors Fenner. Jimmy describes Mabel as "Sheila's second cousin, twice removed—and twice isn't far enough." Adds Sheila, in a bit of an understatement, "She talks a bit too much." Mabel is a secondary role, and Angela, in her few scenes, adds more than sufficient zest to the film. However, the brightest performance is offered by Kendall, the sadly forgotten British comedienne. Her character is at once well-intentioned and capricious, and Kendall's acting is altogether charming.

Angela and Kendall both look smashing in their Pierre Balmain evening gowns. But in Kendall's case looks were deceiving, and the result was a happy experience neither for Angela nor her fellow cast members. "We all knew Kay Kendall was dying of leukemia," she explained. "Everyone, that is, except for Kay, who did not know. It was difficult trying to be funny when you knew a brilliant light was about to be extinguished." Kendall died the following year, at age thirty-three.

During this period, Angela was not so much an actress as a paid professional hired to appear on-screen—to show up on time, know her lines, and give a performance. That was it. Her name, and reputation as a two-time Oscar nominee, kept her in the running for parts. But it was difficult for her to seek out more substantial roles, to make demands of the powers that be to cast her in parts that would exploit her untapped talents. Of this period in her professional life, Angela recalled, "I wasn't moving forward."

The Reluctant Debutante serves as proof of Angela's celluloid stagnation. While receiving decent billing—fifth, after Harrison, Kendall, Saxon, and Dee—her character is little more than a plot device. And this was the best she could do on celluloid during the 1950s!

As a result, there was little special about Angela on-screen—a fact of which she was very much aware. By 1961, she was fed up. She conceded, "As far as the movies are concerned, I've had it. I've done a lot of puttering around in Hollywood, and the movie people never were really interested in what I could or couldn't do."

Years later, she added, "Hollywood simply defeated me! It was stock-company time, and I was never allowed to spread my wings. But my heart was ever hopeful. I had this absolute conviction that I wanted to sing and dance and move on a stage. I wanted to reveal grace. . . . I just had the feeling that I could take off like a bird if given half the chance."

During the 1950s, Angela first became quite active outside the movies. Even before her MGM contract expired, she was appearing on radio. In 1948, for example, she and Brian Aherne starred in W. Somerset Maugham's *Of Human Bondage*, broadcast on *The NBC University Theatre*. The following year, she starred in the same series in Jane Austen's *Pride and Prejudice*.

She also did summer theater in 1952. And during the decade, she was cast in almost two dozen television dramas. Most were episodes of anthologized series, which were broadcast live. "In those days," Angela remembered, "they used to hire you and pay you about a thousand dollars and your airfare. You'd go to New York, you'd rehearse for two weeks, and then you'd do the show."

The decline of the Hollywood studio system was impacting on even the top motion picture stars. During those early years, the biggest movie actors appeared in live television dramas. Humphrey Bogart, Lauren Bacall, James Cagney, Joan Crawford, Joan Fontaine, Henry Fonda, Mickey Rooney, Ann Sheridan, Claire Trevor, Margaret Sullavan, Ginger Rogers, and Fredric March were but a few of the movie names who acted on such shows as *Robert Montgomery Presents*, *Revlon Mirror Theatre*, *Ford Theatre*, *Producers Showcase*, and *Studio One*. Because the studios were no longer signing fledgling actors to seven-year contracts, the likes of Jack Lemmon, Joanne Woodward, Paul Newman, James Dean, Grace Kelly, and Peter Falk (followed a decade later by Robert Redford, Robert Duvall, and Martin Sheen) appeared on television before finding big-screen stardom.

As early as 1950, Angela starred on *Robert Montgomery Presents* in an adaptation of A. J. Cronin's *The Citadel*. "Angela Lansbury was apparantly present for her name value only," wrote the *Vari-*

ety critic, "since her role as Montgomery's wife was far below her talents."

Some of her notices in the trade papers were respectful. Of 1953's *Dreams Never Die*, on *Revlon Mirror Theater*, the *Variety* critic noted Angela "is properly hysterical" as a woman framed for her husband's murder. *Variety* wrote of her 1953 appearance in *The Ming Lama*, a ten-cent reworking of *The Maltese Falcon* on *Ford Theatre*, "As a glamour-puss killer, Miss Lansbury plays the part so well a looker has to work hard to build up hate for her." But none of her projects were particularly memorable.

Two stand out as more prestigious than the other jobs. Angela appeared with Ronald Colman in *String of Beads*, presented in 1954 on *Four Star Playhouse*. The show was directed by gifted screen designer William Cameron Menzies and based on an original story by W. Somerset Maugham. It was the story of a governess whose stock in the world rises after a gem expert judges her strand of pearls to be of high value. Wrote *Variety*, "Angela Lansbury is excellent as the governess, projecting the proper and rather subtle shadings into her role." Angela was reunited with her first leading man, Charles Boyer, in 1955's *Madeira, Madeira*, another *Four Star Playhouse* entry. In the story, Boyer's character investigates the drowning of a friend. A clever *Variety* critic observed, "Angela Lansbury is very good as the femme who drives men to dunk."

Not all of Angela 1950s television appearances were in dramatic series. She was introduced as "Hollywood's lovely Miss Angela Lansbury" when guest-starring on *The George Gobel Show*. The comedy between the two plays on the differences between Angela-the-British-sophisticate and Georgie-the-Midwestern-provincial. Furthermore, she is a head taller than "Lonesome George," and he refers to her as "great big you."

Angela was also a regular on *Pantomime Quiz*, a popular prime-time game show in which teams of celebrities played charades. "For nine weeks over a summer we did charades," Angela remembered, "and I can't do charades at all!"

Angela's work in live television took her to New York, where, as she explained, "I began to get the smell of Broadway. I liked it and I didn't like it. It was a pull-me, push-me feeling between the

New York theater and California. I adored living in California. It was very hard for me to live in New York."

By far her most important credit of the decade in any medium was to be New York–related, and it would portend Angela's future. On April 12, 1957, Angela debuted on Broadway at the Henry Miller Theatre in Georges Feydeau and Maurice Desvallieres' classical French bedroom farce *Hotel Paradiso*. Indeed, years later Angela observed, "If I hadn't got out and gone to the stage in *Hotel Paradiso*, I think my whole career would have fizzled out."

"I was afraid of Broadway until this happened to me," she frankly revealed during the play's run. "When this Broadway offer came to me, it was a challenge—and my husband and I talked it over. We agreed that I ought to try it."

Angela was in good professional company. Her director was Peter Glenville, an old friend of Angela and Peter's, who had first directed at the Old Vic in 1944. Glenville, who had adapted the play from the original French, had earlier helmed a British production of *Hotel Paradiso* and later would film it, in both cases with Alec Guinness in the lead. Heading this production's cast was Bert Lahr, the popular stage and screen comic.

Hotel Paradiso is a frenzied burlesque, set in Paris, that chronicles the comical plight of Benedict Boniface (Lahr), a henpecked mollycoddle who seeks out a fleabag lodging for a one-night dalliance with his best friend's beautiful wife, the captivating Marcelle Cot (played by Angela in a heavy blond wig and wide straw hat).

The play—and Angela—earned excellent reviews, with Angela showing that she could be a superb farceur. "Although *Hotel Paradiso* was written in 1886, there is life in the old farce yet," wrote Brooks Atkinson, who went on to describe the performances of Angela and her fellow actors collectively as "wildly funny." Richard Watts Jr. wrote, "Angela Lansbury reveals surprising humorous gusto." John McClain noted that Angela "proves to be a statuesque and highly becoming performer with a fine sense of comedy." John Chapman added, "It would be difficult to find a more alluring and straight-faced comedienne than Angela Lansbury to tempt the erring Lahr. . . . It is a joy to watch her throw a fit or a faint." Noted Walter Kerr, "Angela Lansbury, ravishing in that flattop hairdo that made the Gibson Girl glorious . . . generally demonstrates that she is a very crisp chick with a snappish line."

Screenwriter DeWitt Bodeen, accompanied by pioneer screen actress Dorothy Gish, saw Angela in *Hotel Paradiso*. They were both awed by what Bodeen described as her "skillfull stage deportment. Dorothy couldn't get over the way she utilized the 'Gibson bend,' assuming a slanting stance while the other comedians like Bert Lahr cavorted." Bodeen added that Angela seemed "much like Margaret Dumont remaining perfectly composed in the midst of the Marx Brothers' shenanigans."

Angela settled in New York for the play's run, subletting an apartment in an East Fiftieth Street duplex brownstone. "I adore comedy," she explained while movers and telephone company personnel were readying her lodging. "Such a change after the harpies and heavies Hollywood cast me in. This play was offered me on a platter. I was steeped in domesticity when Peter [Glenville] called me. I hopped a plane and with only three weeks of rehearsals opened in Washington. When we came to Broadway, I was scared spitless.

"There's only one thing on my mind now—literally," she half-joked. "That's my wig. Can you imagine that topped off with the wide straw hat, heavy with roses I wear in the second act, and summer's soaring temperatures? I won't worry about it for a few months more."

Angela later explained, during the run of the play, "[This is] the kind of acting I've never done before—comedy at a fast pace, with all of us opening and shutting doors and running up and down stairs, in Paris in 1910. At first one of our problems was how to rush around like that and have breath enough to say our lines. But we're used to it now." And she also added, "I never dreamed it would catch on like this. This is a real fling for Mum. I would have turned my back on it in a wink, but my husband, friends, and Peter Glenville, our director, said simply, 'You must do it.' Still, it took one heck of a push to persuade myself to leave my family and our home in California. Broadway has always been a bright light way off in the future, but I finally brought it down to the present."

She added prophetically, "But although *Paradiso* is strenuous work, I'm already looking forward to more stage roles. I'd love to brush up on my singing and dancing and do a musical."

As in her early days as an MGM contract player, Angela remained something of a homebody, choosing the serenity of her apartment over the din of New York nightlife. She did not move with the theater crowd, hanging out until the wee hours at Downey's, Gallagher's, the 21 Club, or the Stork Club. "Until my two younger children arrived in New York—the oldest is in school in California—I felt completely lost in the city," she said. "I was just happy to find refuge in my dressing room every evening."

However, Angela did not have to cope with feeling lost in New York for long, nor did she suffer playing in *Hotel Paradiso* throughout the hot city summer. The show closed in June after 108 performances.

Angela eventually came to acknowledge that a portion of her work in the 1950s did bring lasting rewards. Appearing in live television dramas prepared her for the rigors of performing onstage. Even more important than that, working with such a brilliant comic actor as Bert Lahr would prove invaluable throughout the remainder of her career. Years later, she sent Lahr a Christmas card inscribed, "To Bert—who has taught me all I know." "He taught me about the craft of comedy," Angela told the actor's son and biographer, John Lahr. "He taught me about the signposts and props that hold up a funny situation and how you build it. The rules have to do with movement. I can never forget him."

Angela's next Broadway role came in 1960, when she demonstrated that she could play high drama as deftly as farce. Producer David Merrick brought her back to New York to star in the Broadway version of Lancashire-born Shelagh Delaney's five-character play *A Taste of Honey*, directed by Tony Richardson and George Devine, which opened at the Lyceum Theatre on October 4. At first, Angela passed on the role. "I read the script, said it's a wonderful, great part, but thank you very much—*no!*" Angela recalled. "My husband read it, liked it tremendously. . . . Peter [Glenville] had some business with my husband and during a conversation said, 'Angela's crazy not to play this part.' Well, I knew damn well he was right. My decision was for domestic reasons."

By the time Merrick flew to Hollywood to convince her that she was right for the part, the pump had been primed for Angela to give in and play it. She returned to New York, this time subletting a furnished apartment on Fifth Avenue.

A Taste of Honey is a slice-of-life play about Josephine, a troubled Lancashire teen (played by thirty-one-year-old Joan Plowright). Angela's character was becoming all too familiar to her: a miserable mother. She described this one as "a very sad woman." Her name is Helen, and she is the mother of Josephine. "I took this [role] only from the actress's point of view that such parts don't come along often," Angela explained during the show's run. "Gives me a great deal of satisfaction to play this." She also added that she knew, and understood, these types of women. "They're not freaks or unusual by any means, but this woman isn't easy to do. It takes a drive I've never been called on to produce before."

Helen might have been an aging version of Nancy in *Gaslight*. She is tawdry, alcoholic, self-involved; she has "always pulled her hand away" from her daughter. Helen shows what theater critic Howard Taubman described as a "cheerful and brittle indifference" to Josephine as she becomes involved with a crude, one-eyed male "friend" (Nigel Davenport). Meanwhile, Josephine is impregnated by a black sailor (Billy Dee Williams) passing through Lancashire and ends up being cared for not by Helen but by Geoffrey (Andrew Ray), a gay—contemporary descriptions of this character used the term "effeminite"—art student.

Delaney wrote *A Taste of Honey* when she was nineteen; it had premiered at the Theatre Royal in London's East End in May 1958. Taubman wrote that the play "is an evocation of disenchantment done with touching honesty. At its base, however, there is an unfaltering sense of the dignity of life. Throughout, the writing has the plainness of truth, irradiated by poetry as vagrantly as a drab environment may light up a meaning. Miss Delaney's achievement is remarkable."

While Joan Plowright earned superlatives as the play's focus, Angela's performance was not overlooked. Noted Taubman, "Angela Lansbury plays the mother with quicksilver that does not conceal the seaminess of her life."

Robert Coleman disliked the play, describing it as a "primitive shocker." But he too applauded Angela. After praising Plowright, he referred to Angela as "another first-rater" and "properly flashy as the errant mom." However, he went on to add, "She's been directed to deliver most of her lines to the audience, which is sometimes disconcerting."

Even when Angela earned a less-than-laudatory notice, blame for her performance was placed elsewhere. Richard Watts Jr. commented, "I believe it is an error to have Angela Lansbury portray the mother with so much striving for humor and sympathy. There is a larger hint of evil in the woman than the production seems willing to admit."

The New York run of *A Taste of Honey* was followed by an anticlimactic road tour, organized by David Merrick. While playing Cincinnati, Angela endured one of her most disconcerting onstage experiences. The show was booked into the Shubert Theater, which she described as "a barn of a place." Between twenty-five and thirty people came to see the show per performance. "They disregarded us," she noted. "They just kind of watched." However, even this ordeal did not negate the fact that the show had a successful, 376-performance run on Broadway.

Little did Angela know at this time that her professional salvation was to come in the theater. Until she reinvented herself as the star of *Mame* on Broadway in 1966, she was to appear in over a dozen movies. Most—but not all—would add pitifully little to her career.

9

Elvis's Mother

Most of Angela's screen roles were so undistinguished that critics often lumped her together with other cast members. Back in the 1940s, in his review of *The Private Affairs of Bel Ami*, Bosley Crowther included her as one on "the whole list of love-laden ladies and fancifully costumed gents [who act] as posily and pompously as they are compelled to talk. Ann Dvorak, Angela Lansbury, Katherine Emery—the whole lot of them are as utterly artificial as the obviously paint-and-pasteboard sets." Two decades later, in his *Blue Hawaii* critique, Howard Thompson noted, "Roland Winters, Angela Lansbury, John Archer and Howard Mc-Near peer in from the sidelines."

The sad fact is that Angela has never been given that great screen role. She would have memorable stage roles and star in a long-running TV series, but celluloid superstardom was to elude her.

Nonetheless, almost two decades into her movie career, Angela felt she was finally learning the ins and outs of screen acting. "You know, some actors are very quick to catch on to where their key light should be," she recalled, "but I didn't become aware of myself in relation to the camera until the early 1960s. I began to understand that I shouldn't be photographed with directional lighting. The more light you throw on me, the better. I'd been spoiled by people like Harry Stradling and Joe Ruttenberg, who would never let a scene go by without me looking as good as possible. But I would hesitate to say to a cameraman, 'That's a bad angle for me,' because it's sometimes more telling to look slightly ravaged if a scene demands it."

When Angela was an MGM contract player, she had yearned to become a glamorous leading lady. Instead, she was usually considered a character performer. As the years passed, character actresses did become bona fide movie stars; in 1981, Angela described Ellen Burstyn as "the consummate actress, capable of weaving a character in front of your very eyes. She has depths which the average leading actress would never think of." The same might have been said of Angela. But roles for actresses of any age—and, in particular, those of an advancing age—were becoming rare to the point of extinction.

While the quality of Angela's parts did improve somewhat in the 1960s, the quality of her films—with several exceptions—did not. For this reason, Pauline Kael was to label her a "picture redeemer." Most generally, Angela was cast as mothers who were at best self-centered and at worst downright evil. In 1958, she had played an upper-crust, self-absorbed mom in *The Reluctant Debutante;* she repeated this characterization during the following decade in *Blue Hawaii* and *The World of Henry Orient.* In *Harlow* (as in *Gypsy,* which she was to play in London and on Broadway during the 1970s), she was the consummate stage mother. She had already played a neurotic mom onstage in *A Taste of Honey:* in *All Fall Down,* she would be a domineering mother bent on stifling the instincts of her children; she would play the bad mom to the extreme in *The Manchurian Candidate,* where her character quite literally was the Mother from Hell.

This typecasting even carried over to television. In the 1960s, Angela's TV appearances were far less frequent than during the previous decade. But one of her best roles in this medium came in 1963, in an episode of *The Eleventh Hour* titled "Something Crazy's Going on in the Back Room." The scenario centers on Donald (Don Grady), a bright but alienated teen who has been suspended from school after breaking fourteen windows in the school library. His grades are "pretty bad." He has been hanging around with an unsavory crowd and is headed for far worse.

Donald and his relations comprise the flip side of the idealized nuclear families depicted on *Ozzie & Harriet* and *Father Knows Best*. Angela plays his mother, a crass, neurotic nag in denial. She refers to her brood as "just the average American family—normal" as she constantly calls Donald "dumbbell" and browbeats her weary husband (Martin Balsam). Despite his long hours toiling in the family store, she tells him, "If it hadn't been for me, we'd still be living south of the gashouse." Donald, his parents, and siblings—an older sister (Tuesday Weld) and brother (Roy Thinnes)—end up in family therapy, where their problems are predictably aired and resolved by the finale.

Angela plays her role to the hilt, giving a performance as fine as any in her movies. She is especially memorable near the end of the show, in a monologue in which her character concedes her insecurities.

Angela's first screen role at this juncture of her career was in *Season of Passion*, a British-Australian production also known as *Summer of the 17th Doll*, which was actually made in 1959. Her costars are Anne Baxter, Ernest Borgnine, and John Mills. The latter pair play friends who work as sugarcane cutters in northern Australia. Each year, during the off-season, they head to Sydney for rest and relaxation with their girlfriends. Only this time around, assorted romantic and dramatic complications make up the story. Angela's role is Pearl, a straitlaced widow who becomes a reluctant substitute for Mills's girlfriend, who had married while he was away.

Angela received good notices for her performance. Wrote the *Variety* critic, "Miss Lansbury brings a comic and sometimes sad dignity to bear on the role." The film was not bad, but it did nothing for Angela's career. However, she recalled, "I enjoyed working with Anne Baxter. She reminded me of me. I thought she was a very, very good actress who never made it as an major film star. Yet she took the roles that came her way because she loved to act."

Angela was barely visible in *A Breath of Scandal*, based on Ferenc Molnár's 1920s play *Olympia*. The director was veteran Michael Curtiz, and the cast included Sophia Loren, John Gavin, and Maurice Chevalier. The setting is Austria in 1907. Loren stars as a free-spirited princess who is set to wed another member of royalty in an arranged marriage. Angela plays the snooty Lina, who schemes to gum up the marriage. She need not have worried, however, as the princess meets and grudgingly falls for a handsome, persistent American mining engineer (Gavin).

The story is meant to be a gentle yet pointed satire of clashing cultures, but it's directed and played like a typical 1950s–60s Hollywood comic confection. Its highlight: a shot of Loren's nude back, très risqué for a film released in 1960.

As for Angela, the best that can be said is that she was given the chance to wear a few lavish period costumes. "Michael Curtiz was a very good director," she recalled, "but he spoke with a thick Hungarian accent. I don't think Sophia Loren understood a single word he said on the set.

"Oh, well. It was nice to film in Vienna."

Next came what must be, in retrospect, one of Angela's most bizarre screen roles: the wealthy, possessive mother of a desexed Elvis Presley in *Blue Hawaii*, released in 1961. Elvis plays Chad Gates, who returns to the islands after having been discharged from the army. Sarah Lee Gates (Angela) is a snobbish flower of the South who calls her son "Chadwick" and refers to his native pals as "nasty little beach boys." She orders Chad to "associate yourself with the finer elements," "have a responsible position with [her husband's] Great Southern Hawaiian Fruit Company," and "marry a girl of your own class." However, the young man has other ideas.

Blue Hawaii is a piece of Elvis Presley fluff in which Angela does all she can with her narrow role, making Sarah Lee Gates a campy Southern belle caricature and a refugee from a Tennessee Williams play. "That was the lowest, darling," was her comment on the film. On another occasion, she added, "Elvis was twenty-six. It's a jolt, I can tell you, for a woman of thirty-five to be asked to play his mother. But I did it. I was desperate! Elvis was unfailingly polite. I remember, he was into karate at the time. Between takes he would break bricks with his hand."

Angela was good as a sarcastic, sadistic wife in the otherwise miserable 1963 release *In the Cool of the Day*. Even its producer, John Houseman, described the film as a "banal story of upper-middle-class Anglo-American adultery." One time, when asked about this film, Angela acknowledged that it was too awful to recall, and that in fact she has totally erased it from her memory.

For the record, Angela plays obnoxious Sybil Logan, who lays her myriad frustrations on her nice-guy husband (Peter Finch). It is no wonder that he falls in love with pretty, vulnerable Jane Fonda, wife of a business associate (Arthur Hill, who two decades later would play a key role in the *Murder, She Wrote* pilot). Angela rises above this turgid material, making Sybil a fully developed, albeit thoroughly dislikable, character. Indeed, her performance and the attractive on-location filming in Greece are the sole reasons for watching the film. A nostalgic note: in Angela's first appearance on-screen, her character is listening to a record of her former MGM costar Judy Garland singing "Over the Rainbow."

A much happier experience came in *The World of Henry Orient*, a 1964 release that might be programmed on a double bill with the 1994 New Zealand feature *Heavenly Creatures* as films contrasting the manner in which early 1960s and early 1990s movies portray intense friendships between young teenage girls. Both sets of kids are obsessed with celebrities. Both create fantasy worlds that only they share. In the 1960s film, the kids are sweet innocents, while in the 1990s film they first develop a sexual relationship and then hatch an odious murder scheme.

In *The World of Henry Orient*, Angela is the on-again, off-again mom of poor little rich girl Valerie Boyd (Tippy Walker), who begins a fast friendship with new schoolmate Marian Gilbert (Merrie Spaeth). Val eventually develops a crush on Henry Orient (Peter Sellers), a jerky, womanizing avante-garde pianist.

A somewhat filled-out Angela shows up an hour into the film. Her Isabel Boyd is a stiff, short-tempered elitist, completely devoid of maternal instincts, who is carrying on an affair with a handsome younger man and before the final credits is bedded by

Henry as well. "What a dreadful woman," Marian's mother ever-so-rightly observes.

Val is just a nutty fourteen-year-old with a schoolgirl infatuation. But in Isabel's dirty mind, her daughter is a nymphet capable of carrying on a sexual liaison with a man several decades her senior. Isabel projects her own guilty feelings onto her daughter when she calls Val a "little tart." Her nice-guy husband (Tom Bosley, who would later support Angela on *Murder, She Wrote*) is often absent as he jet-sets around the world for his job. He catches Isabel in an adulterous lie, leading to his becoming full-time single parent to Val.

Angela's role is one that by now she could act in her sleep, but she plays Isabel Boyd with the same grit she employed in *The Manchurian Candidate*. She described working on *The World of Henry Orient* as "a singularly riveting and memorable experience. We did a lot of improvisation. Made it up as we went along. That was one of the few times I've ever done that."

Her next film, also released in 1964, was a respectable outing: *Dear Heart*, a comedy-drama about two lost people finding each other. Unfortunately, neither is played by Angela. Instead, she is Phyllis, an Altoona, Pennsylvania, widow betrothed to traveling salesman Harry Mork (Glenn Ford), who wishes to settle down after many years on the road. A tentative romance begins between Harry and Evie Jackson (Geraldine Page), an Ohio postmistress in New York City for a convention.

Yet again, Angela's role is small: she makes her first appearance on screen almost 97 minutes into the 114-minute film. By that time, it's clear that Harry and Evie are suited to one another, so Phyllis must be made into a less-than-attractive character. Her voice might drive any husband batty if it were the first thing he heard each morning. Her idea of a marriage is twin beds. She wants to live in a hotel and be waited on, just the opposite of what Harry needs. What's more, Harry realizes that if he weds Phyllis, he will be destined to mediate endless arguments between her and her freeloading college-age son.

Angela might have played Phyllis as a coarse caricature, but instead acts the role with just the right subtlety. After all, Phyllis is no villainess, just a woman on a different wavelength from Harry. Despite her thoughtful performance, *Dear Heart* did not further Angela's career. "I relished the opportunity to work with Geraldine Page" was her recollection of the film.

Angela was one of a parade of stars, alphabetically from Carroll Baker to Ed Wynn, cast in George Stevens's 1965 biblical epic *The Greatest Story Ever Told*, a somber depiction of the life of Christ. Her role is by far the smallest of her career, with practically all of her footage ending up on the cutting room floor. For her performance in this film, Angela might be in the running for an award for Biggest Nonappearance by a Star Name in a Motion Picture. If you quite literally blink, you will miss Angela; she is in two brief shots on a darkened stairway in a scene in which Pontius Pilate (Telly Savalas) interrogates Christ (Max von Sydow). "Imagine a young Jessica Fletcher married to Kojak, and you begin to get the picture," Angela quipped. But in reality, Angela is seen fleetingly in the shadows and speaks not a word. She might as well have been an extra.

It was back to playing mothers in *Harlow*, one of two 1965 screen biographies of the legendary platinum blonde. One starred Carroll Baker; the other, Carol Lynley. Angela was in the Baker version. Her Mama Jean Bello is mostly ineffectual. "He's a good man. He just dreams too big," she rationalizes to daughter Jean of her loafer husband, Jean's stepfather, as he wastes the young actress's hard-earned money.

Angela is practically invisible in *Harlow*, and she was not exaggerating when she observed, "I could have played it competently with my hands tied behind my back." Several years later, after *Mame* had made her a superstar, Angela related to Christopher Isherwood at a party, with tongue firmly planted in cheek, "I told [producer] Joe Levine I'd do *Harlow* again—but this time *I* get to play Harlow!"

In *The Amorous Adventures of Moll Flanders*, based on the Daniel Defoe book and a playful comedy in the manner of *Tom Jones*, Angela was reunited with her now-aging MGM costar, George Sanders. She played Lady Blystone, employer of the title character (played by Kim Novak). The film, released in 1965, was shot just after the closing of Angela's first Broadway musical, the ill-fated *Anyone Can Whistle*. She described it as "a romp, which was just what the doctor ordered to get me through my disappointment."

Of 1966's *Mister Buddwing*, all Angela could say was, "*Mame* was just around the corner!" James Garner starred as a man who awakens in New York's Central Park with amnesia. Angela appears in an all-too-brief cameo at the opening; Garner's character rings up a telephone number he finds on his person, only to reach a drowsy, blowsy Angela, who erroneously thinks he is her drunken husband. For this role, Angela wore a padded foam-rubber skin diver's foundation, which made her appear fifty pounds heavier.

Angela's three exemplary screen roles during this period came in *The Dark at the Top of the Stairs* (released in 1960), *All Fall Down* (1962), and most memorably, *The Manchurian Candidate* (1962). For the latter, she won her third and, to date, final Best Supporting Actress Oscar nomination.

Angela described *The Dark at the Top of the Stairs* and *All Fall Down* as films that taxed her "emotionally and physically and broke my heart with pride, but only appealed to a small, rather special audience."

In *The Dark at the Top of the Stairs*, Angela finally had a good (albeit brief) role in an outstanding film. It was based on William Inge's Pulitzer Prize–winning play, whose theme was the need to face up to life; it was directed by Delbert Mann, who was to work with Angela in *Dear Heart* and *Mister Buddwing*. Her character, Mavis Pruitt, was talked about but never seen in the play. "They added this heartbreaking, sympathetic woman to the film," Angela said. "Just two scenes, really."

Set during the 1920s, the film is essentially an essay about a troubled Oklahoma family. Rubin Flood (Robert Preston) is a larger-than-life traveling salesman languishing in a failing relationship with his unresponsive wife, Cora (Dorothy McGuire). He is employed by a saddlery that is about to go under because the automobile is rapidly making horse travel extinct. He loses his job, yet cannot confide this to the self-involved Cora. Meanwhile, their daughter Reenie (Shirley Knight) falls in love with an ill-fated

Jewish boy (Lee Kinsolving). Other clan members include their fearful, mama's-boy son (Robert Eyer) and Cora's insensitive sister (Eve Arden).

"Life is closing in on me," Rubin exclaims. He seeks solace in his friendship with Mavis, a widow who operates a small beauty parlor. She is a woman to whom he can pour out his heart. She knows and understands him and has come to quietly love him. "You're good to me, Mavis," Rubin tells her. "You're good for me." What they share is a deep friendship, one that will never segue into an affair because Rubin is, after all, a "family man."

There is a sadness and poignancy to Mavis, and Angela offers a touching, tender performance. She indeed appears in two scenes, each beautifully played, in a movie filled with beautifully played scenes. Her first is with Preston, and her second is with McGuire.

Angela was equally compelling in a far more substantial role in *All Fall Down*. The director, John Frankenheimer, saw and admired her performance in *The Dark at the Top of the Stairs*, which led to her casting. Her role was that of yet another unsympathetic mother. Noted John Houseman, the film's producer, "*All Fall Down* was an intriguing, sensitive novel [written by James Leo Herlihy] that had been received with critical approval and moderate sales. It was suggested to me by William Inge, whom I had known during the years of his Broadway fame. As his star dimmed and he became subject to discouragement amounting to melancholia, he became eager to move to California to work in films and seemed particularly well suited to deal with this story of a neurotic Midwestern family."

All Fall Down is a psychological study of the dysfunctional Willart clan: the troublesome, womanizing, forever drifting Berry-Berry (Warren Beatty), who constantly challenges the law and becomes bitterly hostile whenever any of his lovers tries to domesticate him; his idealistic and inexperienced kid brother, sixteen-year-old Clinton (Brandon de Wilde), who idolizes Berry-Berry; Annabel (Angela), their irritating, possessive mother; and Ralph (Karl Malden), their superficially amiable, semi-alcoholic father.

Berry-Berry arrives at their home in Cleveland and immediately becomes involved with the charming and beautiful Echo O'Brien (Eva Marie Saint), the daughter of Annabel's "very oldest friend." Echo falls in love with Berry-Berry, but he is unable to reciprocate her feelings. Upon learning she is pregnant, Berry-Berry panics and leaves her. She, in turn, sets out on an ill-fated car ride that ends in her death. Clinton in particular has been captivated by Echo, over whom he has developed an adolescent crush. His illusions about his brother shattered, he decides to kill Berry-Berry. But when Berry-Berry breaks down and sobs in his presence, Clinton sees how pitiful his brother truly is. He leaves Berry-Berry to his misery.

For Angela, the filming of *All Fall Down* was not without friction. John Houseman recalled that within forty-eight hours of the start of filming he and Frankenheimer were "locked in a fearful dispute. He rushed into my office from the set after the second day's shooting and announced that my friend Angela Lansbury was 'impossible,' that he could not direct her and that the part must be recast immediately. I disagreed. It got to the point where he announced that if she didn't leave the picture, *he* would. I stood firm. Forty-eight hours later they had become inseparable, and he refused to make his next film, *Manchurian Candidate*, without her."

Noted Angela, "One thinks of John [Frankenheimer] as an action director, but he was so much more than that. He attempted to get under the skin of the characters, and he got some fascinating performances out of all of us. Annabel was a very difficult part for me, and I give high credit to John for that performance. In the book she had almost bohemian overtones . . . all sorts of character facets which we really didn't get time to explore in the picture."

Aspects that were explored are Annabel's small-mindedness and hysteria. Clinton continually fills notebooks with conversations he overhears. Ralph thinks Clinton is a budding Theodore Dreiser. But to Annabel, "it's not normal." Clinton says he is tired and wishes to go to bed, but to Annabel this is proof that he has contracted a disease—possibly malaria. "Do you think I went to all this agony for myself," she complains after preparing

Baby Angela and her "Irish Beauty" actress mother, Moyna MacGill.
(*Boston University Photo Services*)

Angela poses in a school uniform with her parents, Edgar Lansbury (who died when she was nine years old) and Moyna MacGill. *(Boston University Photo Services)*

HILDA MOORE – MOYNA MACGILL
tell how they care for their skin

During the 1920s, Moyna was a prominent actress on the London stage. Here, she is in a 1927 celebrity endorsement for cold cream, above, and, right, pictured in a glamour photo.

Angela, padded to make her look plump, in her screen debut in *Gaslight*, with Charles Boyer.

In *The Picture of Dorian Gray*, Angela sang "Goodbye Little Yellow Bird," a song she reprised decades later in an episode of *Murder, She Wrote*.

While Angela is the focus of this scene from *National Velvet*, she is surrounded by the film's real stars, Mickey Rooney and Elizabeth Taylor. Also pictured are Juanita Quigley and Donald Crisp, left, and Anne Revere, right.

On-screen, Angela was to become typecast as villainesses and "other women." Em, her character in *The Harvey Girls*, appears to be unamused by gun-toting Susan Bradley (Judy Garland).

Angela posed with Spencer Tracy, Katharine Hepburn, and Van Johnson, left to right, in a publicity shot from *State of the Union*.

Despite Angela's reputation for lacking glamour in her days as an MGM contract player, she displays a trim midriff while playing Semadar in *Samson and Delilah*. She is pictured with Victor Mature, left, and William Farnum.

Angela in an MGM publicity portrait.

Angela and her new husband, Peter Shaw, toast their happiness on their wedding day. Note the MGM logo in the center. *(Boston University Photo Services)*

Angela enjoys a nitecap with, left to right, playwright-director Reginald Denham, first husband of Moyna MacGill; Angela's half sister Isolde; and Denham's playwright wife, Mary Orr. *(Boston University Photo Services)*

During the summer of 1952, Angela appeared in summer stock in upstate New York, starring in a production of *Affairs of State*. Travelling with her was her infant son, Anthony Shaw.

SACANDAGA SUMMER THEATER
SACANDAGA PARK, N.Y.

Phone Northville 335

ILONA MASSEY

IN

"ANGEL IN PARIS"

With

KIRK ALYN and JOHN MALCOLM

———————

NEXT WEEK

ANGELA LANSBURY

in the New York Comedy Hit

"AFFAIRS OF STATE"

an elaborate Christmas celebration that is wanted neither by Clinton nor Ralph.

Clinton has left school and is working in a car wash. Annabel asks him, "How'd the work go today?" He responds, "Okay." Her retort: "Is that all you can say, 'okay'?" Now she has an opening for a lecture on why he would be better off back in school, "like other boys." And, for that matter, "it wouldn't hurt you to go to church either. I guess that's asking too much." Annabel is not finished. "I don't know what young people want today. You're just stubborn. That's all that's the matter with any of you."

Even more telling is her blatant incestuous feeling for Berry-Berry. Upon his arrival home, Frankenheimer's camera lingers on Annabel as she slowly rises from the dinner table. A very unmotherly look is on her face as she approaches him and gives him a very unmotherly kiss. Echo is the kind of woman any mother would want for a daughter-in-law. But when she and Berry-Berry begin their relationship, Annabel commences her carping. "It hurts me to realize that Berry-Berry's in love," she says. She begins dropping remarks that Echo, never married at thirty-one, is older than Berry-Berry. Finally, plain as day, Annabel states that she is bothered that her son is in love with "someone else."

Upon Echo's tragic death, Ralph and Clinton point accusing fingers at Berry-Berry. Annabel will hear none of it. "I love him, you hear," she rages. "I love him. I don't care what he's done. I'll love him always. Forever."

Ultimately, Berry-Berry is shown to be the victim of a mother whose feelings he can neither understand nor reciprocate. Every time he abuses a woman, whether she be Echo, a whore in Florida, or a schoolteacher who picks him up while he is pumping gas, Berry-Berry is venting his rage at his mother. "I hate life," he tells Clinton, adding soon afterward, "I guess you know I hate her guts."

All Fall Down earned some exemplary reviews, with Angela's performance not singled out but rather cited along with those of her costars. Wrote Arthur Schlesinger, "To judge by *All Fall Down*, one of the best domestic movies in a decade, Hollywood at last seems to have learned its Freudian lesson so well that it no longer needs to spell it out. . . . John Houseman . . . has put together an extraordinary production."

Unfortunately, the film, an MGM release, was mismarketed by the studio's sales department. *All Fall Down* is a complex drama of the British "kitchen-sink" school that should have opened in a few big-city art-house-style theaters, where it could have been allowed to develop a following among viewers attracted to this sort of material. In fact, John Houseman claimed that he was made just such a promise. However, the studio responded to the abundance of publicity surrounding Beatty, who was attracting attention by hyping himself as the new Marlon Brando/James Dean. In addition, one of their prestige projects, a big-budget remake of *The Four Horsemen of the Apocalypse,* had performed poorly at the box office. So *All Fall Down* was rushed into dozens of oversize movie houses, in small and medium-sized markets as well as larger cities, as a substitute for the failing epic. (Coincidentally, Angela had accepted a job dubbing the voice of another performer, Swedish star Ingrid Thulin, in *Four Horsemen.* "It was kept secret for many years," Angela revealed two decades later.)

This exhibition strategy ended up dooming *All Fall Down* to financial failure. For this reason, it did not boost Angela's screen career. But it did lead to Frankenheimer's casting her in the role that was to become her enduring cinematic triumph.

10

"Raymond, Why Do You Always Have to Look as If Your Head Were About to Come to a Point?"

Angela's second film with John Frankenheimer was *The Manchurian Candidate*, based on a book by Richard Condon. Frankenheimer described the book as one of the best he ever read. "I just couldn't put it down, and after I had read it," remembered the filmmaker. "I thought, 'I've just got to make a film of it.' It had great social and political significance for me at the time, and it has certainly been—unfortunately—a horribly prophetic film."

For, indeed, what remains most chilling about *The Manchurian Candidate* is that this fictional chronicle of a plot to assassinate an American politician premiered a full twelve months before the murder of John F. Kennedy.

Again, Angela is not the star of the show but rather a supporting player. And, again, she plays the mother of an actor (Laurence Harvey) who could more realistically have been a sibling; Angela was just fifteen days under three years Harvey's senior. And, yet again, she played an out-of-touch mother—but this one was entirely different from Annabel Willart in *All Fall Down*, or for that matter any of her other selfish celluloid moms.

The story centers on two men, members of an army patrol captured during the Korean war. One, Congressional Medal of Honor winner Raymond Shaw (Harvey), has been brainwashed into becoming a deadly, robotlike killer. The other, Shaw's superior officer, Bennett Marco (Frank Sinatra), is plagued by recurring nightmares relating to the sham and eventually grasps how Shaw has been indoctrinated just in time to prevent the assassination.

On one level, the film is an exercise in Cold War paranoia. The "enemy" is personified by the sinister Yen Lo (Khigh Dhiegh), an imposing Oriental with nary a hair on his head. He is a brainwashing expert, from Moscow's "Pavlov Institute." As he tests his handiwork, he orders Raymond to kill as if he were casually dictating a memo to a secretary.

Angela's supporting role is nonetheless the showiest in the film. She gives a scorching performance, literally spitting out her dialogue as Raymond's coolly calculating, patronizing, and power-mad mother: a dragon lady of major proportion whom she was to aptly describe as "a real Messalina of ladies" and "a good example of unadulterated evil." This character is given no first name; she is most often referred to as Raymond's mother. Her husband—Raymond's stepfather—is Sen. John Iselin (James Gregory), a McCarthyesque caricature who cannot remember the number of communists he continually alleges have infiltrated the Defense Department. Iselin is the puppet of his wife, who is a formidable creation from both political and psychological perspectives. "I keep telling you not to think," she commands Iselin. "You just keep yelling point of order . . . I'll do the rest."

She first appears on-screen as Raymond arrives home from Korea. She pushes her way through a throng of dignitaries and, in a flash, has a photographer snap a picture of Raymond under a banner labeled "Johnny Iselin's Boy." Raymond expresses his loathing for her publicity-seeking, and her warped psychology immediately becomes apparent as she pronounces, "Raymond, I'm your mother. You know I want nothing for myself. You know my entire life is devoted to helping you, and to helping Johnny. My boys. My two little boys." Throughout the film, Angela makes the character spine-chillingly sharp and sarcastic as she harangues Raymond with lines like "Go get yourself a drink or a tranquilizer or something" and "Raymond, why do you always have to look as if your head were about to come to a point?"

The plan is for Raymond-the-killing-machine to be handed over to an American operative working for the communists. This agent proves to be none other than Dear Old Mom—a woman who, ironically, is active with different American "patriotic organizations," and who dubs anyone who does not agree with her a communist. In this regard, she and Senator Iselin are broadly drawn characters who satirize 1950s-style anticommunist hysteria.

All along, she has been jockeying to secure her husband her party's vice-presidential nomination in the upcoming election. As the presidential nominee begins his speech in Madison Square Garden at the climax of the party convention, the plan is for Raymond to assassinate him—thus giving John Iselin the top spot on the ticket. "You are to shoot the presidential nominee through the head," she tells Raymond, "and Johnny will rise gallantly to his feet."

Angela's key scene comes near the finale, when her character gives Raymond his orders. Most of the dialogue in the three-minute, forty-three-second sequence is hers, and her performance is gritty, raw, positively electric—arguably her best-ever acting on celluloid. The sequence ends with Mamma promising to get back at the Russians for taking away the soul of her son. In what might be considered a follow-through on the mother-son relationship previously explored by Angela and Frankenheimer in *All Fall Down*, Mamma then kisses Raymond on the forehead, the cheek—and the lips. "And you know," Angela explained, "we shot that scene only once. It just all came together. We rehearsed a lot but finally shot it in one take."

The Manchurian Candidate was almost not produced. "There was some opposition from United Artists because [studio president] Arthur Krim wanted to be ambassador to Israel, and he didn't think that President Kennedy would want it made," recalled Frankenheimer. "It turned out that [Frank] Sinatra was very friendly with Kennedy. President Kennedy asked Sinatra what he was gonna do next, and Sinatra said, I want to do *The Manchurian Candidate*. And the president said, 'God, I love that book. Who's gonna play the mother?' " (Ironically, the actress cast as the fictional ex–Mrs. Shaw/current Mrs. Iselin was a real-life Mrs. Shaw—Mrs. *Peter* Shaw!)

The kudos Angela earned for playing this role were far-reaching. The story goes that veteran screen actress Mary Astor, who also had a home in Malibu, would frequently see Angela at the local grocery store. The two had never met. But after seeing the film, Astor approached Angela and told her, "I just want you to know that I think you gave one helluva performance."

Angela earned her third Best Supporting Actress Oscar nomination. Her rivals were Mary Badham *(To Kill a Mockingbird)*, Patty Duke *(The Miracle Worker)*, Shirley Knight *(Sweet Bird of Youth)* and Thelma Ritter *(Birdman of Alcatraz)*. Duke was the winner.

Despite some fine reviews—the *Variety* critic began his notice by observing, "Every once in a rare while a film comes along that 'works' in all departments, with story, production and performance so well blended that the end effect is one of nearly complete satisfaction"—*The Manchurian Candidate* was a box-office disappointment. The powers-that-be at United Artists did not recognize what they had in the film, and so it was not marketed shrewdly.

After the JFK assassination, the film was withdrawn from circulation. For a long time, it was common knowledge that Sinatra, who purportedly owned a piece of the film, was responsible. Angela, however, maintained that "nobody knows what really happened, whether it was United Artists or [producer] Howard Koch or a slip of bookkeeping." Whatever the reason for the film's unavailability, it nonetheless developed quite a reputation. "The movie went from failure to classic without passing through success," noted its screenwriter, George Axelrod.

During the spring of 1988—at the end of Angela's fourth season playing Jessica Fletcher on *Murder, She Wrote*—*The Manchurian Candidate* was reissued theatrically to promote its video release. The twenty-six-year-old film ended up earning raves, and box-office profits, and was as entertaining and riveting as any new film to hit movie screens that year.

Film journalist Peter Biskind called it "a wonderful piece of Cold War kitsch." Sol Louis Siegel described it as "one of the most emotionally disorienting movies ever made; other directors are still trying to match its split-second ability to turn shrieks of delight into gasps of horror." Peter Travers added, "And words are puny to describe Angela Lansbury's acting. . . . Lansbury creates a modern-age Lady Macbeth with the skill of a sorceress. It's an astonishing, engulfing performance." And from Roger Ebert: "The depths to which the Lansbury character will sink in this movie must be seen to be believed, and the actress generates a smothering 'momism' that defines the type." The performance served as a jolting reminder to those who only knew Angela from *Murder, She Wrote* that she was capable of brilliantly playing the most hissable villain.

In fact, of all the scoundrels Angela has played over the decades—and that includes the depraved Mrs. Lovett in *Sweeney Todd*—the character of Raymond Shaw's mother is the most odious. Nine years after the film's release, Angela was to describe her as "a woman so destroyed by evil [that] she appears to be disintegrating before your eyes."

"From an artistic point of view, I love these parts," she had explained years earlier. "You see, I lack guts in my own life. I lack fire and meanness—so I love playing it in screen roles. I am rather a sensitive person, and I think you have to be a sensitive person to play it nasty. It isn't true that you have to be one to play one. I have seen real bitches in Hollywood play soft, sentimental roles so beautifully I wept."

On another occasion, she discussed the manner in which she dealt with playing heavies. "I have my own approach, and it has to do with me—Angela—being a very sensitive person. I'm very, very sensitive to people giving me the cold shoulder, or telling me where to get off. And therefore I can imagine it so well that I can act it out. It can be so acutely hurtful to me that I know how to turn it around and do it to someone else."

11

Angela Can Whistle

When Angela was a young MGM contract player, a fan magazine interviewer asked her whether she preferred singing or dramatic roles. "I do prefer the straight dramatic type," Angela responded, "but I like to sing a song just for fun."

Little did she know that, two decades later, she would finally be allowed to display her vocal talents in a professional venue befitting her abilities. Angela would then be singing more than a song, and it would be more than just for fun. The end result would be the major show business stardom that had long eluded her.

In 1964, Angela appeared in her first Broadway musical, *Anyone Can Whistle*, which was to be a sojourn along the path to that stardom. The show, originally titled *The Natives Are Restless* and then *Sideshow*, also featured Harry Guardino, Gabriel Dell, and Lee Remick (with whom Angela had appeared in *The Long Hot Summer* and would later costar as mother and daughter in the made-for-television movie *The Gift of Love: A Christmas Story*). It was to to be a daunting experience.

To begin with, *Anyone Can Whistle* (which opened April 4 at the Majestic Theatre) earned mostly unfavorable reviews and closed after nine performances. (By coincidence, opening three days later at the Alvin Theater was *High Spirits*, a musical adaptation of Noël Coward's *Blithe Spirit*. The show featured Bea Lillie, whose comedy style had had such an impact on Angela when she was an unknown acting student.)

Whatever the quality of *Anyone Can Whistle*, its subject matter did not augur for an evening of escapism for Broadway audiences. This could be gleaned from the subhead above critic Howard Taubman's review of the show: "Musical at Majestic Is About Madness."

Anyone Can Whistle was a combination of fantasy and moralism. Its point was that society is innately corrupt, with the greatest promise for its redemption coming from within those whom society judges to be insane. These are the people who make others uneasy because of their attempts to lead individualistic lives.

The setting is a town in decay, lorded over by a glamorously powerful but crooked mayoress, Cora Hoover Hooper (Angela), and her henchmen. Other characters include a practical-minded but repressed nurse (Remick) and a free-spirited newcomer (Guardino), who is thought to be a doctor but actually is a potential patient in the town's mental institution, Dr. Detmold's Cookie Jar, "a sanitarium for the socially pressured." Along the way there is the marvel—which is actually a fake miracle, instigated by the mayoress and her cronies to bring tourists to the town—of having water mysteriously pour from a rock.

The creative powers behind the show, Arthur Laurents (who wrote the book and staged it) and Stephen Sondheim (who wrote the music and lyrics), were attempting to expand the boundaries of the musical theater via this potentially explosive and controversial subject matter. Indeed, they referred to the show as "a comedic attack on conformity," with Sondheim claiming it was the first musical to utilize "musical-comedy style for nontraditional subject matter."

But the bottom line was that *Anyone Can Whistle* was a decidedly uncommercial venture at a time when the hit Broadway musicals—*Funny Girl, Fiddler on the Roof, Oliver!, Hello, Dolly!*—were more traditional in their formats. But as Taubman observed, Laurents and Sondheim "have aimed for originality, and for that one respects them. Their trouble is that they have taken an idea with possibilities and have pounded it into a pulp."

Continued the critic, "If *Anyone Can Whistle* didn't know it was in difficulties, it should have listened to itself. It starts virtually in full cry and keeps shouting at the top of its voice most of the evening. The performers yell rather than talk and run rather than walk. This insistence on high pressure cannot cover up the sloppiness of the book and the lack of laughter in the lines. It works best when there is dancing."

Added Walter Kerr, "*Anyone Can Whistle* is an exasperating musical comedy. It is exasperating because it isn't very musical. . . . It is exasperating because it isn't very comical."

Additionally, Laurents and Sondheim cast performers who had no history of appearing in musicals. "I do think that what they were looking for, in that piece, were actors, which is clear from the casting," recalled Lee Remick. "They wanted actors. And it was, to be sure, the experience that put Steve on to the idea of not having actors singing ever again, because although Angela could sing it very well, I couldn't do it full justice at that time. And Harry Guardino couldn't sing, as well. We couldn't handle it or sustain it. Angela always could."

The first Angela heard of the show was when she received what she later would describe as a "lovely letter." It read, "Dear Miss Lansbury, My friend Stephen Sondheim and I have written a musical and we wondered if you had ever thought of appearing on the musical stage. Have you ever done any singing? Would you be interested in talking to us about it? Sincerely, Arthur Laurents." Angela felt the project was worth checking out, so she requested its script. "So I read it," she recalled, "and I really didn't know what to make of it. I thought it was nuts, crackers. But there was something about it that sort of appealed to me."

Laurents, Sondheim, and coproducer Kermit Bloomgarden came to Los Angeles to audition Angela. Beforehand, she was coached by Herbert Greene, the show's musical director and vocal arranger. Angela explained that Greene "had this extraordinary system of making anyone a singer by doing a curious thing of pressing his fingers on your throat, releasing the tension in the larynx, and then somehow you sang." For her audition, Angela performed "A Foggy Day in London Town." She was hired.

Anyone Can Whistle was in trouble even before it came to Broadway. Some of Laurents's ideas, which sounded great in his script, did not come off when produced onstage. During re-hearsals, he was forced to do major rewrites. Musical numbers were added, while others were dropped.

During the first performance on the road in Philadelphia, a fire broke out in the ladies' room, and smoke wafted throughout the theater. The following night, one of the actors overran the stage, landing in the orchestra pit. The only casualty—for the mo-ment—was a slightly dented instrument. But then the musician who played the instrument suffered a heart attack. He was carted off to the hospital, where he died. Just when the cast and crew thought nothing more could happen, one of the cast members, Henry Lascoe, also had a heart attack and died.

Aside from the growing belief that joining the *Anyone Can Whistle* company meant signing your own death warrant, there was the additional problem of mounting a musical with nonmusical performers. Throughout the entire rehearsal period, out-of-town tryout, and even into the New York run, Lee Remick suffered from tonsillitis; she had her tonsils removed several weeks after the show closed. Harry Guardino also experienced problems in lend-ing his voice to the musical stage; eventually, he talked his songs.

Despite Remick's and Guardino's lack of musical experience, it was Angela who became the scapegoat for the show's problems. "They were going to fire Angela in Philadelphia because the whole show didn't work," recalled theatrical agent Charles Adams Baker, who added, "They said, 'Oh, Angela's a movie star; she can't do this.' And she was superb—but they were going to fire her!"

Angela herself was considering quitting the show because she and Laurents differed over his approach to directing and their conceptions of her character. She wanted to explore Cora's vul-nerability, while he was more interested in her playing the role as an outright villainess: a reincarnation of Raymond Shaw's mother, the role she had played two years earlier in *The Manchurian Candidate*. Angela was also bothered by what she perceived as Sondheim's inability to make decisions. Reportedly, Nancy Walker had already been invited to replace her.

Continued Baker, "I took Peter Glenville down because he was a client of mine and a friend of Angela's, and I said, 'Somebody has got to pull some weight around here.' We all went and had drinks after the matinee, and Peter, who is terribly authoritative and very Oxonian, told them, 'You have discovered the newest musical-comedy queen!' And they said, 'You mean Lee Remick?' 'No,' he said, 'Angela Lansbury.' "

Angela did earn some good notices for her work in *Anyone Can Whistle*. Howard Taubman wrote, "Angela Lansbury as the Mayoress appears with four volatile, tap-dancing pages, and there is promise of life in the decrepit town. But Miss Lansbury doesn't get around to waking the town and the show until the third act." Richard Watts Jr. remarked, "Angela Lansbury is vigorous and bouncing as the grasping lady mayor, and, if I am not otherwise certain about her performance, it is because I was never sure what the role was supposed to be." Walter Kerr described her as "a creature who can toss her head, her arms, and her shapely legs until the sparkle from her bracelets and the sparkle from her earrings seem one and the same sparkle."

Musically, *Anyone Can Whistle* was ahead of its time. And many things ahead of their time are met with resistance. Back in 1964, success for a Broadway musical meant the audience had to leave the theater humming the score. Plus, individual songs had to catch on with the public to the extent that they would become immediate standards and be recorded by the popular singers of the day. Such was not the case with *Anyone Can Whistle*.

Observed John Chapman, "This book and the lack of a melody I could whistle impeded my enjoyment of the last two acts, which didn't quite fulfill the high promise of the joyously daffy first act." Recalled Herbert Greene, "I thought the music was grubby and ugly, so I designed an orchestra that was so unusual that it would make the music sound as though there was something really going on. There were, I think, six cellos, four horns, five clarinets, three percussion, and six brass—whatever the hell, I forget now, but it *forced* us to orchestrate in an innovative way. The music was less interesting than it sounded; now it's considered a kind of classic."

Despite Greene's seeming to take credit for Sondheim's innovations, the score does contain classic Sondheim elements that would be utilized in his subsequent work. Norman Nadel, one of the few critics who liked the show, wrote, "Sondheim's music and lyrics deserve an entire review in themselves. . . . His overture is shaped of intriguing mild dissonances, with scant, pleasantly tantalizing fragments of theme started in short, irregular phrases. . . . The blending of lyrics, melody, dance rhythms and orchestral texture is remarkable; the lyrics are more clever than the spoken dialogue."

Despite the failure of *Anyone Can Whistle*, Angela had at least proved to herself that she could handle a musical role onstage. She sang with a clear and consistently strong voice, and had the show become a hit, it would certainly have established her as a musical force. Unfortunately, well-reviewed performances in flops are quickly forgotten, or—as happened in this situation—they become legends and are remembered years later in late-night conversations among theater buffs.

Upon the closing of *Anyone Can Whistle*, Angela became, as she explained, "desperately unhappy for quite a long period of time. We poured our hearts and souls into it, and here my forward motion came to a halt." She added, "I'd proven myself to producers. I could sing. The show had enhanced my musical talents. I was ready to go to battle again."

12

Open a New Window

Before she opened in *Mame*, Angela explained, "I always fancied I had a sexy singing voice, but no one would ever let me use it. When *Whistle* was offered to me, I grabbed it. It was a magnificent failure, but if it hadn't been for *Whistle*, I wouldn't be playing *Mame*."

Twenty years later, Angela explained of her pre-*Mame* career, "All those years I had this vision that someday I'd blossom forth, that I'd show everybody what I was really capable of. I could see myself singing, dancing, carrying on, being the life of the party, hogging the limelight—the works. Nobody knew—not even my family. But *I* knew."

The show was based on *Auntie Mame*, by Patrick Dennis, which had previously been a bestselling novel, a play, and a film. The musicalized *Mame* featured a book by Jerome Lawrence and Robert E. Lee, with music and lyrics by Jerry Herman (whose previous smash hit—*Hello, Dolly!*—was simultaneously playing on Broadway). It opened at the Winter Garden on May 24, 1966. It was to be among the most momentous dates in Angela's life.

Unlike *Anyone Can Whistle*, *Mame* did not try to be innovative, but was simply good old-fashioned entertainment.

The show's book is in many ways faithful to the original. Why change a story that had proven successful with millions of readers and viewers? The first scene begins during the Roaring Twenties. The heroine is lovably unconventional, irrepressible Mame Dennis, an upper-crust Manhattanite described by Angela as "a wise woman, a teacher . . . she's capricious but honest. She's a realist."

Mame's orphaned nephew, Patrick, comes to live with her in her swanky Beekman Place apartment. Against the wishes of the stuffy banker whose job is to look after Patrick's interests, Mame enrolls him in an avant-garde school. She eventually loses her fortune in the stock market crash and weds Beauregard Jackson Picket Burnside, a wealthy Southern aristocrat. After his death, she returns to New York only to find that college student Patrick has grown up to become a snob. He is engaged to wed Gloria Upson, an airhead of a debutante whose parents are vile racists. Some shrewd manipulation on Mame's part ends Patrick's engagement and gets him back in touch with his childhood values. He ends up marrying Pegeen, a likable interior decorator, and at the finale Mame is set to take Patrick and Pegeen's young son on a trip around the world—bringing the plot full circle.

In order to ensure success, the show's producers, Robert Fryer, Lawrence "Jimmy" Carr, and Sylvia and Joseph Harris, wanted to cast one of the Broadway musical's leading lights in the pivotal title role. Before rehearsals began, reports circulated regarding the possible *Mame* stars. The logical first choice was Rosalind Russell, who had played the non-musical Mame on stage and screen and previously had starred in the Broadway musical comedy hit *Wonderful Town*. Russell, however, declined. "I don't like to eat last week's stew," she declared, telling the show's producers, "It's not for me anymore. I've done it, I have to move along."

The legendary Mary Martin was choice number two. Producer Fryer flew off to Martin's home in Brazil to pitch the part to her. She accepted and was announced as the show's lead. However, she soon backed out, allegedly having second thoughts about playing a role so closely associated with another star. Ethel Merman was asked, and she too would have made an excellent Mame Dennis. But she refused because she did not wish to make the long-term commitment necessary for a hit Broadway show.

Next, a who's who of performers either were considered or politicked for the role. The process could be likened to the casting of Scarlett O'Hara in *Gone With the Wind*. The list of potential Mames was lengthy: Eve Arden; Patrice Munsel; Bette Davis; Katharine Hepburn; Greer Garson; Lauren Bacall; Susan Hayward; Arlene Francis; Tammy Grimes; Constance Bennett; Ann Sothern; Doris Day; Ginger Rogers; Olivia de Havilland; Lucille Ball; Irene Dunne; Beatrice Lillie; Julie Harris; Margaret Leighton; Elaine Stritch; Lena Horne; Jane Morgan; Geraldine Page; Dinah Shore; Maggie Smith; Georgia Brown; Kitty Carlisle; Nanette Fabray; Gisele MacKenzie; Simone Signoret; Dolores Gray; Janet Gaynor; Phyllis Diller; Lisa Kirk; Barbara Cook; Kaye Ballard; Judy Garland ... John Hallowell asserted in *Life* magazine, in a profile of Angela accompanying a photo spread on the show, "Not even Damon Runyon at his improbable best could have invented a Broadway gambler crazy enough to lay money that the winner ... would turn out to be that perennial also-ran, Angela Lansbury."

It was summer, 1965. Angela was approaching her fortieth birthday. While considered a solid and reliable performer, she had never, ever been top-billed in a movie or onstage. But she knew she would be a great Mame. Upon news of Martin's leaving the show, she approached Jerome Lawrence, an old pal with a house close to hers and Peter's in Malibu. This cautious first step led to Angela's flying to New York to convince Jerry Herman that she was perfect for the part. While sitting around and conversing in Herman's Greenwich Village apartment, it dawned on the composer that before him was the new Mame Dennis. "Suddenly, just listening to her make small talk, it was *boom*, she had me," Herman explained. "I loved her: she *was* Mame. She had her shoes off, and she was like dancing around the room, and I was at the piano teaching her two songs from *Mame* that none of the other ladies had even heard." If Herman had any reservations about Angela, it didn't hurt that he fondly recalled her performance in *Anyone Can Whistle*.

Angela agreed to audition for the part, which many other established stars would shun as being beneath them. The following day, she performed for Joshua Logan, who was set to direct the show, and other behind-the-scenes powers. "Out there in the house sat all these important figures," Angela said. "At least I had Jerry Herman at the piano. And the two songs he'd taught me. So I sang. In the middle Mr. Logan said, 'I can't see your face.' " Angela ceased singing, with a look of horror spreading across her face. "Mr. Logan asked somebody with the work light to mask it with a script," she continued, "and point it right at me. It was a damn good thing I was used to movies, with all those lights in my face. I started again. Mr. Logan stopped me. 'I still can't see you.' So up they all come onstage right up for a good close *look*, for God's sake. It was summer, all very hot, and they were holding raincoats and wearing dark glasses—a regular lineup. I did the songs again. Then they said, 'Goodbye,' 'Thank you.' That was all."

Dejected, Angela flew back to Hollywood. Rumors still swirled over who would be cast. "When it seemed that they had turned her down," recalled Hurd Hatfield, "she would plant some more roses." Added Angela, "I went out and bought six red rose-bushes and planted them. I don't cover my disappointments. You can't do that—I just clear them out." But she still hoped that somehow the role would be hers, and her heart would pound at each ring of the telephone. "There we'd be, scared together, for bloomin' months, [with fourteen-year-old son] Anthony coming in with surfboards and sand and dogs and cats and me by that god-damn phone."

The problem, it seemed, was that Logan had balked at her casting. Angela explained, "But, as it turned out, the writers and composer weren't really getting along with Josh Logan, and they brought in another director, Gene Saks, and again I auditioned." To do so, Angela returned to New York.

Angela felt her audition went well. Saks, however, was cordial but noncommittal. So what was the problem? Angela felt that the time had finally come for her to be chosen or be gone. "So in the morning, I said, 'Right, this is it,' " she recalled. "I told the pro-ducers, 'I am going back to California and unless you tell me—let's face it, I have prostrated myself—*now*, yes or no, that's the end of it.

"That very afternoon Jimmy Carr came to my hotel and said,

'We are offering you *Mame*. It's official.' " The date was November 19, 1965. As Jerry Herman explained, all of the show's decision-makers had agreed to cast "a new lady, a fresh lady."

Angela was exhilarated as she flew back to California. Finally, at the age of forty, when other actresses were making the transition from lead to secondary roles, she had reversed the pattern to become the star of the show. Angela's contract stipulated that she play Mame Dennis for a minimum of two years, or more than eight hundred performances.

To prepare for the rigors of playing Mame Dennis, as well as to acquire the character's sleek physique, Angela undertook a strenuous routine of exercise and diet. The photos published in *Life* show a svelte Angela looking as if she had just got off a StairMaster. Sporting a boyish bob hairdo, she dominates every photograph as she leads chorus lines of singer-dancers, performs with her supporting cast, and (in a nice touch for the character) clings to a paper moon. Finally, she is depicted alone, sitting on a chair, "vamping, turbaned and swaddled in about a dozen little foxes." And there she is on the magazine's cover, beside the headline "Auntie Mame's Newest Exploit a Musical Smash" and caption "Flicking her stogie, ANGELA LANSBURY whoops it up as Mame."

Indeed, in *Mame* Angela was onstage for almost the entire show. She had ample opportunity to demonstrate her abilities as a dramatic actress, comedienne, singer, and dancer (doing a Charleston, a tango, and a cakewalk). One reporter even noted that she "moves with the coordinated feminine looseness of a conditioned dancer." Observed the actress Cathleen Nesbitt, "Angela is the only star I have ever seen who could dance as well as the best dancer in the chorus—and if you have seen the average musical-comedy star just 'getting away with it' in front of the chorus line, you will appreciate what fantastic work that must have meant."

During the run of *Mame*, Angela tore a tendon while dancing. But there was no way she was going to rest. She missed only two performances. When she came back, her dance steps were adjusted and she took cortisone for the injury. Later, as she was about to leave the show, she declared, "I've stayed in training like an athlete. Playing Mame is like being a track star. People out front have no idea of the endurance you need, just as I had no idea of what happens to the star of a smash Broadway musical. No one could have told me."

Several years later, Angela explained that "to me energy is the key to youthfulness. It's when one's tired, when one doesn't continue to generate that sort of force and energy—that's when one's old. The actor's job is to rev himself up at a given time of the evening to suddenly take on a whole new life force, a whole new set of physical characteristics, and it takes energy to do this."

Additionally, in any previous role in any medium, Angela had never really been afforded the opportunity to be out-and-out glamorous. One simply could not consider her role in, say, *Samson and Delilah* as the epitome of elegance.

"Hell, I want all the glamour there is," she told *Life*. "I've been starving for it for years!" In *Mame*, Angela ran through twenty-plus costume changes, in which she enthralled audiences by donning costume designer Robert MacKintosh's striking outfits. For her entrance, she wore yellow evening pajamas striped with gold paillettes; at the curtain call, she was garbed in an extravagant white gown, banded with white mink that surged out from the slick bodice into a train. Walter Kerr observed that Angela "looks as though Augustus John were being kept backstage to paint her in fresh oils for each entrance." Despite her being bedecked in such attire, Angela kept in mind her primary role onstage. "The real trick," she recalled, "is to come on again in a stunning dress and not get a round of applause but get on with the scene, at least as far as I'm concerned."

Angela added, "I worked at it very hard and made [Mame] a graceful and intelligent woman. She was a bit of an ass on occasions—she made some rather funny mistakes with her nephew, but she did it with a sense of realism. I played it in total belief that what I was doing was not funny at all. Well—it worked. . . . I didn't take any theatrical license. I didn't play to the audience. I didn't do any of the things one associates with musical comedy actresses. I don't care whether a show has music or is a straight drama—to me it's all theater."

Despite being surrounded by talented actors in choice supporting roles—notably Bea Arthur as Mame's "bosom buddy," the actress Vera Charles; Frankie Michaels as young Patrick; and Jane Connell as Mame's employee, the goofy, spinsterish Agnes Gooch—*Mame* was Angela's show. She delighted audiences performing Jerry Herman's tuneful songs—"We Need a Little Christmas" (which Mame performs with young Patrick, Agnes, and Ito, Mame's butler); "My Best Girl" (a duet with Patrick); "Bosom Buddies" (a duet with Vera); "If He Walked Into My Life" (a solo, in which she speculates if she is the cause of the grown-up Patrick's blunders); and "Open a New Window" (performed while Mame and Patrick walked to the top of a beautiful staircase, at which point the scenery was stripped away and the characters were carried into the next scene).

Recalled Angela, "When Jerry Herman heard me sing 'Open a New Window,' he said to me, 'Angela, from now on you may call yourself a singer.' . . . He couldn't have helped more if he gave me one of those Oscars I've always just missed."

If Kay Thompson, Roger Edens, and Arthur Freed could see her now!

Mame played in Philadelphia and Boston before opening to raves at the Winter Garden Theatre. The opening-night performance was capped by a standing ovation, and an enormous—and well-earned—bouquet of roses. Wrote columnist Earl Wilson, "It was the biggest, maddest, wildest evening at the refurbished Winter Garden." The performance was followed by a party at the Rainbow Room atop the RCA Building. At the celebration, Angela told an interviewer, "It's impossible to sum up the work of many years. . . . Can you imagine how I feel? . . . I just want to know Broadway audiences. I just want to share with them what I feel onstage. . . . I was a closet dancer. I sang and danced but nobody ever knew it. . . . I finally came out of the closet."

"This star vehicle deserves its star, and vice is very much versa," declared critic Stanley Kauffmann. "No one can be surprised to learn that Angela Lansbury is an accomplished actress, but not all of us may know that she has an adequate singing voice, can dance trimly, and can combine all these matters into musical *performance*. In short, Miss Lansbury is a singing-dancing actress, not a singer or dancer who also acts. (Somewhat surprisingly, there is even more character color in her singing than in her spoken dialogue.) In this marathon role she has wit, poise, warmth."

Kauffmann concluded his review by noting that "*Mame* does its job well with plenty of effective theatrical sentiment, laughs and vitality.

"And with Miss Lansbury."

Wrote Norman Nadel, "In charm, in poise and certainly in vitality, Angela Lansbury is the match of any previous Mame. . . . Though she is not a singer in the grand sense, she can project a song with accuracy, appeal and an infinite warmth of personality. Also, Miss Lansbury is inherently a lady, just as some famous women of the theater inherently are not. She can—and does—jitterbug without upsetting that delicately balanced quality of feminine gentility. I don't mean that she lacks the hellfire essential to Mame, but whereas it might blaze in others, it glows in her."

Added Walter Kerr, "*Mame* isn't a trailblazing musical, any more than Miss Lansbury is a powerhouse personality. But we knew both of these things before we went into the Winter Garden. What is looked for in retracing such familiar material is simply a substantial and professional friendliness, and what we want from Miss Lansbury is her own quality, which is that of the fastest girl in high school who also turned out to be nice. We get it."

It was not without irony that Rex Reed declared that Angela brought "the Broadway stage about as close to an MGM musical as the Broadway stage is likely to get."

Not all critics were lavish in their praise. Wrote Douglas Watt, "Miss Lansbury has her qualities—grace, charm, hoydenish good looks, a haystack hairdo and, primarily, cheer—but she is not constituted to take over an entire show and that is what she has been asked to do."

But Angela was to prove him and other naysayers wrong. She was up to the task of playing Mame; certainly, her becoming Broadway's newest luminary meant hard, grueling work. Reported Rosalind Russell, in her autobiography, Angela "worked like a dog, and I've heard she was fine. I believe it, she's a good actress."

"I'll have a glass of burgundy . . . for blood," Angela told a reporter interviewing her in her Hotel Dorset suite before the show's premiere. "I need blood for all this hyperactivity. I don't know where Auntie Mame gets her go-go. It's exhausting. I'm on a real food kick, tea with honey, gelatin and asparagus tips . . . and steak. I survived the London blitz, just the beginning. Quite possibly I can survive this."

Soon after the opening, Angela candidly admitted, "I don't know how successful I really am. But *Mame* is a smash and people keep saying, 'You're the toast of Broadway now.' It worries me a little. They will expect me to change. They tell me, 'You should dress like Mame and get around like her.' Rosalind Russell does. She always looks every inch the great star she is. But I cannot do it."

She added, "Don't misunderstand me, I love what I'm doing. I love Mame. I wouldn't have known what to do with all this twenty years ago. But now I feel as though everyone in New York is my friend."

If that last sentiment was a generalization, the Tony Award voters considered Angela much more than a friend (or, in the spirit of *Mame*, bosom buddy). She was nominated for her first Tony as Best Actress in a Musical. Her competition was tough: Barbara Harris *(On a Clear Day You Can See Forever)*, Julie Harris *(Skyscraper)*, and especially Gwen Verdon *(Sweet Charity)*.

Less than a month after *Mame* opened, Angela found herself in the Tony Award winner's circle; her victory prevented Verdon (who had already won three awards, for *Can-Can, Damn Yankees,* and *New Girl in Town*) from becoming the all-time winner. Also victorious were Frankie Michaels (Best Featured Actor in a Musical) and Bea Arthur (Best Featured Actress in a Musical). However, *Man of La Mancha* bested *Mame* as Best Musical.

A little over two decades earlier, a starry-eyed teenager named Angela Lansbury would stand in front of Sardi's and dream her youthful dreams of fame as an entertainer. Now, the management of that fabled theatrical eatery had moved her portrait, an Al Hirschfeld drawing from her *A Taste of Honey* days, from an inside wall to a far more prominent place near the door.

And Angela had to become accustomed to passersby referring to her as Mame as often as they would call her by her given name. "Suddenly, after years of beating her brains out," observed husband Peter, "Angie's really a star."

"It was like everything you've ever read about—the front table at Sardi's, like living on another planet," Angela later recalled of her stint as the star of *Mame*. "Everyone loves you, everyone loves the success and enjoys it as much as you do. And it lasts as long as you are on that stage and as long as you keep coming out of that stage door. I know I am Mame forever to a lot of people. I'm part of their furniture. They say, 'That was really it, girl. You really had it then.' They don't want you to do anything else and burst that bubble."

During the run of the show, Angela was determined not to forsake other media, and to show audiences across the nation what New Yorkers were coming to know. In November 1966, she guested on Perry Como's Thanksgiving television special; two years earlier, she had appeared on Como's Christmas program. The *Variety* critic captured the essence of Angela's changed status in show business when he wrote, "Miss Lansbury delivered the song-and-dance stuff with an ease and charm that might have surprised some, her filmic forte having been in the drama groove."

Angela also appeared as a "mystery guest" in a special feature of the TV game show *What's My Line* in which the show's panelists donned masks and attempted to guess the identity of a celebrity guest. She signed in as "Angela 'Mame' Lansbury." She was wearing a shimmery striped dress and large, jeweled dangle earrings; as she walked onto the stage, someone in the audience yelled, "Wow!" To fool the panelists, Angela faked a high-pitched baby voice, similar to a low-class British Betty Boop. In trying to determine her identity, panelist Bennett Cerf asked, "When you appear in pictures, is it your wont to raise your lovely voice in song?" Tellingly, Angela answered with a terse "No." Soon, Pia Lindstrom—the daughter of Ingrid Bergman—identified her.

Cerf asked Angela to "sing a line of 'Mame'," to advertise the show. Angela responded, "If I'm allowed to, I'll sing the whole first act." Cerf countered, "Just the first line of 'Mame' "—meaning what had come to be the show's anthem, its potent title song, which closed the first act. A confused Angela said, "The first line . . . eh." Cerf responded, "She doesn't know it!" After additional moments of confusion, Angela finally sang the line and quickly added, "You see, I don't sing it so I don't know the words."

This awkward interlude was redeemed when Angela reminded Lindstrom that she had met her on the set of *Gaslight*, when Lindstrom was "a little, tiny girl," and host John Daly informed the audience of Angela's three Academy Award nominations and the fact that she was taking one of her rare nights off to appear on *What's My Line* to appeal for public contributions to the Muscular Dystrophy Association of America.

At the televised 1968 Academy Awards ceremony, Angela was the focal point of the *Thoroughly Modern Millie* production number, backed by the Ronald Field Dancers. She brought down the house as she was lowered from the ceiling inside a large birdcage. For once, Angela was playing to an audience of her peers. But she was no longer Angela Lansbury, supporting actress struggling to win roles; she now was Angela Lansbury, glamorous Broadway star. Whether it was a fleeting stardom or not, Angela was loving the opportunity to return to Hollywood under such enviable circumstances.

"Even Joan Crawford cheered," began a *Los Angeles Times* article describing the event. This somewhat catty remark referred to the actress, then sixty-eight years old, who over two decades earlier had briefly dated Peter Shaw.

"We'd all grown up together," Angela remembered of that special Oscar-night audience, "and there they were, and there I was." Three years later, she was to tell TV talk-show host David Frost that this was the most exciting audience for whom she had ever played.

Angela and former brother-in-law Peter Ustinov cohosted the 1968 Tony Awards. That evening, public recognition came from Jack Benny, who declared that she "has always been one of our finest actresses." Angela looked smashing in shimmering teardrop earrings and a pastel blue satin sheath covered in chiffon, and her bright eyes and charm were a perfect match for Ustinov's droll wit. Angela was not exaggerating when she introduced Jerry Herman as "very dear to me" and "my talented and very dear friend." The following year, she returned to the Tonys to present a special award to her *Reluctant Debutante* costar, Rex Harrison.

In February 1973, Angela was a guest on television's *The Julie Andrews Hour;* the pair saluted great ladies of show business, including Mae West, Sophie Tucker, Ethel Merman, Judy Garland, Carmen Miranda, Eleanor Powell, Helen Morgan, and the Dolly Sisters. A month later, Angela opened the forty-fifth Academy Awards as the centerpiece of an elaborate, Las Vegas–style production number saluting moviemaking. The routine ended with Angela alone onstage, singing, "Make a little magic. That's what it's all about."

Over the years, Angela was to make frequent Tony Award show appearances. Of her hosting chores in 1987, television critic Kay Gardella wrote, "The real winner at Sunday night's Tony Awards was Angela Lansbury. Slimmed down to perfection and decked out in a stunning Bob Mackie gown, the star of CBS's *Murder, She Wrote* stole the show."

Angela played Mame through August 1967, when she took a two-week vacation and was replaced by Celeste Holm (who was to go on to play Mame in the road company). In March 1968, while closing out her Broadway stay in *Mame,* Angela was honored by Harvard University's Hasty Pudding Club as its Woman of the Year. Angela's contract terminated at the end of the show's second season, at which point the coveted role went to Janis Paige (who was in turn replaced by Sheila Smith, Jane Morgan, and Ann Miller).

Angela must have been thrilled when, in June, she opened in *Mame* at the Los Angeles Music Center. She had just completed a seven-week run in San Francisco and was to appear in Los Angeles for a similar length of time.

During the San Francisco run, Herb Caen, that city's longtime connoisseur of taste, observed, "In a more romantic era, [Angela] would have been thrown into a carriage by ardent young men after her opening night and hauled around town, à la Sarah Bernhardt and Adelina Patti." Nonetheless, her performance in Los Angeles was to be an even greater triumph. On her opening night, an audience of 3,243—just about twice as large as the capacity of the most spacious Broadway theater—stood up upon the finale and gave her what was reported to be a twenty-minute ovation. In fact, James Doolittle, director of the city's Greek and Huntington Hartford theaters, dubbed Angela's show nothing less than "the most exciting opening in the history of theater in Los Angeles. There was an electricity I've never felt before."

Upon the Broadway bow of *Mame*, Norman Nadel predicted, "It probably will run longer on Broadway than *Auntie Mame*, which lasted for 637 performances." He was correct. *Mame* lit up Broadway for 1,508 performances, closing in January 1970.

During her run as Mame Dennis, Angela Lansbury, New Star, was finally able to describe herself as "the most fulfilled person you've met in many long years."

As her time as Mame Dennis was nearing its close, she exclaimed, "I think of it all as a beautiful dream. . . . I probably have sung 'Open a New Window, Open a New Door' over eight hundred times, and yet with every audience I feel I am communicating, telling them something I want them to know. Mame does people so much good. She always has a new horizon, and she wants to give the greatest gift, love of life and living." Several years later, she recalled that playing Mame was "like a marathon race that never stopped. The marvelous thing was that—except for getting a little bit bored and tired by the prospect of doing it each night—while I was actually onstage, I generated so much energy I was never tired. . . . When you know the audience adores you if you lift your little finger, you're going to he happy as a lark out there doing it."

Mame would have been a perfect vehicle for Angela when it was brought to the screen in 1974. Four years earlier, Warner Bros.–Seven Arts purchased its screen rights for $3.5 million— then the second-highest amount paid for a movie property, after the $5 million the same studio shelled out for *My Fair Lady*. Upon the purchase, word was out that Elizabeth Taylor—between tense separations and passionate reconciliations with Richard Burton—

was interested in making her musical debut as Mame Dennis; she was allegedly disappointed at not having been signed to star in the screen version of *Hello, Dolly!* "Well," observed Robert E. Lee, "if they put a lot of dancers in front of Miss Taylor and then she emerges momentarily, they might just squeak by—but I seriously doubt it. It would bear no resemblance to any book by Patrick Dennis or the musical we wrote." Liz did not get the role.

Angela was given a fifty-fifty shot at winning the part. An unidentified industry figure was quoted as declaring that Angela had "sort of infected us with herself; she's a comeback girl, particularly after [the Los Angeles] opening night. They like her fighting." John Frankenheimer, who had directed Angela on-screen in *All Fall Down* and *The Manchurian Candidate*, was more to the point: "It will be *ludicrous* if they don't put her in the movie *Mame*." Added Lee, "We sold *Mame*, we don't have a say, but *of course* Angela is our first choice—she's *inside* the character. . . . Angela *is* Mame."

Bea Arthur and Jane Connell were signed to re-create their respective roles as Vera Charles and Agnes Gooch. But Lucille Ball—one of the names originally bandied about when the show was first being cast—was hired to star. Ironically, in his column following Angela's 1966 opening-night triumph, Earl Wilson pointed out, "There were those who thought that Lucille Ball should play [Mame]. But Herman preferred somebody less comedic."

With regularity over the years, Broadway actors who are not major movie stars have not been cast on-screen in roles they played to great acclaim on the stage. On occasion, a more gracious movie name would back out of such assignments. Robert Preston seemed inseparable from his stage character of Harold Hill in *The Music Man*. But when it came time for Warner Bros. to cast the role, they turned to Cary Grant.

Grant had seen the show several times on Broadway, was fond of the role, and would have loved to play it. But Grant respected the validity of Preston re-creating the part. His reported response was that if the studio did not award the role to the man who could play it best—Robert Preston—he would not even bother to see the film when it was released. Preston ended up starring as Harold Hill on-screen.

Lucille Ball had a longtime desire to play Mame, and she had no intention of allowing the role to be given away to Angela or anyone else. The powers at Warner felt that, unlike Angela, Ball was a known box-office commodity; her most recent film, the 1968 family comedy *Yours, Mine and Ours*, in which she starred with Henry Fonda, had been a surprise hit with audiences. Additionally, Ball felt that starring in such a prestigious property as *Mame* would position her to continue her movie career once she ended her long-running TV series *Here's Lucy*.

So despite the acclaim Angela had earned playing Mame Dennis onstage, it was just as if she were back at MGM, losing coveted parts to Ava Gardner or Lana Turner. In fact, even after Ball was injured in a skiing accident, delaying the project for a year, no request was made for Angela to come in as replacement. However, Ball's mishap did result in Gene Saks replacing the original director, George Cukor, who had gone on to make *Travels With My Aunt*—by coincidence, a project in which he briefly considered casting Angela.

Ball had supposedly craved the role of Mame ever since she had seen Rosalind Russell in the 1958 screen version. In Mame Dennis, she perceived a comic character as memorable as Lucy Ricardo. Public declarations had been made regarding Angela's playing *Mame* on-screen. In 1968, she signed a two-year contract to appear in another Broadway musical, *Dear World*. "I'm sure something could be worked out," Angela noted, if the movie were to go into production with *Dear World* still on the boards. A December 1969 Joyce Haber "Hollywood" column was even headlined, "Mame's [Angela] Ready If Warner Is."

In a move atypical to the Lucy that we love, Ball gave a self-serving quote to the press, claiming that Angela did not want to do the movie version of *Mame* because she had become weary of playing the character. "Actually, I didn't want to [play Mame Dennis]," Lucy said. "Besides, I had broken my leg in a ski accident and felt apprehensive about fulfilling my commitment. The only reason I went through with it was that I felt obligated after having given my word to the producer. Now I'm thrilled to have done it." Ball added, "I put myself down and tried to talk them [producers Robert Fryer and James Cresson] into signing Angela Lansbury for the title role. But Angela would have nothing to do with it. I guess she had her fill of the part. Besides, she was in Ireland taking care of her son."

"I honestly don't know where Lucy ever got such an idea," Angela remarked. It so happened that, during the summer of 1972, as *Mame* was being filmed on the West Coast, Angela was back East touring the show on the "Music Fair" circuit.

"I wanted to make the film of *Mame* in the worst way," she continued. "But I was, quite simply, never asked. By the way, did anyone ask Julie Andrews to do *My Fair Lady*?"

Andrews (as Robert Preston in *The Music Man* and Angela in *Mame*) had expertly played a beloved stage role: Eliza Doolittle. When it came time for the screen version, the actress had as yet never appeared on-screen. As a result, the powers at (yet again) Warner Bros. felt it best to cast a known screen commodity: Audrey Hepburn. Hepburn gave a delightful performance as Eliza, but her singing voice was dubbed by Marni Nixon. Sentiment against her casting was one of the reasons she did not earn a 1964 Best Actress Academy Award nomination for her performance. Her costar, Rex Harrison, who had played Henry Higgins on the stage, not only won a nomination but walked home with the statue.

The year's Best Actress Oscar winner was none other than Julie Andrews, for her debut performance in *Mary Poppins*.

Logically, why would a performer be disinterested in re-creating on celluloid the role that brought her stardom onstage? It simply makes no sense that Angela would not have wanted to play Mame in the movies, even if she had already performed the role a thousand times—which she actually had!

Ever the diplomat, Angela explained, "As for Lucille Ball, I think she made those remarks out of a mistaken sense of kindness. She came to see me twice at the Winter Garden, and I know this woman was sincere in the things she said to me. She really dug the part and loved my performance.

"Look, I think she was in a position to be offered the part, and I think she ran with the ball, no pun. I don't blame Lucy a bit. I'd have done the same thing. And she's got Bea Arthur, one of the most skillful funny women who ever tottered on two feet. I had her for almost two years with me, and Jane Connell as Gooch.

"But when I see those billboards and Lucy with that cigarette holder clenched between her teeth, I must admit I do wince. I think she plays Auntie Mame. I played Mame Dennis. Of course we are totally different, and so are our approaches to Mame. I like to think I have a little more warmth. But I have no doubt it will be a success, and people who haven't been out in years will leave their TV sets to see Lucy in the movies."

At another juncture, Angela observed, regarding Lucille Ball's casting, "They felt they needed a big name. They didn't trust my name to carry it. It was one of my bitterest disappointments. I never saw the movie; what I did was keep working like crazy. Listen, my dear, I have paid my dues."

There also were reports of Ball feuding with Beatrice Arthur during the filming. "I'm not going to say a lot of things I guess people want me to say," Arthur told columnist Earl Wilson. "It was lovely working with Angela and it was lovely and trying working with Lucy." She added, "Lucille is a very determined lady. She wanted me for the movie. She kept saying, 'I'll go to Bill Paley.' [Paley was in charge at CBS, where Arthur was starring in the hit TV series *Maude*.] She said, 'I won't do it without Bea.' She wants to work with professionals. We came on the set one day and she said, 'Where's your nail polish?' I said, 'I don't think my character would wear nail polish.' She thinks I goofed in not wearing nail polish, but she had enough respect for me to let me not wear nail polish."

Ball, meanwhile, complained that Arthur was "a difficult lady to talk to, and I'm not about to stretch myself for her. She's having a hard enough time adjusting. She's used to doing her work without having to account for anything. If you start a deep conversation with her, she'll fall asleep on you!"

Ball exercised damage control with regard to a claim that she had attempted to have Arthur fired. "Radie Harris started that story in her column in the *Hollywood Reporter,* just to attract attention," Ball claimed. "I *chose* Bea before I had a director or anything. I had seen Bea as Vera Charles in Angela Lansbury's company, and she was the greatest Vera Charles in the world. We wrapped the whole production around Bea Arthur."

When Angela first learned that she was being passed over, she tried to rationalize away her disappointment. In a June 1970 interview, Angela noted, "A lot of people are upset I'm not doing the film of *Mame*. I can only say I'm very relieved. The night I left the show, a lady in the orchestra I liked very much told me, 'Don't let them eat you up. Be yourself.' At the time I thought, 'Who's them?' and now I know. 'Them' are the people who want me to be Mame, to be all of the time what I was for two hours onstage each night: a little pocket of happiness. However, there are several realities, and one must live with them. One reality is that I am not *Mame* and I'm living with it and so must other people, the people who can only take from you. It's really rather difficult to explain."

Angela knew quite well what it was like to be typecast; for years, she had been playing variations on the role of the shrew, or the bitchy mom. Perhaps when she made this statement, she somehow feared being typecast as Mame Dennis. However, one cannot imagine that had she been asked, Angela would for a moment have turned down the screen version of *Mame*. She admitted as much in 1979: "You bet it was a disappointment. At the time I was terribly careful not to let it hurt me too much. I forced myself to take it lightly. But looking back, I do honestly believe if I had done it, we could have made it one super movie."

One can only speculate what might have happened if Angela had indeed played Mame on-screen. Would she finally have become a full-fledged movie star? Would she have won her first Oscar after three unsuccessful nominations? Whatever the case, it truly is a shame that she did not star in the movie. For one thing, it would have been nice to have a public record of her *Mame* performance. For another, without Angela the film ended up a critical and box-office disaster.

Even if Lucille Ball had not campaigned to play Mame Dennis on-screen, an actress other than Angela might have been cast. Judy Garland biographer Al DiOrio wrote, "Until her death (in 1969), there were many rumors that she was the actress wanted most for the motion picture version (which, of course, has now been filmed starring Judy's good friend Lucille Ball)." Garland, an unsuccessful candidate for originating the role, desperately wanted to replace Angela when she left the show. Garland loved the score, and indeed she might have made a formidable Mame. In her younger days, she would certainly have been an easy match for the rigors of the role; however, by early 1968, about the time that Angela was preparing to leave the Broadway run of *Mame*, Garland was in London with her new husband, Mickey Deans, a discotheque manager. Deans had arranged a booking for his bride at a London cabaret for a three-week engagement, and there Garland suffered the worst failure of her long show-business career. Her once rich voice was cracking, she forgot the lyrics to many of her numbers, and often she didn't arrive at the club until long after she was due onstage. Audiences lost patience with her and booed and tossed food, forks, and napkins at the stage. Despite that horrid fiasco, she still considered herself a queen among musical performers and was heartbroken when beaten by Janis Paige as Angela's replacement.

Such are the ups and downs of show business. Back in the early 1950s, when Angela's career was at a low ebb, she had been Paige's summer-stock replacement in *Remains to Be Seen*. In the mid-1940s, Garland was one of MGM's bright lights, starring in many a memorable film, while Angela was a supporting player struggling for better roles—and being hissed in public for being so nasty to Judy in *The Harvey Girls*.

Whether Judy Garland would have gotten the screen role of *Mame*, and what she would have done with it, remain subjects for conjecture. The possibility of her winning the role seems slim when considering the odds of a studio obtaining insurance on Garland, whose erratic behavior and fragile health were widely publicized.

But one thing is certain: the actress who was cast was decidedly too old for the part. To cover her wrinkles, Lucille Ball, at age sixty-three, was shot in soft focus. The result was at best visually garish, at worst ludicrous.

Observed film critic Pauline Kael, "[Ball] throws up her arms, in their red giant-bat-wing sleeves, crying out, 'Listen, everybody!' and she really seems to think she's a fun person. But we in the audience are not thinking of fun; we're thinking of age and self-deception. When [Vera] asks her, 'How old do you think I am?' and Mame answers, 'Somewhere between forty and death,' one may feel a shudder in the audience. How can a woman well over sixty say a line like that, with the cameraman using every lying device he knows and still unable to hide the blurred eyes?"

Vincent Canby added that Ball's "face alternately looks beatific—all a religious glow—or like something sculptured from melting vanilla ice cream."

Then there was the matter of her singing. "I knew I couldn't improve on Angela Lansbury's interpretation," explained Ball. "And so I asked, 'How can I be different?' They told me to give it my own brand of honesty and sincerity. They impressed upon me that it wasn't important if I didn't sing or dance so great."

But different isn't necessarily better—or even good—and it is no understatement to observe that Ball's singing was less than great. "The sound is somewhere between a bark, a croak, and a quaver, and it doesn't quite match the movement of the lips," quipped Kael. "Did Lucille Ball sync her own singing in *Mame*, or did Dick Cavett dub it for her?"

The studio-generated publicity on the film was that it was "one of the great entertainments in the history of motion pictures." But Leonard Maltin called it "hopelessly out-of-date," noting that it will "embarrass even those who love Lucy. Calling Fred and Ethel Mertz!"

Perhaps what had captivated Broadway in 1966 had become "hopelessly out-of-date" by 1974. The world had changed so much in eight years. Nonetheless, it would have been interesting to see Angela (and not Lucy) playing Mame on the screen, recreating the role that had cemented her stardom forever.

At the same time, *Mame* did not prove to be a celluloid springboard for Lucille Ball. In fact, it was her final screen role.

Angela followed *Mame* with another Broadway musical, *Dear World*, which opened at the Mark Hellinger Theatre on February 6, 1969. In it, she was reunited with the *Mame* team of Lawrence-Lee-Herman. And she reportedly earned the highest salary to date of any Broadway star in history.

However, *Dear World* was a troubled production. Angela would describe the experience as "one of the most difficult . . . I've had in the theater." When the show had been in rehearsal for two and a half weeks, Peter Glenville replaced director Lucia Victor. Explained Jerry Herman, "I, Miss Lansbury, Mr. Lee, and Mr. Lawrence differed with Miss Victor over the interpretation. We felt it was not going in the direction we thought it should. Miss Victor's resignation was amicable." By the time the show came to Broadway, Glenville had been replaced by Joe Layton, who received official credit as director-choreographer.

During its tryout in Boston, Angela insisted on assorted behind-the-scenes changes, much to the chagrin of her fellow cast members. In spite of the inconvenience to herself and others, Angela firmly believed these adjustments were necessary to the show's survival. *Dear World* had been set to open on December 26, 1968. Prior to its actual February opening, the show played a reported record number of previews—fifty-seven, during six weeks.

Thematically, the show was closer to *Anyone Can Whistle* than *Mame*. Both are well-intentioned social commentaries on the state of society. *Dear World* was a musical version of the Jean Giraudoux allegorical comedy-fantasy *The Madwoman of Chaillot* (of which a production, adapted from the French by Maurice Valency, ran with great success on Broadway during the 1948–49 season). Angela, bedecked in a red wig, had the part of the seventy-five-year-old main character, who calls herself the Countess Aurelia: an eccentric old lady who symbolizes sanity in an insane society, and who rescues Paris after the discovery of a wealth of oil underneath the city. A group of nasty, moneyed capitalists scheme to blow up the City of Light and make off with the riches. But all is saved when the countess, with the help of her companions (the Madwoman of Montmartre and the Madwoman of the Flea Market, played respectively by Jane Connell and Carmen Matthews), lures the predators through a secret entrance into the sewers beneath the city and shuts the door behind them.

Giraudoux wrote his pithy social commentary during the early 1940s, while living in neutral Switzerland where he had sought asylum after the Nazis invaded and occupied Paris. So intent was he to have his play produced once the war ended that, in 1942, he made an unusual transatlantic telephone call to French producer-actor Louis Jouvet, who was in Rio de Janeiro, to explain the work. *"The Madwoman of Chaillot* will be ready for you when you return to Paris," he told Jouvet. Before Giraudoux died in 1944, he inscribed a copy of the completed play to Jouvet with a bold prophecy: *"The Madwoman of Chaillot* was presented on October 15, 1945, by Louis Jouvet at the Théâtre de l'Athénée." His prediction was fulfilled just two months later than he anticipated, when the play premiered at the Athénée on December 19, 1945.

Although World War II had ended well over twenty years before the opening of *Dear World*, the symbolism in the Giraudoux play was still potent. But Jerry Herman's take on the original was dissatisfying. It was no exaggeration when, upon its opening, critic Richard L. Coe described *Dear World* as a "much-battered" musical that "limped into port at the Mark Hellinger Theater."

By this time, it was becoming apparent that, even when critics did not like her show, Angela seemed incapable of garnering bad reviews. Richard Watts Jr. noted, "So much hard work and so many weeks of industrious previews have gone into the making of *Dear World* that it would have been poetic justice if it could have turned out to be a brilliant show. But the melancholy truth, it seems to me, is that the musical comedy . . . is, despite a picturesque performance by Angela Lansbury, disappointingly mediocre. . . . The mad countess is so buried in grotesque makeup that there is little of the handsome Miss Lansbury left, but her skill and vitality are still there, and she is the evening's major blessing."

John Chapman described Angela's performance as "captivating. . . . She may dodder as she sets about saving Paris from the

Bad People, but she sings with authority, as usual, and she can cut a frisky caper." Clive Barnes called her work "magnificent," adding, "And for most of the time [the show] stubbornly refuses to get off the ground, except when it is gracefully flounced up airborne by a delicate kick from the adorable Miss Lansbury, who not only can make magic out of nothing but has to."

Walter Kerr, on the other hand, was intrigued by the show: "Quite often I think there is something strangely authentic, in a rich legitimate sense, about it." But he added most tellingly, "But for one minor miracle I suspect that *Dear World* would never have seen the gloom of day. The minor miracle is Miss Lansbury, and whether or not the musical itself is worth seeing—for it is extraordinarily tenuous—no connoisseur of musical comedy can afford to miss Miss Lansbury's performance. It is lovely."

Kerr observed that Angela "comes on looking like Bette Davis in silks." He was not the only critic to compare her appearance to that of Davis. Martin Gottfried noted that she "plays it looking like after it happened to Baby Jane."

Concluded Kerr, "So there it is. Certainly not a great musical. Scarcely a mediocre musical. And whether it is worth seeing will depend entirely on whether you want to treasure the memory of Angela Lansbury. It is a memory worth treasuring in an evening that seems destined to be forgotten."

Unlike his scores for *Hello, Dolly!* and *Mame*, Jerry Herman's music did not catch on with the public. Indeed, his lyrics—which describe the size of a dream as being more important than the size of a fist and, in the style of a Hallmark card, wish our "dear world" to get well soon—were as vapid as they were sincere and sweet.

And Angela did not catch on in the role of a septuagenarian. In retrospect, she observed that "people wouldn't accept me as an old lady; I had to force myself on audiences because they wanted another Mame." Still, in addition to her positive reviews, she received compliments for her performance from some very special places. While on a two-week trip to New York, Noël Coward saw her in *Dear World*. "Angela Lansbury brilliant," he wrote in his diary.

But because of all the trouble surrounding the production, Angela reportedly wanted out of *Dear World* almost as soon as it opened. Producer Alexander Cohen refused to close the show unless the weekly box office dipped below $51,000. In its opening week, *Dear World* took in $74,000 in a house with a potential gross of $104,000.

While Angela won her second Tony Award—her competition was Maria Karnilova *(Zorba)*, Dorothy Loudon *(The Fig Leaves Are Falling)*, and Jill O'Hara *(Promises, Promises)*—the show lasted just 132 performances. Afterward, Angela observed, "Playing that 'lovely old crock,' as somebody called me in *Dear World*, was pretty depressing for six months." But she denied ever wanting out of her contract: "I always believed in the show. I never wavered. And I never, never said that I wanted out. When we started previews in New York, we were a mess!"

Angela closed out this stage of her theatrical career with an even bigger disappointment: *Prettybelle*. The show was based on Jean Arnold's *The Rape of Prettybelle*, a novel that reviewer Phoebe Adams likened to a sow's ear, "with apologies to all decent hardworking pigs."

Prettybelle was staged by top Broadway musical talents including Gower Champion, with music by Jule Styne and book and lyrics by Bob Merrill. However, this one didn't even make it to Broadway. It was scheduled to open at the Majestic Theatre on March 15, 1971, but producer Alexander Cohen withdrew it during its scheduled five-week Boston run. "I have decided that the show is not in shape for Broadway," Cohen tersely noted in a press statement.

"I really thought we had something big in *Prettybelle*, a biting musical about the South, rednecks, and magnolia blossoms, plus Gower Champion," Angela recalled. But she also admitted, "When you are in a project like that, you get so immersed in it that you don't realize you are going too far. We just didn't realize how far out we were."

Angela starred as Prettybelle Sweet, a small-town Southern belle with myriad problems. She is an alcoholic. She is a schizophrenic. She has just been widowed. Her sheriff husband, Leroy Sweet, was your standard Southern racist cracker; flashbacks show Leroy (played by Mark Dawson) killing blacks, instigating fights with Chicanos, and whoring in New Orleans. The musical number about the latter is titled "New Orleans Poon." Furthermore, Prettybelle's mother-in-law is senile, and her daughter is ugly and weighs two hundred pounds.

To assuage her guilt over her husband's racism, Prettybelle donates money to the NAACP and allows herself to be sexually assaulted by the kind of men whom her husband despised, including a Chicano delivery boy and a black servant. These carnal adventures end up ripping apart the social foundation of her town.

"It had a lot of civil rights overtones," Angela remembered. "It was a little late for that, and we couldn't circumvent the basic horror of the subject. It didn't seem possible to temper it with humor. So we scuttled it."

But the show's problems were more succinctly stated by the *Variety* critic: "Foremost of the difficulties are Bob Merrill's choppy, aimless, vulgar and unfunny book and lyrics." As usual, Angela emerged unscathed. "Miss Lansbury is pretty and supple," continued the *Variety* scribe, "as she proves in a sexy solo number, 'When I'm Drunk,' in the middle of the second act. She's a game trouper in the service of poor material with this collection of ethnic slams and four-letter words."

Local critic Kevin Kelly described *Prettybelle* as "pretty bad," despite its intention to take a serious look at "the shriveled spirit in the South." Samuel Hirsch opined that the show "wants to please but can't quite make up its mind exactly how to go about it," adding that "Miss Lansbury is poised and beautiful, completely at home on that stage. She plays the looney lady's wide-eyed, blank stare with bewitching charm." Elliot Norton observed that the show was "likely to offend some, to irritate others and to bewilder at least a few playgoers of good will. For it is always blunt, sometimes cruel, is often bitter." However, he felt that if Champion could "bring it into sharp focus and give it a little more muscle," the show would have a chance to succeed.

Apparently, producer Cohen thought otherwise.

13

A Bitch and a Witch

"Mine was a career that might have petered out if it had not been for *The Manchurian Candidate*," Angela once explained. Unfortunately, all of the acclaim Angela earned for her work in the film did not lead to another screen role of similar stature. In fairness, she did not accept all parts offered her. She turned down the role of the title character, an aging British soap opera actress/lesbian, in the film version of *The Killing of Sister George*, based on a play by Frank Marcus, which came to the screen in 1968. Beryl Reid eventually played the part.

"But, corny as it sounds," Angela told columnist Earl Wilson, "I don't want to destroy the image I've created for myself in *Mame*. It was not an easy decision to make." Years later she explained, "I just didn't want to play a gay woman at that time."

She also refused the role of Nurse Ratched in *One Flew Over the Cuckoo's Nest*, a part that won Louise Fletcher an Academy Award in 1975. In that instance, she was in good company. Anne Bancroft, Colleen Dewhurst, Ellen Burstyn, and Geraldine Page reportedly turned down the role, as well. "I just couldn't stand that character," Angela declared. "You know, a character becomes very personal. You have to live with it. During the course of the shooting, we were going to be six or eight weeks in a mental institution in northern California with real inmates. I couldn't have taken that. I'm too sensitive. I didn't want to treat people the way she had to treat them.

"Plus, I know how tough it is to live down that kind of image. Louise Fletcher had a hard time getting another part after doing that film."

Meanwhile, other projects did not come to fruition. In 1971, George Cukor was planning to film Graham Greene's *Travels With My Aunt*. Katharine Hepburn was set to play the title character, a robust, eccentric women in her seventies. After Hepburn insisted on rewriting the screenplay, she was fired and the conception of the character was altered to suit a younger actress. Cukor fleetingly considered Angela for the role before settling on Maggie Smith, who went on to earn an Academy Award nomination.

Another project was *The Widower*, to be directed by Alan Pakula. "After I read [Alvin Sargent's script], I just sat and cried," Angela said. "This is a kind of woman I've never played."

The character was Lila Fisher, a shy, aging, terminally ill spinster who blossoms upon becoming romantically involved with an awkward young man. The project, retitled *Love and Pain (and the Whole Damn Thing)*, was eventually made with—again—Maggie Smith. While the role had outstanding dramatic possibilities, the film ended up a failure, with its distributor, Columbia Pictures, unceremoniously dumping it onto the marketplace.

Angela was to remain ever hopeful of winning a screen role equal to her stage role in *Mame*. Referring again to that might-have-been celluloid version of the show, she declared, "I could've paid off in the right movie, and oddly enough, I think I could've done it with *Mame* if they had let me play the lady I played on Broadway." She also added, "But that movie I envisioned will never be made, so maybe there's another one in my future that will give me the kind of screen recognition I wanted."

But the sad fact was that good roles in good films were not to come Angela's way. "I have never been offered a really good part in Hollywood since I did *Mame*," Angela observed in 1979 as she was set to open on Broadway in *Sweeney Todd*. "It's just interesting. It doesn't matter. It doesn't matter." As Angela carted off her fourth Tony Award, husband Peter observed, "Angela hasn't done her best in films but she will now." But as far as the movies were concerned, she was never given the opportunity.

As far back as 1974, critic Gene Siskel astutely observed, "When the movie industry and its screenwriters decide they want to make pictures about a strong woman, about, if you will, a Joanne Woodward character who *doesn't* have a mental breakdown every reel, then they will seek out Angela Lansbury, and she will respond by making some very good films."

In the years immediately after she conquered Broadway, Angela did appear in two additional features. The first, released in 1970, was *Something for Everyone*, directed by Hal Prince and adapted by Hugh Wheeler from Harry Kressing's comic novel *The Cook*. It was filmed mostly on location in Fuessen, Bavaria, and in Neuschwanstein, the dream castle of mad Ludwig of Bavaria. The second film came out the following year and was something else altogether: Disney's *Bedknobs and Broomsticks*, made by the same people (producer-coscreenwriter Bill Walsh, coscreenwriter Don DaGradi, director Robert Stevenson, and composers Richard M. and Robert B. Sherman) who created the smash hit *Mary Poppins*. In fact, the star of that film, Julie Andrews, turned down the role that Angela was to play.

In retrospect, *Something for Everyone* and *Bedknobs and Broomsticks* are transitional roles for Angela. In the former, her character is a sexual creature who dresses in revealing costumes and shares several romantic interludes with handsome costar Michael York. In the latter, she is sexless—after all, *Bedknobs and Broomsticks* is fashioned for children. But the lingering image of Angela in the film is that of a mature actress ready to be cast in older character roles—this despite the fact that she had played so many such parts early on in her career.

Unfortunately, neither film added punch to her career.

When *Something for Everyone* premiered, Angela had been away from movies for three and a half years. In the interim, she had become queen of the musical stage in *Mame* and won two Tony Awards, for *Mame* and *Dear World*. Not surprisingly, when Angela was asked which medium had been kinder to her, movies or theater, her quick response was "the stage," adding that "I only want to keep my foot in the door of pictures. On Broadway you just bury yourself. It's a lovely way to be buried, but you must also do movies and television."

Angela was to refer to *Something for Everyone* as "Hal's [Prince] first picture, and I enjoyed doing it. The German scenery was terrific."

While being filmed, *Something for Everyone* was called *The Rook* (rather than the novel's title, *The Cook*). At one point during preproduction, it was also known as *The Dreamers*. Angela starred as decadent, near-penniless widow Countess Herthe von Ornstein, a vestige of Old World, Middle European royalty. World War II has long been over. The countess describes the time as "the bad new days."

Countess von Ornstein is the personification of Eurotrash. In her first appearance on-screen, she is seen reading *Vogue* magazine through sunglasses and is soon puffing on a cigarette. "Every now and then mother gets delusions of vanished grandeur," observes her plump, precocious sixteen-year- old daughter. The countess humorlessly notes, "When your world is gone, you're your own ghost." That world, however, was one of upper-class excess, with a tinge of obliviousness to everything around her. She laments that she can no longer afford strawberries for breakfast. "I suppose they're too expensive," she notes. "How extraordinary to have to concern oneself about the price of strawberries. My husband always had our own flown in, from Corinthia, Hungary, wherever they were the most perfect. Even the war never stopped the flow. Until, of course, those horrible weeks at the end." Later, the countess describes Nazis as "boring," adding, "One merely snubbed them, and that was that."

Enter pretty-boy Conrad Ludwig (Michael York), an enigmatic symbol of evil, whom Angela was to describe during the shooting as "a very interesting fellow." Via various forms of chicanery—from seduction to subtle manipulation to murder—Conrad steers his way into the Ornstein household. He starts out as footman and ends up as the countess's lover. And he orchestrates the courtship of the countess's callow son and the alienated daughter of the Pleschkes, a crass nouveau-riche couple. All the in-laws might benefit from such a union. The countess would come into some much-needed wealth, while the Pleschkes would marry their daughter into the titled class.

What no one knows is that Conrad has seduced both son and daughter.

While Angela is first-billed in *Something for Everyone*, Conrad is the film's main character. But she offers a solid performance, as usual, playing the countess with clipped dialogue. She amusingly rolls her *r*'s as she speaks the line, "We must all look our most ravishing for the great event tomorrow."

And indeed she does look terrific, especially in the nifty black Florence Klotz–designed dress she wears during a party. Countess von Ornstein is Angela's sexiest-ever screen role, a fact that is never more apparent than when she dons a revealing negligee and tells Conrad, "I should know by now that you know how to do everything perfectly."

"It's going to be interesting to see how I'm accepted in it," Angela noted before the film's release. In fact, she was certain that she and York "had a good one on our hands." Explained the actor later on, "Like all the best comedies, even black ones, the film had serious overtones. Conrad was the 1970s version of the New Man—greedy, opportunistic, materialistic, and downright immoral. Against him, the old orders—aristocratic, political, moral, whatever—had no protection."

Unfortunately, the film was a box-office failure. But, like *The Picture of Dorian Gray*, *Something for Everyone* has since become something of a cult film. "I think it gets better and better," Angela observed of the film's growing reputation.

Bedknobs and Broomsticks provided Angela her first lead role in a screen musical. "It's all peaches and cream," she said before it went into production, "an introduction for me to movie audiences singing and dancing, which turned the corner for me." The film is set at a time and place that were quite familiar to Angela's life: England in 1940, as that country was being bombarded by Nazi warplanes. It opens in just the sort of small village to which Angela might have been evacuated had it been decided by Moyna that Angela would leave London to escape the blitz, rather than remain in the city and study acting. Angela plays Miss Price, an unmarried, middle-aged villager, garbed in duffel coat and powder blue tam as the film opens, who reluctantly takes in three such children just arrived from London. Enough years had passed since those tragic times, so it was perfectly acceptable for the story of Miss Price and the children to be set to music and even include some comically polite, only slightly menacing Nazis.

Miss Price is an eccentric. She lives alone in a big house, with only a scruffy black cat she calls Cosmic Creepers. She eats boring, healthy foods rather than sausages or strawberry jam. She studies witchcraft at a correspondence college and has just qualified as an "apprentice witch." Because of the war, the school is shut down. Miss Price is thus unable to receive her final witchcraft lesson. She seeks out the school's headmaster, Emelius Browne (David Tomlinson), who is actually an inept magician, then searches for the information she needs to master a particular spell.

All of this allows Angela to fly through the sky on a broom and then, with the children, on a bed. The characters interact with animated creations. "It is not an acting role," Angela noted, "it's a performing role. There's a difference. The techniques used in shooting a Disney picture are specific and quite unique. They pre-plan every shot. There's no room for improvisations . . . the trick is to make it seem alive and fresh and improvisational." Angela does get to dance a bit and to sing a series of songs that collectively are as forgettable as those for *Mary Poppins* are memorable. This time, no one would dare suggest that her voice be dubbed. While *Bedknobs and Broomsticks* remains an engaging film, especially for children, it did not catapult Angela to movie stardom the way *Mary Poppins* launched Julie Andrews.

Although she was not allowed to let her hair down during the filming, Angela popped a few bobby pins during an appearance on *The David Frost Show* at the time of the film's release. The talk show host asked her, "What do you do in *Bedknobs and Broomsticks?*" Angela quickly responded, "I thought you were going to say what do I do in bed." This resulted in much laughter from the studio audience. "Wow," Angela added, " . . . another night."

At this phase of her career, Angela made a few revealing comments on the pitfalls of her newfound (and long-sought-after) stardom: "My way of dodging the trap is to delete the word *star* from my consciousness and go on with it. Certain truths are beginning to filter through, and some of them are rather uncomfortable. For instance, it's very hard for an 'actress'—in quotes, because deep down to my toes I love to act . . . to be a star. The battle against you by yourself is endless. Do I do star parts or parts I want to do as an actress?"

She added, "To put it another way, I got up this morning to come here and do an interview. My first instinct was to be a star, all dressed up. I put on false eyelashes. Then I looked into the mirror and I thought, 'Who are you fooling? Yourself?' So I decided to hell with the eyelashes and I haven't dressed up either."

14

The Window Breaks

"I have a split life, and being an actress is a very small part of it," Angela explained in 1961. "My role as a mother always comes first with me, and the making of a good life. That to me is number one. . . . I find myself wanting to stay home all the time. Living the life of an actress has always been difficult for me. If I feel I'm going to sacrifice the children to it in any way, I don't want any part of it."

During the 1960–61 Broadway season, Angela played the meaty role of the alcoholic, self-centered mother of Joan Plowright in Shelagh Delaney's play *A Taste of Honey*. "I felt it was a provocative, fascinating part," she recalled a couple of years later. "I didn't want to leave my family and go to New York, but I couldn't resist the part." During the play's run, eight-year-old Anthony and seven-year-old Deirdre came to live with Angela in New York. "However, I'm afraid the only parties the children had over the holidays here were for grown-ups," Angela noted in January 1961. "They haven't made any friends here, to speak of, because they have a tutor and aren't in school with other children. So, for Christmas dinner together, we all went out to a very gemütlich restaurant and had a lovely time. But it's at home that they have birthday parties, with people their own age."

In 1966, when Angela was starring in *Mame*, she declared, "Without Peter and the children, I feel like half a pair of scissors. Without this other part of my life, the theater is very hollow for me. As soon as the curtain comes down, I'm alone. Right? When I'm alone in New York, I feel incomplete. A career alone would be a form of purgatory for me."

Reported gossip columnist Sheilah Graham in December 1964, " 'By hook or by crook I'll be home for Christmas,' said Angela Lansbury to her twelve-year-old son Anthony and eleven-year-old daughter Deirdre, before she took off for London to star with Kim Novak and Richard Johnson in *The Amorous Adventures of Moll Flanders*. To which her son replied, 'You'd better be.' " Continued Graham, "It seemed to me that I am always seeing Angie in Europe, or New York, hardly ever in Hollywood. 'But I have made only two films in London,' she assured me. 'The last one was two years ago, *In the Cool of the Day*. I saw you in Vienna three or four years before that— *A Breath of Scandal*, remember, with Sophia Loren. . . . Oh, yes, I saw you in Paris when I was in *The Reluctant Debutante* with Rex Harrison and Kay Kendall.' "

These revealing quotes and anecdotes mirror Angela's mindset during the late 1950s and early 1960s. She most certainly was aware of her responsibilities to her children. She loved them and wanted only the best for them. So with this in mind, motherhood was her "number one" priority. Yet at the same time she was an actress. While she had not yet reached the professional level she attained after starring in *Mame*, she was a known commodity in the acting community. Understandably, it would be difficult for her to resist accepting a potentially interesting or lucrative role.

It would be unfair to label Angela as hypocritical for her conflicting feelings regarding career versus motherhood. The point is simply that choosing one over the other was a real dilemma for her during this period.

Add to the mix the fact that Anthony and Deirdre were not the children of anonymous working parents. On one level, they were as average as a movie actress's kids could be. In 1963, Angela told an interviewer that Deirdre was planning to be a jazz pianist. "When she plays, she sounds like someone in a hotel cocktail lounge. I'm green with envy. Anthony will probably be a creative person of some sort, but he could fool me. They are not at all impressed that their mother is a movie star. In fact, my little boy wants me to take off my makeup as soon as I come in from the studio."

How different were the reactions of her children to their mother's return from the theater than her own childhood experiences with Moyna. As a youngster, Angela equated the sweet smell of greasepaint with the glamour of stage acting. To her son, the makeup meant mother was working away from home. Mother was busy with her job and was often too distracted to take an interest in daily family activities.

Regarding her philosophy of child rearing, Angela explained, "I'm not a professional mother. I don't bring up my kids by the book. I feel they're individuals, and I try to treat them as such. I tell them that they do not, and should not, have to conform to the dictates of a group.

"Playing all these driven mothers as I have on the screen has made me stop and think. I say to myself, 'Am I guilty of any of these things?' I think I have been guilty of a few. I know I am oversolicitous. And we really do our children an injustice by worrying and fussing over them. Children should have disappointments. And it is the sweetest thing in the world to see a child getting over a disappointment."

But the fact remained that Anthony and Deirdre's mother was one of the chosen few: first a working actress, then a Broadway star, but always a celebrity.

It is no easy task for the children of celebrities to establish their own identities, to find their places in a world in which their parents receive exorbitant attention from strangers.

For this reason, Angela and Peter had decided to deemphasize Angela's celebrity by keeping their children away from movie sets, dressing rooms, and the backstage theatrical atmosphere. Nonetheless, this parenting strategy backfired. "If I had let them be around me in the dressing-room part of my life," Angela later concluded, "they wouldn't have seen me as this rather overblown person who is stared at on the street. If they had known that people always did say, 'Oh, look, there's Angela Lansbury,' they would have understood there was nothing peculiar about it."

She added on another occasion, "One of the hardest things about success is that those nearest you often misunderstand a great deal of it. The way they apply your success to themselves is distorted, and no matter how hard you try to keep things separated, the success that's imposed on you spills into your children's lives in a bad way."

Angela did not mean to be an inattentive parent. When the children were young, they could easily travel with their mother when she was on a job. Once it was certain that *Hotel Paradiso* would not immediately close, five-year-old Anthony and four-year-old Deirdre joined their mother in New York. Observed reporter Helen Ormsbee, who had come to Angela's East Fiftieth Street apartment for an interview, "By now Deirdre and Anthony had come downstairs, ready to eat. The little girl, whose eyes were like her mother's, was pointing out her dollhouse, which stood across the room in a prominent spot. . . . Anthony, in a plaid shirt and tan shorts, came over to exhibit the pictures he had been drawing with colored crayons that morning." Stepson David, then thirteen, had remained in Los Angeles with his father. While Angela was working, Deirdre and Anthony were in the care of her secretary and the children's governess, a young woman named Miss Fyfe.

"Oh, she's a second mother to them," Angela told the journalist. "I was at Idlewild airport at seven-fifteen in the morning to meet the three of them, when their plane came in from the Coast."

This arrangement might have worked when Anthony and Deirdre were younger. But as they matured, the frantic pace of Angela's career would have dire consequences on the children. When she returned to New York to appear in *A Taste of Honey*, she told gossip columnist Cindy Adams, "I didn't start them in school because I believe we'll finish out the season, but comes a [newspaper] strike or bad weather of if there's a war in Cuba—you never know how long the play will run. So, they have a tutor. Besides, the East grades them differently. They're taught all sorts of things like [New York] history that they don't need. This way they're neck and neck with California curriculum—we hope! It requires push to make them work three hours daily at home, but that's Jane's doing. She's combination secretary-governess-companion. Been with me for years. Sees that all runs smoothly."

What Angela was not taking into account was that grade-school children need more than a tutor to teach them their ABC's. They need a stable and consistent home life. They need the security of familiar surroundings, where they can develop friendships and social skills. And they do not need "second mothers" (or, for that matter, "second fathers") to fix their dinners and reassure them when they scrape their knees.

By the time Angela became the toast of Broadway in *Mame*, Anthony and Deirdre had already entered their teen years. She then told an interviewer, "I was raised in a kitchen, and that's where we gather at home. . . . That's where you can talk. Kitchen conversations would reduce juvenile delinquency." Yet the reality was that Angela was spending too much time away from home to be around for many meaningful "kitchen conversations." A harbinger of things to come occurred at the tail end of the *Mame* opening night. After Angela's triumph onstage, followed by the Rainbow Room gala, Anthony had to be taken to the hospital. Reportedly, he had developed a severely swollen finger and had to have a ring removed.

If only such minor mishaps were to be the extent of his difficulties.

Upon the end of the school year, fourteen-year-old Anthony and thirteen-year-old Deirdre came to New York to be with Angela. "I think I've got my kids into the Dalton school," she told an interviewer. "Do you know it? It seems very nice. It's very hard on teenagers to change schools this way. They're a little upset but very gutsy."

While gutsiness is a positive attribute, the children were still taken away from what should have been a solid home environment and placed in a transient one. In 1973, Angela observed that, in all of her years of living in New York and performing on Broadway, "I never had a home there. Home was always in Malibu and I was never there, either." Later on, she admitted, "Frankly, I wish I had spent more time with my family. . . . Both my children, but particularly my son, became involved with drugs."

Despite the sojourn to New York when Angela was in *Mame*, the two youngsters spent the greater part of this period at their home in Malibu. Here they found themselves submerged in a world of hedonism and escapism. Add to this the temper of the era: this was the beginning of the late 1960s, a time of major cultural upheaval in America; a mismanaged and unpopular war was being fought thousands of miles away in Vietnam; and a "turn on, tune in and drop out"/"don't trust anyone over thirty" mentality existed among the young.

So it should not have been a shock when fifteen-year-old Anthony began using cocaine and heroin, eventually becoming an addict. Deirdre too experimented with drugs.

When Angela was lighting up Broadway in *Mame*, the sad fact was that Anthony and Deirdre were just plain lighting up. "My children's generation was the first to be so confused by reality," Angela observed. "The sixties was a bad time to find yourself.

"The artificiality and the tinsel of Broadway and Hollywood had never taken me in, but it takes in other people. People assume you are Mame Dennis, not Angela Lansbury. That's one helluva thing to live up to for an actress. For the kids who glorify you up to an extreme point, it's tragedy. I, as an actress, know what I'm doing, but they don't. I know teenage kids here in New York who suffered terribly because they related to this shining woman, Mame Dennis, blowing a golden bugle onstage. It drove them off their nuts. They haunted me. It sounds ridiculous, but they were hooked on the character of Mame, not on the real Lansbury.

"No, I've never had that feeling. My saving grace is that I'm an absolute stick-in-the-mud. But my own children, Anthony and Deirdre, were disoriented."

Angela added, "That really shocked me because I didn't think it could happen to my own. Even in Hollywood we'd lived simply. After all, I'd never been taken in by the unrealities. And I was their age when I arrived, just seventeen. And when I was eighteen, how well I remember celebrating my birthday, October sixteenth, on the set of *Gaslight* with Ingrid Bergman."

But the world had become a more perplexing place in the intervening years. According to Angela, her son's "two closest friends ended up dying of overdoses. It was a terrible scene. Charles Manson and his followers were always hanging around, and, yes, Deirdre got to know them."

Despite her success in *Mame*, Angela was tormented by the private and personal agony of Anthony's situation. As Angela would return to her dressing room after taking curtain calls, Anthony, when in New York, would be waiting for her to solicit drug money.

"Whenever the curtain goes up, I really feel super," Angela explained. "I suppose you could say it doesn't really matter how you feel before, but I've gone on with some dark scenes being played out in my personal life."

Angela might be all smiles while onstage. But the curtain, each night, would eventually go down, and for Angela that meant going back to dealing with her son. "How well I remember the temptation to say to Tony, 'How can you kick your father and me in the face after all the patience and understanding we have given you?' " she said. "Then you realize that he's not doing this to get at you. When he was lucid, we always talked about his recovery. . . . He tried everything, psychiatry, weeks in a hospital . . ."

By the time he was nineteen, Anthony had been cured. "I played God with drugs. Then suddenly I couldn't control it anymore," explained the tall, bushy-haired young man in a lengthy and revealing 1971 interview, while accompanying Angela to the London premiere of *Bedknobs and Broomsticks*. "If I can help other kids by what I've been through, then I'll have done some good. I'm cured. Both my parents were absolutely incredible. They stood by me completely."

He added:

It began as a slow buildup through soft drugs. I was always curious. I guess ninety-nine percent of young people are curious these days, and that's half the trouble. . . . Thinking back, the depths I sank to were really quite horrifying. Everyone tells you it's a terrible thing, and disgusting, and that you're killing yourself. But while you're into it doing it, nothing registers.

At the time it's fantastic, and you get something out of it. But the most dreadful part is when you wake up in the morning and know you've got to find forty dollars for a fix. I knew that by noon I'd be sick. That was the cost of my habit. . . . To get the money I did absolutely everything, from sex to virtual robbery. It was nothing to be proud of. If I had sat down and thought what a bastard I was, I don't think I could have stood it. I'd go to the theater and beg my mother for cash to buy the drugs I needed. . . . There were so many bad things I did, I don't like to think about it, even now.

At the time of this interview, scars were still noticeable on Anthony's arms.

Added Angela, "I've never talked about this before. It was a terrible time for all of us, but now I don't mind discussing it. It's over. I think he's marvelous because he kicked the habit himself.

"It's a happy day for all of us. Anthony did it alone. True, we stood by him. But however much support parents give their children in this kind of trouble, in the end the kids have to get through it themselves. We tried everything, including psychiatry. We went through all that. Anthony spent several weeks in a hospital and finally came to our home in Ireland."

Angela and Peter had concluded that it was time for the family to come together and escape the excesses of fast-lane life in Hollywood and New York. The Shaws asked friends to find them real estate in Ireland, which led to the purchase of their house in County Cork. In their remodeling of the property, Angela and Peter transformed this home into a special place: a family place, where Angela, Peter, and the children could live a more cozy, anonymous lifestyle. This necessitated (at least for the time being, although she didn't know it then) Angela's abandonment of her career.

Angela described the purchase of the Ireland property as "like

going back to the grass roots": a healthy and necessary mind-set
for this juncture of her life. It allowed her to step back in time because, as she was quick to observe, Ireland was forty or fifty years
behind the rest of Europe. An idyllic prewar innocence could still
be found there: an innocence that Angela remembered from her
childhood surroundings. She explained, "Being the star of *Mame*
was a joy, but there was also unhappiness"—and the cause of that
unhappiness, Angela knew, had best be acknowledged and handled.

It would have been difficult for her to go this route alone. And
to her good fortune, unlike her widowed mother, she did not have
to go it alone.

"During this difficult period," Angela remembered, "my husband was the backbone—he was *there*. What is more, he gave up
his own career, which was an incredible thing to do." By that time,
Peter had left MGM and gone to work for William Morris. "He
gave it all up so he could be with us."

Years after the crisis had passed, Angela observed, "Peter and
I have been through the kinds of rough times that either tear people apart or make them closer. Our bond is so tremendous that
nothing can break it."

When Anthony arrived in Ireland, he had to be carried off the
airplane on a stretcher. According to Angela, part of her son's cure
was "a complete change of environment. There were no tempta-
tions, no pushers, no memories, none of the high-powered living
of Los Angeles and New York. He was able to reeducate his re-
flexes in a quiet, peaceful atmosphere. I've never tried drugs myself, perhaps because I was chicken. But I was a chain-smoker for
years and it was hard enough to get over that. My interests were
my work. I never felt the need for drugs. They're mostly the result of boredom among kids today. The frightening thing is that
kids are getting into it so young."

Angela later remembered, "The children needed me. Their
father, who had also left his job, and I were determined to make
a home where the family could be together and have a new beginning.

"I seriously believed I would never go back to work again."

These were tough years for Angela. The Shaws' Malibu

home—its address was 24818 Pacific Coast Highway—was destroyed in a September 1970 brushfire that devastated more than
one hundred thousand acres in Los Angeles County. All the family's belongings were lost, including treasured artifacts from Angela's career: diaries, letters, newspaper and magazine clippings,
photos, and other memorabilia. "I put two metal files in the
Japanese pond, thinking a fire wouldn't travel across water, stupid
me," Angela said. "Everything went—passports, the children's
birth certificates, everything. I've been through unbelievable red
tape having everything duplicated."

Angela and Peter received commiseration from friends and
colleagues. "Darlings Angela and Peter," wrote Joan Crawford,
Peter's old flame, "I am so sorry to hear of the disaster of your
home in Malibu. I want you to know that my thoughts are with
you. I am sure your wonderful spirit and courage will help you to
overcome your losses."

Gower Champion offered assistance: "We can only stand by
helplessly, and hope that if there is anything we can do for you,
that someone else might not be able to do, that you will not hesitate to call on us."

And from Rex Reed: "When I think of all the photographs
and all those paintings of Angie and all the personal things that
can never be replaced—I could die. It all seems so unreal, but here
we are, in an unreal world where nothing should surprise anyone
anymore. . . . You must have tremendous courage to go on, start
all over, and never look back."

"We feel extremely sympathetic to you," wrote Mary and
Reginald Denham. "We realize what a shocking blow this must be
to you. The only bright thing we can think of to say to you is a
cliché many of your friends must have already said: 'Thank God
you weren't in it.' "

"The year 1970 was a bad one for us," Angela said in 1974.
"The sadness! If you dwell on it, you wouldn't stop crying for a
week. It's still lurking there."

To add to the family's woes, Peter underwent major surgery: a
hipbone implant, to help alleviate an arthritic condition. Stepson
David did military service in Vietnam, as a combat photographer:

a frightening experience for any parent. He left for Southeast Asia while Angela was starring in *Mame* in San Francisco. "One simply hopes . . . ," she said at the time. "We had a lot of fun together before he left." After his return home, Angela recalled, her voice quivering, "He was in an army film unit. . . . It was horrible."

To top it off, a broken hip kept Angela's beloved mother, Moyna, incapacitated for months. Then she contracted throat cancer, resulting in the removal of her voice box. "Do you know what it means for an actress to lose her voice?" Angela asked. Moyna died in Santa Monica on November 25, 1975, at the age of seventy-nine. Her ashes were scattered amid the heather in a valley nearby the Shaws' Ireland home.

When in the United States, Angela and Peter chose to stay in New York; they took an apartment opposite Lincoln Center. "I don't like California anymore," she said in 1977. "I lived there for twenty-five years, brought our children up there. We lived out the whole 1950s indulgent kind of life, with big houses, swimming pools, all the status symbols. Now it's just like a whole page of my life which is turned. It's past. It bears no relation to reality for me anymore."

Even though life in County Cork had proven to be a godsend for the Shaw family, Angela realized that her absence from the boards would be temporary. While in Ireland, she went to London to work with Dame Peggy Ashcroft in a 1972 Royal Shakespeare Company production of Edward Albee's *All Over*. And a year later, she starred in the London revival of *Gypsy*. She did this only when she was absolutely certain that Anthony and Deirdre's lives were back in order.

Anthony went on to study acting in London at the Webber-Douglas School of Singing and Dramatic Art, Angela's alma mater. He was dialogue director for Angela's London production of *Gypsy*, teaching the British actors their American accents. He became assistant stage manager and Keir Dullea's understudy in a London stage production of *Bus Stop*, starring Angela's old professional cohort Lee Remick.

Dullea reportedly became angered because Remick was receiving the lion's share of billing on the marquee of the Phoenix Theatre, and one Friday evening he refused to go onstage. Reported the *London Daily Express,* "A twenty-four-year-old understudy with virtually no stage experience had to take his place fifteen minutes before the curtain." That understudy was of course Anthony, billed as Anthony Pullen. "This boy has the makings of a star," noted Alfred Marks, another actor in the cast. Before the final curtain fell, Marks and his fellow cast members applauded Anthony, who also received an ovation from the audience.

Stardom as an actor was not meant to be for Anthony. However, he did two seasons of repertory in England; toured in the United States in revivals of *Gypsy* (with his mother) and *Cabaret;* and had small roles in several films, including *A Bridge Too Far* and *The Spy Who Loved Me.* In the latter, he was billed as Anthony Pullen. He became Anthony Pullen-Shaw when he appeared in the NBC miniseries *The Martian Chronicles* and was Anthony Shaw in the NBC miniseries *World War III,* produced by his uncle Bruce Lansbury.

In 1982, Anthony opened on Broadway with his mother in *A Little Family Business* and eventually became a dialogue coach on *Murder, She Wrote.* It was with motherly love that Angela playfully observed of her son's job on the TV series, "He knows me well. If I start getting naughty, he'll rap me over the knuckles." Way back in 1975, when Anthony was at Webber Douglas, Angela observed, "My own opinion is that he'll be a good director. I think he has a critical facility. He's a good selector and I think he'd be a good director." So it was not unexpected when, thirteen years later, Anthony directed the first of many *Murder, She Wrote* episodes. In more recent years, he has been directing one of every three of the show's episodes.

Anthony also directed Angela in the 1992 made-for-television movie *Mrs. 'Arris Goes to Paris.* It seemed fitting when, at one point in the story, Angela's Mrs. Harris observes, "A child is the most important thing in the world."

By this time, Anthony and his wife, Lee, had made Angela and Peter grandparents three times over. Their offspring are named Peter, Katherine, and Ian. Peter—his full name is Peter John

Shaw—was the firstborn, coming into the world in December 1982, just as Angela and Anthony were completing previews of *A Little Family Business*. Grandma Angela described the baby's birth as "one of the most exciting things that's ever happened to me."

Deirdre—known as DD or DeeDee by her family—became interested in art and studied acting in New York with Stella Adler. In 1978, she was living with her photographer husband, Rene Volpi, on Bleecker Street in Greenwich Village. However, Deirdre was not destined for a career on stage or screen. This could have been foretold by a comment she made at age sixteen: "I hate faking all that show-biz happiness." However, Deirdre did at one point tour with her mother in *Gypsy* and also did some modeling in New York.

By the time she was in her early thirties, Deirdre was operating a restaurant in Italy with a new husband, Vincenzo Dattarra. She remained in Italy for a number of years. By the early 1990s, she had returned to Los Angeles where she and her husband manage Positano, a Santa Monica restaurant.

Prior to his army service, David Shaw was Angela's West Coast representative. Afterward, he married, went into the building business, becoming a contractor, and during Angela's *Murder, She Wrote* success began running his stepmother's production company, Corymore.

"I sometimes find it hard to believe we lived through the nightmare, that Tony overcame all his problems," Angela recalled in 1979. "And the fact that he and Deirdre are doing so splendidly now is, well, it's like a miracle."

But as the years passed, the horror of those times—and what she might have done to change them—remained in her thoughts. In a 1985 television interview with Barbara Walters, Angela was brought to tears as she recalled her heartache. "Sometimes I say, what could I have done?" she observed in 1992. "I was at home a great deal during [Anthony's] early years until he was thirteen. But then there were great stretches of time when I was gone.

"I don't know how to tell anybody how to do it differently. But perhaps I should have made it my business to be more accessible to my kids."

15

Moyna

Early on in her career, when Angela would be complimented on her *Gaslight* and *The Picture of Dorian Gray* Academy Award nominations, among her other achievements, she was inclined to respond, "Oh, Moyna is responsible for that."

As they settled in for Angela's run on *Murder, She Wrote*, she and Peter purchased a three-bedroom house in the exclusive Brentwood district of Los Angeles. On a wall near the living room sofa hung a striking portrait. "That's my mother, Moyna MacGill," Angela once told a visitor. "A true Irish beauty, wasn't she?"

Angela may have become expert at playing bitchy mothers on stage and screen. But Moyna was no role model for any of these characters. "My mother has always had a wonderful spiritual quality—sensitivity, an understanding of people," Angela observed in 1961. "When she is working, she has a sense of well-being and accomplishment."

"I was never rejected," Angela recalled of her childhood two years later. "Mom's a lot of fun." Indeed, both Hurd Hatfield and Maggie Williams, who first met Moyna back when Angela was beginning her Hollywood career, have described Moyna as being funny and charming.

In her later years, despite an occasional stage or screen role, Moyna had for all intents and purposes retired from acting.

"Moyna and I used to sit in her apartment in New York, which Angela got for her," recalled Hurd Hatfield. "We'd paint and draw, you know. I loved Moyna. She was really a big loss for Angela."

Despite her own fame as an actress, Moyna became so inextricably linked with her daughter that she was described in her *New York Times* obituary as "one of Britain's most popular actresses and the mother of Angela Lansbury." Another actress mother might have wallowed in jealousy over being so tied to a successful child. Not Moyna—at least until the last years of her life. Moyna was always delighted over her daughter's accomplishments. Hurd Hatfield escorted her to Angela's opening-night performance in *Mame*. "She came and visited me on Long Island," remembered Hatfield. "I drove her in to the opening. That was a wonderful evening. Moyna was very proud."

However, the superstardom Angela earned in *Mame* far eclipsed any of Moyna's professional accomplishments. Reportedly, in her final years, Moyna sometimes strayed from the role of doting mom.

Years after Moyna's death, *People* magazine reported that Angela "anguished over a rift with her mother, who evidently became ill and irrationally jealous over her daughter's success."

But how irrational were those feelings? In 1973, Moyna told Leonard Lyons, "Being the mother of successful children was a novelty at first, but then it wore off and became a bore." One can understand her frustration given the context of the quote. It is excerpted from an item, published in Lyons's *New York Post* gossip column, in which Angela is cited for her upcoming London opening in *Gypsy* and brother Edgar is cited for the screen version of *Godspell* (which he had produced, and which had just opened the Cannes Film Festival) and *Gypsy* (of which he was one of the producers). Moyna is referred to only as "Mrs. Lansbury." She is without a first name. By then, her own career on the London stage, appearing with John Gielgud, Basil Rathbone, and Herbert Marshall, was remembered only by a small number of theater buffs and historians.

Some of the old-timers still appreciated Moyna. Less than a month after Moyna's death, upon Angela's opening in *Hamlet*,

John Gielgud dropped her a note in which he referred to Moyna as "an old and sweet link broken." But to a gossip columnist solely concerned with the present, and a younger generation without a sense of history, the half-century-old accomplishments of an aged actress could easily be overlooked in favor of the latest opening happenings.

Even when Moyna's career was acknowledged, it was some-times trivialized. In 1973, columnist Ken Nixon erroneously re-ported, "[During the 1920s, MacGill] appeared on [*sic*] one or two plays—once with Gerald Du Maurier—but never had a big suc-cess." Such misrepresentations must have been quite hurtful to Moyna, who was in an ever-weakening state of health.

For her part, Angela would not let others' viewpoints cloud her devotion to her mother, and her appreciation of Moyna as a role model. Days before the *Gypsy* opening, Angela compared Moyna to the character she was about to play: Rose, the domi-neering stage mother of Gypsy Rose Lee and June Havoc. "My own mother, bless her, was a woman who certainly pushed, though nothing like Rose did—but she arranged for auditions, she coached me for the stage," Angela said. "We all need encourage-ment. We all need someone to tell us, 'Yes, yes, you can do it.'" On another occasion Angela added, "It was because of Moyna that I started off right. She never stressed the need for a formal edu-cation. I was in drama school when I was twelve. I think she truly recognized the embryo actress in me at a very early age. Very early.

"Her sense of humor and her encouragement were of a nature which never put any limit on what I could achieve. Her philoso-phy of life was extraordinary, and she imbued me with that at an early age, this notion of understanding that one was the master of one's fate."

Over the years, books, newspapers, and the airwaves have been filled with accounts of the problems of famous children, and chil-dren of the famous, as they mature to adulthood. Anthony and Deirdre's drug usage seems almost manageable when compared to the fate of one of Angela's distant relatives. In October 1933, Robert B. Mantell Jr., twenty-one-year-old son of her Shake-

spearean-actor uncle and aunt (who also was an actress), committed suicide. As revealingly reported in the *New York Times*, the suicide, "for which friends told the police the motive apparently was
discouragement over his career as an actor, took place on the eve
of his mother's returning to the stage." The younger Mantell had
"faced a mirror in his home . . . and fired a pistol bullet into his
head."

Given the status of their elders in the theatrical (not to mention political) world, Angela and her siblings might have struggled
in the shadows to develop their identities and senses of self-worth.
"We all grew up under the glow of Grandfather," Angela once
commented. "When I went back to London, it was as his granddaughter." Another time, when Moyna was still living, Angela offered special insight into what it was like to have an actress
mother when she declared, "I never thought I was pretty. I was always self-conscious. I had a very beautiful mother. She's still beautiful. Maybe the psychiatrists would say that's why I felt that way
about myself. I like the way I look now more than I did when I
was younger. I think I've grown into myself. I found a style that's
right for me. In the past, I always felt I had to look like someone
else. Now I can look like me."

Whatever self-assurance Angela and her siblings possessed
was due in no small part to Moyna's parenting skills. Recalling
their childhood in 1966, Bruce Lansbury noted, "Mother went to
special pains to allow us to develop independently." Added
brother Edgar, "Maybe that's why we're so well-disposed to each
other now."

Moyna's success as a parent—and this without benefit of a parenting partner—permitted her children not only to get along as
adults but to fondly recall their childhoods. "I remember Bruce
had a great flair for dress," remembered Angela, with no small bit
of big-sisterly fondness. "He owned a waistcoat at twelve. Edgar,
on the other hand, was very large with corduroy. Later, he became
Mr. Bill Blass. But Bruce always had better legs than Edgar."

In the early years, Moyna, Angela, Edgar, and Bruce were an
especially solidly knit family. "To become a part of Angie's life,
you have to be accepted by her family," Peter Shaw wrote in 1950,

less than a year after he and Angela married. Several evenings after they had met, Peter was invited to dinner. "A table for two in front of a roaring fireplace? Soft lights and sweet music? Dan Cupid should live so long! . . . [Moyna and the twins] were all on their best behavior, and believe me—so was I! I had a feeling there was a strong union here, and anyone, to crash it, must pass an acid test of four." Peter noted that Moyna had the good sense eventually to withdraw to the next room. "But Bruce and Edgar, bless their little black hearts, allowed me a fat fifteen minutes alone with their sister!"

As the years passed, the Lansbury siblings remained especially close. "The years have brought each of us supreme success," Edgar observed on one occasion, "but we did not become different enough to be strangers to one another." In 1971, it was announced that Angela would star in and Edgar would coproduce a musical titled *Sister* (which later in its evolution was known as *Glorianna*), about evangelist Aimee Semple McPherson, with a book by Paul Zindel and music by Al Carmines. Even though the project never came to fruition, Angela and Edgar were able to joke and fondly chide one another during a press conference. "Brother is one hell of a better producer than he ever was an actor in *Little Red Riding Hood*," Angela noted, referring to a Christmastime skit in which they appeared as children. "He simply could not get his fangs together."

In 1981, Angela's nephew Michael Lansbury told her, "You know, I recognize Moyna in some of your characterizations."

"Yes, that's quite true," Angela responded, "but it's also the Irish in us, an attitude laced with a sense of humor about ourselves. Moyna had this quality of seeming to make an ass of herself in the most charming and funny way. Always putting herself down. She couldn't accept a compliment, though she was such a great beauty until the day she died. She always had that mantle around her neck of being the great, great beauty. I was fascinated by her as a child and bowed to that, not by dint of what she did, but the way she was, her manner. And it's this marvelous Irish which I've inherited, and for an actress it's a marvelous quality to have up your sleeve. I reveal it sometimes onstage without realizing it with a turn of my head, a motion of my body, or a way of saying a line."

Ultimately, Angela's unabiding love and respect for Moyna transcended whatever rift may have occurred during Moyna's decline, or for that matter whatever everyday mother-daughter disagreements they may have had over the years.

This adoration is best expressed on the acknowledgments page of *Angela Lansbury's Positive Moves*, her health and fitness book published in 1990. Angela thanked, among others, her son David, her husband Peter, and her family. But the volume was dedicated to a woman who had passed away fifteen years earlier: her mother.

"To Moyna," Angela's inscription reads, "my inspiration then and always."

Angela in a 1950s publicity portrait.

Jessica Fletcher meets Perry Mason: In 1956, Angela costarred with Raymond Burr on the big screen in *Please Murder Me*.

In the 1960s, Angela became typecast as mother-from-hell, most memorably in *All Fall Down* and *The Manchurian Candidate*. Her Annabel Willart is not at all pleased with the developing relationship between son Berry-Berry (Warren Beatty) and Echo O'Brien (Eva Marie Saint) in *All Fall Down*.

Angela had another bitchy role, this time opposite Jane Fonda and Peter Finch in *In the Cool of the Day*. *(The Billy Rose Collection, The New York Public Library for the Performing Arts, Lenox and Tilden Foundations)*

Angela is beginning to show her age—forty—in this scene with Kim Novak, from *The Amorous Adventures of Moll Flanders*. *(© 1965 by Winchester Film Productions Ltd.)*

In the Broadway production of *Mame*, Angela revitalized her career and earned the superstardom she has not relinquished to this day.

Angela–wearing a Bette Davis-style wig–appeared with an aged and ailing Sir Laurence Olivier in the made for television movie *A Talent for Murder*.

Angela recreated her role as Nellie Lovett in *Sweeney Todd* on tour. George Hearn played the title role. *(Photo by Sam Emerson)*

In 1980, Angela starred as a frumpy Miss Marple in the screen version of Agatha Christie's *The Mirror Crack'd* (left). Four years later, she began her long run as the more stylish writer-sleuth Jessica Fletcher on the TV series *Murder, She Wrote* (below). *(Photo below courtesy of Universal Television)*

Angela, as Jessica, is flanked by Tom Bosley, left, and Claude Akins on the *Murder, She Wrote* set.

Angela as Jessica Fletcher, at the harbor in her beloved Cabot Cove.

Angela, all smiles, enjoying her *Murder, She Wrote* success.

16

London Calls

Back in 1961, Angela declared, "I am first and foremost a movie actress, but a movie actress who would hope to work in the theater now and again."

Little did she know that over the next two decades she would spend most of her professional life performing onstage. It would be the ultimate achievement of an actor's life to win one Tony Award; Angela went on to win an remarkable total of four. By 1970, her outlook on the theater had been altered enough for her to observe, "I find that I must go back to the stage as often as I can." For during those nine intervening years, the theater did for Angela what the movies and television had not done. It won her attention from the media and the public as it brought her a major and permanent stardom.

"A stage is a space that *must* be filled to attract and hold the attention of an audience," Angela observed in 1979, after opening in *Sweeney Todd*. She added:

If you are a performer who is given a part that is central to a work of theater, you must be prepared to take that stage and fill it and demand that the audience watch and listen closely to what you have to tell them, because you are going to tell them a story in a certain way that is going to entertain them— transport them out of their seats and take them on a magical mystery tour that, hopefully, will enhance their evening and

maybe a week of their lives. I have always felt that acting is really understanding other human beings, and it has to do with
trusting humanity. Once you have learned this, the audience
will get any message you wish to send them, and when you
feel that the message has been received, it's a heavenly sensa-
tion. One thing I'm *not* is a Method actress. I don't examine
my id or get terribly introspective about a part. I believe that
a character is there on the page of a script. If that character
isn't there, no amount of Method acting is going to bring it
to life. So, it's up to us, the actors, to bring that character off
the page and interpret what a writer has said. It's very basic,
and that's how I approach any part, whether it's in a comedy,
a drama, or a musical.

She also noted, several years later, "I can sense right away
from the dialogue whether the author really understands the lady
he's writing about. If I feel it's true, then I sense that there's room
for me to bring something to it, as well as just saying the words
and getting across what he wrote. That's the difference between
an exciting part and an ordinary one."

And regarding directors (on screen as well as stage), Angela
explained that she wants "much too much, probably. I don't want
to be left on my own. I really look for a great deal of help from
a director, and I'm disappointed when I don't get it. I've lived
through several pictures where I've been thrown on my own resources or instincts by a director who's delighted and thrilled because he hasn't had to do anything about the performance."

Whatever her role, Angela's performances had come to be
highly regarded among her peers for their consistency and self-
control. "I've had [self-control] all my life," she noted when she
was in her late forties. "It's just a part of me. Sometimes I think
it gets in my way and I have to push it aside, this thing of always
maintaining a margin for error and working in a safety zone."

In the early 1970s, Angela's primary safety zone was her family. She may have believed that she would not go back to acting,
but of course she did return. Still, Angela had resolved to avoid her
past mistakes. "I think Angela will never again stop mother-

henning her family so that the old problems never arise," Peter Shaw declared years later, during the early run of *Murder, She Wrote*.

As her family problems were solved, she began yearning to go back to work. Peter urged her to return to the stage, which she did first in the Royal Shakespeare Company's production of Edward Albee's *All Over*, presented at the Aldwych Theatre. The play opened on January 31, 1972, following a six-week rehearsal. It was her hometown stage debut.

All Over is a story of loneliness and misery, and an allegory of the spiritual death of the contemporary American upper classes. Its story unfolds on a single set, the antechamber of the bedroom of a wealthy, aged, dying New Englander. His wife of fifty years (Dame Peggy Ashcroft), his mistress (Angela), his two children, a family friend, an elderly doctor, and a nurse await the inevitable. They have a choice: to reveal their feelings, and their humanity, or to withdraw into indifference. Indeed, as Irving Wardle noted in the *Times* of London, the play consisted of a "two-act deathbed conversation."

What especially appealed to Angela about *All Over* was "the idea that Dame Peggy Ashcroft and I were to sit in two comfortable chairs down front, talking our way through the evening. We were able to indulge in the wonderful nuances of Albee at his most somber and analytical. Yet it was exhausting too. The concentration had to be total for such a long time. Of course the same is true of many plays, but of that one in particular because we moved so little."

She enjoyed working with director Peter Hall. "He spent days with us examining and discussing every phase of our individual roles and the interplay that could develop," Angela said. "As an ensemble piece it was fascinating to play and, I believe, to watch, whether you liked the subject matter or not." And she added, "I think three months is the longest an actor can keep up energy in a straight part, and that's why *All Over* suited me ideally as a short-term engagement. It was a lovely way to come to Britain, although I didn't know how the British critics would receive me."

Angela need not have worried. Yet again, she was lauded for

her performance in a production that was less well received by reviewers. R. B. Marriott noted that the play "is largely a long-winded, banal piece of pretentiousness. . . . We have performances in place of people. Angela Lansbury, most welcome to the stage of her native London, gives a brilliant performance as the mistress." Concluded Irving Wardle, "Albee has wheeled some extremely ponderous equipment into position to deliver banalities. . . . Angela Lansbury, as the mistress, handles the elaborate convolutions of the dialogue with superb expressive variety."

Angela and Peggy Ashcroft became good friends, which led to a slight bit of embarrassment a decade later. Ashcroft received a Best Supporting Actress Oscar nomination in 1984, for her performance in *A Passage to India*. She had come down with the flu and was unable to attend the ceremony. Her costar, Victor Banerjee, had not been nominated; if she won, Ashcroft wanted him to pick up her statue. When her name was called, Banerjee's moment in the limelight disappeared in an instant when Angela came onto the stage for the trophy, thanking the Academy on behalf of Ashcroft for "this incredibly happy, joyous moment."

It was all a misunderstanding. The Academy was unaware of Ashcroft's designation of Banerjee, and so Angela was asked to substitute for her "dear friend." Ashcroft was later offered an apology from Gregory Peck, representing the Academy.

After the run of the Albee play, Angela returned to America to take *Mame* on tour through the summer theater circuit. It played the "Music Fair" theaters operated by producers Lee Guber and Shelly Gross, opening in Camden, New Jersey. When it played the Shady Grove theater outside Washington, D.C., Tricia Nixon Cox and other political notables were in attendance.

A number of original Broadway cast members—including Jane Connell, Willard Waterman, Charles Braswell, and Sab Shimono —joined Angela for this revival. "There is a sense of déjà vu, of going back in time," she explained. "In a way, it's spooky. But in life you seldom get a chance to see history repeat itself."

17

Angela's Turn

'm very torn between legitimate and musical theater," Angela observed in 1972. "I haven't the voice for opera, but I'd like to do a really fascinating play with a character who not only sings, but also is a piece of whole cloth in the acting department. That's what I'm really hoping to find one of these days, because I think the combination of music and drama is the closest the theater can get to the impact of a movie."

Angela was to find just such a role the following year when she was asked to star in a West End, London, revival of *Gypsy*, which had premiered on Broadway fourteen years earlier. Arthur Laurents had written the show's book, with music by Jule Styne and lyrics by Stephen Sondheim. Angela would be playing Rose (a character originated by Ethel Merman, who declined to appear in the production), a quintessential stage mother whose daughters Baby June and Louise were to go on to earn fame as entertainers. The former became actress June Havoc; the latter became the fabled ecdysiast Gypsy Rose Lee, upon whose memoirs the show was based.

At first, Angela courteously turned down the role—after Merman had already done so. As Angela told Laurents, "I really can't play this, Arthur, because this is written in Mermanese." Around that time, *Company* (whose music and lyrics were by Sondheim) opened in London, with Elaine Stritch earning excellent reviews. The *Gypsy* producers, Fritz Holt and Barry M. Brown, approached

Stritch, who agreed to play Mama Rose. However, with Stritch cast as Mama Rose, they were unable to secure adequate capital for the show.

Laurents, who was by this time set to direct the revival, again appealed to Angela. Now she accepted, realizing that she did not have to imitate Merman; instead, she could create an entirely different interpretation of Mama Rose. Angela was not even interested in learning about the person she was playing; when Laurents attempted to relate to her some anecdotes about the real Mama Rose, she cut him off: "Don't tell me anything about that terrible woman!"

"The reason I was interested in directing the show was because we had a different star," Laurents admitted. "Not to denigrate Merman, but I wouldn't have been interested in doing it with Merman in London—you could get a stage manager and do it the way it was done before. But with a new star, you could play the show for different values."

Additionally, here was another opportunity for Angela to sing Sondheim's words, as she performed "Some People," "Small World," "Rose's Turn," and "Everything's Coming Up Roses." "It's artfully constructed," Angela said of the show. "There are very few musical comedies in which the two elements [book and music] are so beautifully interlocked. The first song I sing, 'Some People,' tells you what Rose is about: she doesn't consider it as being alive to stay home and raise the kids in a small town. Her aspirations are higher. The lyrics say all that."

The highlight of the original *Gypsy* was "Everything's Coming Up Roses," in the first act. Laurents had never been satisfied with this, so he restructured and restaged the final, showstopping number, "Rose's Turn," a solo by Rose. Now, it would be performed with the character leaving the proscenium for a runway that lit up. Quite literally, the spotlight would be on Rose: a tragic figure who had messed up her life, and who remains the only family member who fails to achieve the acknowledgment she craves. With these changes, Laurents felt, the second act was even an improvement on the first.

"Rose's Turn," as Angela noted, "contains the entire saga of her life, and of course it's incredible to perform. The fact that it's set to music gives it that extra dramatic lift which an actress so often longs for in a play where there is no music. It's a moment when you want to yell—and you can't just yell, but you can sing and yell. It's sort of a catharsis. It's very wearing and tearing on the person who's doing it, because one has to keep up a certain level of attack. And of course to try to keep melody, to keep tempo, and to keep dramatic intent, is very rough. But you do it, and it's gratifying." Added Laurents, "It's hair-raising, and [it works] because Angie's an actress."

For seven months, Angela was the toast of London. On opening night, May 29, 1973, she received an unusual fifteen-minute standing ovation at the Piccadilly Theatre. On the second night, the *London Observer* reported that "something remarkable" happened: Angela received another standing ovation! "The cheers were provoked, I think, by the show's closing fifteen minutes," wrote Robert Cushman. "[At this point] a light-studded platform has been shunted across the orchestra pit, annihilating the elegance that generally separates a musical from its audience. [Mama Rose] strides onto it to try her own hand as a performer. She falters, weighed down by memories of the past, and her failure is Miss Lansbury's acting and singing triumph. She stops the show. The effect is devastatingly clever, and as moving as anything to be seen in London."

The *Daily Mail* critic declared, "Ethel Merman, you were not missed. The London musical stage belongs to only one woman, from this very second: a rose by any other name is now Angela Lansbury!"

"In twenty years of London theater," remarked the distinguished critic Kenneth Tynan, "I've never seen anything like this."

By that time, Angela and Peter had settled into a flat located at 45 Cadogan Place in the fashionable Belgravia section of London. On the morning after opening night, Rex Reed interviewed her there. "During the ovation last night, when that voice came out of the balcony and screamed, 'Welcome home!' I was momentarily stopped in my tracks," Angela said. "This is my home, you know, even though I sometimes forget I was born here. And

I've always wanted to come back. They never saw *Mame* and they had a chip on their shoulders because I didn't bring it to London, and I didn't know what the reactions would be."

Nevertheless, Angela might have anticipated at least a positive reception from Londoners. Several days before opening night, the *London Observer* noted, "Miss Lansbury is indeed one of the nicer stars we have met," paying her the highest compliment by describing her as a "Seattle broad onstage, in fact gently English off it."

Angela described Rose as

a great acting part. It's a pretty staggering piece of theater. So I had to forget all about Ethel Merman. I've heard her sing the songs countless times at parties, but I never saw the show, luckily, so I approached it just as I would any new role. I tried to find the core of honesty in the part, instead of playing a caricature of the stage mother.

I think my hunch has paid off. . . . *Gypsy* is really about the tragedy of good intentions. The character of Rose is an absolutely stupid woman transfixed by the word *stardom.* That's the only word in her dictionary. The irony is that both of her daughters . . . became extremely successful but not in any of the ways she imagined for them. Neither one of them fulfilled her dreams, but their own. She's a pathetic person, but her guts make her riveting, exciting, and extremely stageworthy, and that's what the audience takes away with them. . . . This role has everything so it's perfect for me. I'm so glad I came to London in it instead of *Mame* because then I would have been forced to go on playing Mame forever and always. This way, London is getting a new look at me and I might bring it to America later. Right now, I want to concentrate on enjoying London, though.

Later on, Angela noted, "They [London critics and audiences] knew I was a serious performer. . . . They allowed me to come in with all my guns blazing and gave me the [London critics'] best actress award, the first time for a musical star. *Gypsy* appealed to their music hall instincts. They still have them over there."

Another source of acknowledgment of Angela's professional accomplishment came two months to the day after she opened in *Gypsy*. On July 29, she was called upon to reflect on her career in one of a series of John Player Lectures at London's National Film Theatre. Afterward, Angela was reunited with her *Gaslight* coperformer Ingrid Bergman, in London to play the title role in a stage version of Somerset Maugham's *The Constant Wife*.

And on November 18, Angela was honored at a special dinner sponsored by the Gallery First Nighters' Club, the proceeds of which aided the Actors' Charitable Trust and Denville Hall. On the menu were a host of imaginatively named delicacies, including Crème de Mame, Truite Fumée aux Chaillot, Suprême de Volaille Rose, and Vacherin Glacé à l'Angela.

Angela certainly was in demand among London's upper crust. At a Woman of the Year charity luncheon held at the Savoy Hotel, she was photographed in the company of the Duchess of Kent, Lady Medawar, the Countess of Airlie, the Marchioness of Lothian, Mrs. Harold Wilson, and Mrs. Derek Parker Bowles.

An interesting trivia note regarding Angela's *Gypsy:* several months after its opening, word got out that the drummer in the orchestra pit was none other than former Beatle Pete Best, who was replaced by Ringo Starr just before the group hit superstardom.

Angela planned to leave *Gypsy* on December 15, to spend a family-style Christmas in Cork before returning to the United States. Upon the announcement, rumor had it that Ethel Merman would be replacing her. "Everyone seems to be so surprised that Ethel would consider the possibility of following anyone," Angela noted. "But they seem to forget that she followed Pearl Bailey in *Hello, Dolly!*" Despite the reports, Merman did not take over for Angela. Dolores Gray did.

Merman, however, certainly maintained an interest in the production. In fact, the minute the curtain went down on Angela's triumphant opening-night performance back in May, Elaine Stritch telephoned Merman (who was then in New York) and offered a detailed and spirited report of Angela's triumph.

The following year, Angela brought *Gypsy* to America. First, she toured with the show across North America for six months.

For her Chicago appearance, she was named winner of the Sarah Siddons Award as actress of the year, besting fifty-one other nominees, among them Geraldine Page, Anne Baxter, Leslie Caron, Maggie Smith, Tammy Grimes, Jessica Tandy, Eve Arden, Barbara Rush, and Jean Simmons. Angela reportedly won by the greatest majority of votes in the award's twenty-six-year history. Her final destination was Broadway, where *Gypsy* opened the New York theater season with a ten-week engagement beginning on September 24.

Angela was welcomed back on Broadway like a Roman general victoriously returning from a far-off war. A half-block-long red "Angela Lansbury in *Gypsy*" sign was placed on the Winter Garden Theatre marquee. There were also smaller signs: "Here She Is, Boys . . . Here She Is, World . . . Here's Angela!"

A bad cold on opening night could not stop Angela. The ovations were reportedly louder and longer than those she had received in London. Still, as she noted, "The warmth of the audience—that doesn't mean a thing. It's difficult to continue in a show unless you have the critics. They're what count." And in a virtual replay of her success in *Mame*, Angela again "had" those New York critics. Louis Snyder wrote that the arrival of *Gypsy* gave "the New York theatrical season its most auspicious opening in years. . . . As Mama Rose, Angela Lansbury carves out a resplendent new niche for herself in Broadway history through a whirlwind, dynamic performance that is both hilarious and moving."

Once more, it was "Rose's Turn" that earned her the most attention. Observed Edwin Wilson, "At the end, Miss Lansbury traverses the bare stage, singing snatches of songs from her past, grabbing at her lost dreams like torn patches of faded cloth. She ends up down front trying to dredge up the words to 'Everything's Coming Up Roses' and suddenly they won't come. Her jaws work silently and then her face contorts into a horrid mask of humiliation, frustration and anger. For many years Miss Lansbury has played in dramatic roles as well as musicals and at this instant everything she has ever done as an actress and a singer comes together. Rose stands before us vulnerable and entire. It is a rare moment."

Invariably, there were the comparisons between Angela and Ethel Merman. "The heart of *Gypsy* is Mama Rose, a woman utterly different from anyone we have ever seen in a musical," wrote Martin Gottfried. "Disregarding Ethel Merman's once-acknowledged ownership of the role, Lansbury created it anew." Noted Howard Kissel, "Ms. Merman's vocal prowess and physical presence suggest the Super Chief barreling along at full speed; Ms. Lansbury's voice, which ranges from a mousy upper register to a tough, gravelly quality deep in the larynx, and her emotional intensity are on a more human scale. The fact that she does not overpower every scene enhances the drama around her. This Rose seems more vulnerable, and in her moments of crisis, more affecting."

Added Clive Barnes, "Her voice has not got the Merman-belt, but she is enchanting, tragic, bewildering and bewildered. Miss Lansbury not only has a personality as big as the Statue of Liberty, but also a small core of nervousness that can make the outrageous real."

Given the flavor of such reviews, it was not surprising that rumors abounded regarding a tiff between Angela and Merman. After all, Merman had first turned down the stage role of Mame Dennis, which made Angela a Broadway star. Now Angela was playing to great acclaim a part originated on Broadway by Merman, who had given a performance considered to be among the greatest in the history of the American stage.

But at least publicly, Merman tried to appear generous in her wishes toward Angela. "During Angela's run I'll be there," she promised. "I wish her luck and I know she'll be great. . . . I've no hard feelings."

She then bared her fangs and added, "I could have done the role if I wanted to. I'm just so glad I created the role so others can copy it. I'll send her an opening night wire and come in to see her when I can."

Days before the New York opening—just as Merman was making her London stage debut in a one-woman show, booked for two weeks at the Palladium—Angela noted, "I can't beat Ethel at the singing game, and I don't think she can beat me at the acting game. So, no contest. But I'm damned concerned because I am going into her territory." Later on, Angela observed, "Ethel figured Rose was her private property, and I had no right to play the role. She told people that, although she was always cordial to me when we met." Then Angela added, "I can understand why she was upset. Critics made comparisons between her and me, which was unfair because we had our own interpretations of the role. Also, I got a Tony and she didn't, although she richly deserved it.

"It disturbed me that she was resentful, because I admired her so," she continued. Yet Angela must surely have made Merman all-too aware of her advanced years when she concluded, "I thought she was great doing 'Heat Wave' [on-screen in 1938] in *Alexander's Ragtime Band,* which I saw as a kid in England. And Ethel Merman in *Annie Get Your Gun* was the greatest performance I have ever seen in the theater. It inspired me to attempt a career in musicals."

But comparisons between Angela and Ethel were inevitable. As Angela had earlier noted, and theater historian Gerald Bordman corroborated, Angela's interpretation of Rose was anything but a "copy" of Merman's. Bordman observed that Angela's characterization was "more humane" than Merman's. Angela was forty-seven years old when she first played the role; Merman was just four years older when she created the part. Yet ironically, Bordman felt compelled to add, "If she seemed at first glance too young and beautiful to be believable, her thoughtful acting and stylish, energetic rendering of the songs quickly won over skeptics."

Gypsy played on the Great White Way for fifteen weeks—120 performances—closing just after the 1975 New Year. A week before the show's closing, an exhausted Angela observed that, as far as she knew, Merman had not come to see her performance. Angela won her third Tony Award, besting Lola Falana (*Doctor Jazz*), Bernadette Peters (*Mack and Mabel*) and Ann Reinking (*Goodtime Charley*) as Best Actress in a Musical. In her acceptance speech, she thanked Merman for creating the role. "Ethel wrote me a very gracious letter, which I got in Ireland," Angela later reported.

In the summer of 1975, Angela—then approaching her fiftieth birthday—took *Gypsy* on the road, touring the summer theater circuit. She reportedly earned $200,000 for the eight-week tour, which took her to the "music fairs" at Valley Forge (Pennsylvania), Painters Mill (Baltimore), Shady Grove (outside Washington, D.C.), and Westbury (Long Island). The tour concluded at the Nanuet (New York) Star Theater and the Cleveland Musicarnival. She was then the highest-salaried actress in the annals of summer theater.

Now that the tour was completed, Angela fulfilled a vow she had made at the beginning of the summer: "I'm going back to Ireland to make raspberry jam and can it."

After her triumph in *Gypsy*, Angela steered her stage career in yet another new direction. In 1974, she noted, "I haven't done the classics yet, but I think I now have the chest and the experience to play Shakespeare." Equally important, she had now obtained the stature to be asked to do Shakespeare in England—and in distinguished company.

Angela was scheduled to open on Broadway in November 1975 in *Scream*, an Arthur Laurents play, in which she would be cast as a Queens, New York, housewife and survivor of Auschwitz who tracks down a former Nazi. Instead, she chose to forgo this venture to play her first Shakespearean role, as Gertrude in a National Theatre Company production of *Hamlet*, directed by Peter Hall and presented at the Old Vic. Her costars were as choice as could be assembled: Albert Finney as Hamlet; Susan Fleetwood as Ophelia; Roland Culver as Polonius; Simon Ward as Laertes; Denis Quilley as Claudius. Cast as the Second Gravedigger was Stephen Rea, still seventeen years away from attaining international prominence in Neil Jordan's *The Crying Game*. A decade later, Rea would share billing on-screen with Angela in *The Company of Wolves*, also directed by Jordan.

This *Hamlet* was an especially meaningful venture for the National Theatre, which had opened twelve years earlier with a production of the play starring Peter O'Toole. It was unique for two reasons: Hall presented the play uncut, in a version lasting four hours, with Finney onstage virtually the entire time; and his set, depicting Elsinore castle, was bare of furniture except for an odd table or chair. The emphasis was not on the physical production but on the beauty of Shakespeare's lines.

Angela had been at her Ireland home when Hall called her and asked, "How would you like to come over and play in Finney's *Hamlet*?" "I said, 'I'll be there,' and then pointed out to him that I had never played Shakespeare," Angela explained. "He said, 'Don't worry. You have a good sense of rhythm. You just have to brush up on your diction a little."

Hamlet opened on December 9. Quite rightly, the critical focus was on Hall's vision of the story and Finney's performance in the title role. Reviewers were divided on Hall's interpretation; his *Hamlet* either was monotonous or the best since Michael Redgrave played the part in 1950.

Angela was an actress in an ensemble, one part of a motor that had been finely tuned by Hall. John Barber called the production "a speedy, vigorous, deeply interesting and blessedly simple revival," adding that Angela, "blonde and fleshy, finely betrays her duplicity in her deep-sunk eyes." On the other end of the scale, Irving Wardle called the production "a ponderous cultural event," noting that he could "recall few productions less coloured by a directorial viewpoint." Wardle wrote that Angela gave "an anonymous performance consisting of an embattled appearance and a poetry voice. It was presumably on Mr. Hall's instructions that her elegy for Ophelia is prefixed by a bloodcurdling 'Aargh!' from offstage."

Regarding Hall's perception of *Hamlet*, Angela later recalled, "Sex never reared its glorious head in that production, and a lot of people felt cheated because they thought they'd get some fireworks." Still, the play was sold out three weeks before its opening, becoming the hottest ticket in London. Angela was to play Gertrude through May 1976.

Sadly, the production was tinged with personal tragedy. During the final run-through before previews, Albert Finney's father died. For an actor playing Hamlet to confront the demise of his own father was an eerie experience. Less than a month earlier, on November 25, Angela was called away from rehearsal to return to Los Angeles for three days upon the death of her mother. The day after the opening—December 10, 1975—Finney wrote Angela a brief, poignant note: "Welcome to Shakespeare, Dear Mother. She would be proud. Love, Albert."

And upon the opening Angela received a card that meant as much to her as any rave review. "We are all so proud," it read. It was signed, "Deirdre, Anthony, David and always your Peter." After his name, Peter added a loving "X."

Overall, however, Gertrude was not to be among Angela's favorite characters. "I find it very trying playing restrained roles," she noted several days before opening as Mrs. Lovett in *Sweeney Todd*. "I had a nice quiet role playing Gertrude in *Hamlet* a couple of years ago in London, and I hated it."

Just as Angela was opening in *Hamlet*, her next stage appearance was announced: the American premieres of Edward Albee's *Counting the Ways* and *Listening*, two one-act plays to be presented at the Hartford Stage Company in Connecticut, with the playwright himself directing. *Counting the Ways* had recently been staged at the National Theatre, with Beryl Reid in Angela's role. *Listening* was written as a radio play and had been presented in England by the BBC. This would be its debut stage presentation.

Angela had already conquered Broadway and London and proved that she could dance and sing onstage. Now, it was time for her to stretch herself again, as she had attempted in *Hamlet*. Her desire was to do plays she felt were interesting, written by playwrights she admired. And the venue needn't necessarily be the bright lights of Broadway or London's West End.

Of *Counting the Ways*, Angela explained, "Edward refers to it as a 'vaudeville.'" Regarding *Listening*, she said, "It's fascinating dialogue, words . . . but I don't know what the hell it's all about, and I won't until I get into rehearsal. Even then, I may not know. I don't think Edward knows himself, but he wants to find out."

Both plays were concerned with the lack of human contact in contemporary society. *Counting the Ways* consisted of a fifty-minute-long series of vaudeville-style skits and one-liners involving the relationship between a husband and wife, with the characters going on to reveal their true natures. They were billed simply as She and He, and William Prince shared the stage with Angela.

Listening was more of a chamber piece, about a trio who come together in a courtyard. They are an older man and woman, respectively a cook and a therapist, who might possibly have known each other in the past, and a catatonic, suicidal young girl. The characters were billed as Woman, Man, and Girl, and were played by Angela, Prince, and Maureen Anderman.

The plays opened on January 28, 1977. *Variety* called the one-acters "a passable night's theatrical fare," dubbing *Counting the Ways* "light, frothy and amusing." Clive Barnes described it as "a jocular duet for a man's piano and a woman's violin." While *Variety* labeled *Listening* "heavy, symbolic and devoid of dramatic action," Barnes was more in tune with Albee's intentions when he noted, "The beauty of Mr. Albee's writing has never been more evident." But the critic felt compelled to add that "what he is saying here tends toward the self-evident and veers toward the nondramatic."

As always, Angela received positive reviews, with *Variety* noting that she was "commanding in unclear roles."

After finishing her work in the Albee plays in May, Angela again took to the summer tent circuit with another *Gypsy* revival, reappearing at many of the venues she had played in 1975. Angela looked forward to the tour. "It's the sort of theatrical outing you never have in New York," she said. "Theater-in-the-round is a gas, a lot of fun. It's very hard work, of course, but it's wonderful. . . . The excitement you can get going in that tent is very heady." What's more, son Anthony (billed as Anthony Pullen) was on tour with her in a small role, making his American stage debut.

Angela again returned to the musical stage in April 1978, when she and Michael Kermoyan replaced vacationing Constance Towers and Yul Brynner for twenty-four performances of *The King and I*, then being revived on Broadway at the Uris Theatre. While Angela took the part as a favor to her friend Peter Guber, the show's producer, she described playing Mrs. Anna as "the chance of a lifetime for me. There will be no more new Rodgers and Hammerstein musicals." In Towers's and Brynner's absence, some of the songs and dances were restaged for Angela and Kermoyan (who was Brynner's understudy), in order to come closer to re-creating the original production numbers. Richard Rodgers himself acted as Angela's vocal coach.

In the original, the character of Anna was the lead, with the King essentially being a supporting role. This changed when the original Anna, the illustrious Gertrude Lawrence, died during the show's run. At that point, the show's focus shifted to Brynner (who had created the role of the King). However, when Angela came on board, there was a refocusing on Anna. In terms of star attractions, one might say that Brynner had been replaced not by Michael Kermoyan but by Angela.

"Miss Lansbury is an actress first and a singer second," noted Clive Barnes, "a combination that works very well in this great classic Rodgers and Hammerstein musical. . . . The role of Anna was written for an intelligent voice rather than a great voice, and Miss Lansbury points up the drama of every song with unobtrusive delicacy."

18

Attending the Tale

Angela's next Broadway appearance came in *Sweeney Todd,* based on an 1847 George Dibdin-Pitt melodrama that over the years had been rewritten frequently (and known as *Sweeney Todd, the Barber of Fleet Street, The Fiend of Fleet Street,* and *The String of Pearls*). Its scenario was most atypical for a Broadway musical. It follows the plight of Benjamin Barker, a London barber unjustly imprisoned and exiled to Australia by the licentious Judge Turpin, who had taken away Barker's wife and daughter. After fifteen years in a "living hell," Barker escapes and returns to London. To retaliate against a society responsible for destroying him and his family, Barker takes the identity of Sweeney Todd and strikes a curious and deadly union with a woman who has fallen in love with him: Nellie Lovett, a cockney baker and retailer of meat pies. He becomes proprietor of "Sweeney Todd's Tonsorial Parlor," located above Mrs. Lovett's pie shop. Pretty soon, Sweeney is using his razors not to shave his customers but to slit their throats. Their bodies are dumped into Mrs. Lovett's store via a trapdoor, with their remains ending up as the fillings in Mrs. Lovett's pies.

Len Cariou was cast as Sweeney Todd. Angela, brandishing a rolling pin and garbed in a stained pinafore, played Mrs. Lovett. The show opened at the Uris Theatre on March 1, 1979. As writer John Gruen described Angela, she was "looking endearingly frumpy, yet filling the stage with her larger-than-life presence."

The show had its genesis in 1973. Stephen Sondheim was in London to rehearse for the West End revival of *Gypsy*. One evening, he attended a performance of a new *Sweeney Todd* interpretation authored by Liverpool playwright Christopher Bond and presented at Joan Littlewood's Theatre Workshop in the Theatre Royal in Stratford.

The original melodrama was one of the most frequently produced plays in the history of British theater. It was rarely staged in London, however; most often it was put on in the provinces. *Sweeney Todd* was filmed twice during the silent-film era, in 1926 (as a ten-minute-long burlesque with G. A. Baughan in the title role) and 1928 (as a feature-length crime drama, with Moore Marriott as Sweeney). Its most famous screen version came in 1936. Titled *Sweeney Todd: The Demon Barber of Fleet Street*, it starred Tod Slaughter, the maestro of Grand Guignol who was the British cinema's last exponent of Victorian melodrama. A forgotten actress named Stella Rho played Mrs. Lovett.

Sondheim, however, was not interested in offering a traditional interpretation. He was energized by Bond's version, in which the title character is not merely a blood-splattered monster but a victim of the inequalities of nineteenth-century British society: a Dickensian time in which abject poverty existed side by side with prosperity, and the law distinguished—often harshly, and without any sense of humanity—between the classes. By Sondheim's way of thinking, *Sweeney Todd* divided humanity into two classifications: those "who get eaten," and those who "get to eat." The dark irony is how through the course of the story those in the latter category switch over to the former—quite literally.

Clive Barnes was to call Bond's *Sweeney Todd* "radical," "almost Brechtian," and "far more serious than any other version" of the story. Originally, this version was supposed to be imported to Broadway. However, producers Richard Barr and Charles Woodward agreed instead to unite with Sondheim, who had envisioned the possibilities of musicalizing the property. After fulfilling his commitment to pen the score for *Pacific Overtures*, Sondheim got to work on the *Sweeney Todd* music, with Hugh Wheeler writing the book.

"For me, what the show is really about is obsession. I was using the story as a metaphor for any kind of obsession," Sondheim told author Craig Zadan (who had been one of the presenters of *Sondheim: A Musical Tribute*, a one-performance show at the Shubert Theatre on March 11, 1973, which had been a benefit for the National Hemophilia Foundation. Angela participated in the event, along with Len Cariou and other Broadway luminaries).

Sondheim added, "What I wanted to write was a horror movie. The whole point of the thing is that it's a background score for a horror film, which is what I intended to do and what it is. All those chords, and that whole kind of harmonic structure . . . the use of electronic sounds and the loud crashing organ has a wonderful Gothic feeling. It had to be unsettling, scary, and very romantic."

Director Harold Prince initially was reluctant to participate in the project. "Are we going to serve meat pies at intermission?" he asked. "I couldn't find what the motor of the show would be. It was only when I realized that the show was about revenge that I knew how to do it."

In 1977, Prince asked Angela to star as Mrs. Lovett. She initially learned of the show upon receiving a wire from Prince while at her Ireland house. Angela recalled, "I didn't know the play at that time, but one grows up knowing the name Sweeney Todd and one is immediately frightened."

Angela knew that Mrs. Lovett was essentially a secondary character, whose actions revolved around those of Sweeney Todd. Nevertheless, she came to understand the importance of the role within the framework of the whole. Nellie Lovett, with her thick braids and grotesque Raggedy Ann–style makeup, was a night-marishly comic character who would play off the intensity created by Sweeney Todd. Both she and Cariou, in fact, were ordered by Sondheim to play their roles to the hilt. "It became clear to me that the part was a key role, and it also represented the only re-lief in the whole piece," Angela noted. "It had the kind of comedic moments which appealed to me because I knew I understood the backgrounds of the piece really well."

In addition, Angela trusted Hugh Wheeler, with whom she had developed a friendship. "Well, Hugh Wheeler . . . felt that he could make the character I play so interesting that it *would* be a starring role."

Finally, Angela knew that in Nellie Lovett, she had found a character as rare as Rose in *Gypsy:* one that would challenge her to incorporate all she knew of dramatic acting and musical theater.

But most appealing of all was the prospect of working on a new Stephen Sondheim musical. "Obviously, I was immediately interested," Angela said, "because my very first musical venture was *Anyone Can Whistle,* which was also composed by Stephen Sondheim. Well, right then and there I fell in love with Steve's work, and although the show folded after only nine performances, it was one of the most exciting theatrical experiences I've ever had."

She added, "The thing I love about Steve Sondheim is the extraordinary wit and intelligence of his lyrics . . . they're lyrics that you can *act,* and when you're singing them, you're *really* portraying a character. He has always demanded and expected a great deal, and I wanted to live up to his standards." At another juncture, Angela credited Sondheim with affording her "incredible musical opportunities."

Noted Sondheim, "*Sweeney Todd* was easy to write the minute we had cast Angela Lansbury—it wasn't a matter of writing for Angela Lansbury, it was a matter of writing for Angela Lansbury as Mrs. Lovett."

Angela began meeting with Sondheim to hear parts of his twenty-five-song score. "The first song he wrote was 'By the Sea,' and he said, 'Angie, I've written you a song in which you have no time to breathe whatsoever.' Steve always took some kind of delight in doing that and presenting one with that kind of challenge and then saying, 'Well, yes, but you can catch your breath here and you can catch your breath there.' And, of course, most of us who have performed his work find that, indeed, there are places to breathe."

The songs Angela sang in *Sweeney Todd* were indeed exacting. In fact, they were similar to operatic arias. They included complex, lengthy lyrics, the type more commonly performed at the Met than the Morosco. "I sing in voices I never used before," Angela noted. "I belt in ranges I never belted in before."

Sweeney Todd was perhaps the most intricate production in which Angela had ever appeared. The behind-the-scenes dynamics—moving the massive scenery, for one thing—were so involved that an out-of-town run would be an impossibility. The show would only be staged at the Uris Theatre where it would play previews and then open.

"Previewing in New York is pretty horrifying," Angela said. "When I started working in front of an audience, I'm not sure that Hal may not have felt that my tendency to go for the comedic at times was ill thought out. I think he was afraid of my going too far when previews began, but, of course, as time went on, it became apparent that it was necessary to give the audience that relief. But we had to do it under the evil eye of the sternest critics, the New York preview audience."

At first, the show was overlong. Audiences did not quite know what to make of it. While they were overwhelmed by the physical production, they responded uneasily to its mixture of music and blood and guts. Then there were technical problems: how to go about making the blood realistically and effectively spout from the victims' necks? During one performance, a weighty bridge accidently toppled onto the stage. It landed perilously close to Angela and Cariou, who barely escaped injury.

"It was never going to hit us and hurt us, but it actually did come to the deck," remembered Cariou. "It was a strange set of circumstances. We were the only two people onstage at the time. We were singing our little hearts out and I heard this strange noise above our heads. I looked up and saw the bridge was in the wrong position. I just gently went downstage and got Angela downstage of it, and we went on with the singing, and then all of a sudden we heard it very gently kind of come to the deck. It was quite extraordinary."

Another predicament centered around one of Angela's costumes, which had to suit the wardrobe of the woman whose meat pies were known as the "worst pies in London." Angela described it as a "very raggedy sort of woolly pullover," adding that "they decided it wasn't dirty enough. So Franne Lee, the designer, took my costume down to the basement of the theater, took a plate of spaghetti, and slammed it onto the front." Right before she went onstage, Angela was handed the sweater. She recalled that it was "stinking of Romano cheese and tomato sauce and old meat. And I nearly threw up."

The show—all honed and sharpened, with ten minutes of music cut from the first act—opened to mainly jubilant reviews. There were a few naysayers. Walter Kerr, for one, felt that the audience was not "lured into sharing" Sondheim's insight into the story. But Douglas Watt was of the majority opinion when he described *Sweeney Todd* as "a staggering theater spectacle and more fun than a graveyard on the night of the annual skeletons' ball." Critics argued if the show qualified as a musical or a Grand Guignol opera. Its creators preferred the term "musical thriller." However, observed Jack Kroll, "Sondheim has been inching closer and closer to pure opera, and *Sweeney Todd* is the closest he's come yet."

Then there was the matter of Angela's performance. Back in 1972, she told an interviewer, "I don't think I've yet hit my zenith." Perhaps she did here.

Angela again found herself the subject of the highest praise. Watt wrote that she was "an endless delight . . . the grandest, funniest, most bewitching witch of a fairy-tale fright you're ever likely to encounter." Noted Howard Kissel, "Angela Lansbury gives one of the most exciting performances of her career . . . she sings with the gusto and earthiness of an English music-hall performer and plays her part with such relish she makes you fall in love with the grotesque."

"In a show that is as demanding as it is unusual," opined John Gruen, "Lansbury finds a droll reality and wit in a character that in other hands might easily founder. Wide-eyed and simple-hearted, she illuminates the grim proceedings with an astonishingly wide comic range, one that makes mayhem of murder and hilarity of the horrific."

Upon the show's opening, Angela admitted, "I have this awful feeling that I am a disservice to a certain kind of show, because the public really expects me to kick up my legs and be the 'old girl' . . . you know, *Mame*. I don't know what they may feel seeing me in something like *Sweeney*. People always expect the familiar."

Perhaps Angela was thinking of the years in which she was wasted at MGM and typecast as characters well beyond her real age when she added, "But one simply can't go around repeating oneself, can one? Anyway, I've always fed on change and diversity, because it's what makes one grow, and believe me, this 'old girl' wants to grow all the time."

Angela played Nellie Lovett for thirteen months, after which she and Cariou were replaced by Dorothy Loudon and George Hearn. "What we were most proud of," remembered Cariou, "was that we were playing a kind of high melodrama in which it's very easy to fall off that very fine line into farce. All during the time we played together, we never did fall off into that abyss and make it not true to the original staging. There's always a danger of doing that when you're doing a play eight times a week, fifty-two weeks a year.

"The onstage Lansbury is consummate," Cariou added. "She's always there, always focused on what the job is, which is very, very difficult to do when you're in a long run of a show. I think the quality of the show was very high because of that."

Angela found herself nominated for yet another Tony Award. Her competition was Tovah Feldshuh (*Sarava*), Alexis Smith (*Platinum*), and again, Dorothy Loudon (*Ballroom*). Angela walked off with her fourth award—one of eight the show won. Cariou too joined her in the winner's circle; also honored were Prince (Director); Wheeler (Book); Eugene Lee (Scenic Design); Franne Lee (Costumes); and of course, Sondheim (Score). *Sweeney Todd* bested *Ballroom, The Best Little Whorehouse in Texas,* and *They're Playing Our Song* as Best Musical.

Furthermore, in December 1979, Angela was honored by *After Dark* magazine with its Ruby Award—named for Ruby Keeler—as Broadway Performer of the Year. Angela had been nominated by the magazine's editors, along with Richard Gere, Gilda Radner, Donna Summer, Jon Voight, and Robin Williams—all but Voight at least a generation younger than she—and was selected winner in a readers' poll. She was presented the award by Dorothy Loudon. "I'm delighted Dorothy will be helping me out in the kitchen," quipped Angela of her *Sweeney Todd* replacement.

In October 1980, Angela opened a ten-month, six-city road tour of *Sweeney Todd* in Washington, D.C. She starred opposite Hearn. The tour was completed the following August in Los Angeles, with stops in between in Philadelphia, Boston, Chicago, and San Francisco. "Mrs. Lovett is a great role for me," she said during the run in Chicago, "and I guess I wanted to bring a piece of the best of Broadway out to the rest of the country. I just felt the big cities should see a really first-class national tour."

A performance was videotaped at the tour's conclusion, which was eventually broadcast on cable television's Entertainment Channel, and then on PBS. This is the sole public record of Angela cavorting in one of her stage musicals. Captured here is the special quality that endeared her to audiences.

Angela performs her numbers with particular relish. In "A Little Priest," in which she offers a variety of "human meat pies" to Sweeney, she takes on an almost giddy playfulness that transports the number several steps beyond what it might have been had it been sung and acted by a less creative actress. In "By the Sea," she attempts to persuade Sweeney to take her away from London. Here, Angela captures the same whimsy, getting carried away and becoming a comical siren.

Contrast this to her performance in *Bedknobs and Broomsticks*. Her character there was almost as eccentric as Nellie Lovett, but working under the confines of the Disney entertainment formula prevented her from bursting forth and shining as she does here.

19

Angela Plays Agatha

After the release of *Bedknobs and Broomsticks* in 1971, Angela did not appear in movies for seven years. She returned as one member of the ensemble cast of *Death on the Nile*, in which former brother-in-law Peter Ustinov played Agatha Christie's crack detective Hercule Poirot. Also featured were Bette Davis, David Niven, Maggie Smith, Jack Warden, George Kennedy, Mia Farrow, and Olivia Hussey.

Angela was in love with both the script and the role she was to play: Mrs. Salome Otterbourne, a novelist "much given to secret tippling and other excesses." Mrs. Otterbourne is an entirely comical character. She has come to Egypt to research her latest book, a grand opus titled *Snow on the Sphinx's Face;* upon introducing herself to Poirot, she refers to him as "Hercules Porridge." Poor Mrs. Otterbourne is fated to become a murder victim. But the outrageousness of the character allowed Angela to play the role as a campy caricature, who does not so much walk as stumble about. A special delight is her impromptu tango with David Niven.

Of her performance in *Death on the Nile*, Angela was to observe, "I nearly knocked myself out of my seat with my vigor and energy. That had come straight from the theater. I felt I was really quite overdrawn, though, and wished somebody had hit me and made me just tone it all down a bit. But people did rather seem to enjoy it, because audiences tend to love a rather theatrical performance. Well, they got it in *Death on the Nile*." For her work in this film, Angela was cited by the National Board of Review as the Best Supporting Actress of 1978.

During this time, Angela became especially friendly with Bette Davis. Of Angela, Davis recalled, "She's a sweetheart. Angela, whom I adore, is fantastically funny. She's a riot. She broke us up time after time. It was almost impossible to play a scene with her without cracking up. She and Niven do a tango that is the funniest thing since Rudolph Valentino." And regarding Davis, Angela remembered, "She once said to me, 'The thing about us, we're character actresses.' She wasn't a great beauty, and she knew that. She was a tremendous role model for me. She simply encouraged my aspirations at not [being] a great beauty."

Angela next appeared in a 1979 remake of Alfred Hitchcock's 1938 classic *The Lady Vanishes*, scripted by George Axelrod. Like *Death on the Nile*, *Lady* was filmed in London. Angela was cast, simply enough, as the lady who vanishes: Miss Froy, a counterespionage agent. The role was originally played by Dame May Whitty—and turned down this time around by Bette Davis.

Although billed above costars Elliott Gould and Cybill Shepherd, she is on-screen only for about a third of the film. "I tried to make [Miss Froy] a real English nanny," Angela said, "and worked very hard on just the right class accent. Also, in this film there is more reason—Miss Froy has been a nanny to a Prussian family—for her to be associated with British Intelligence."

Angela's performance cannot be faulted, but the film is done in by the lack of chemistry between Gould and Shepherd. Of this *Lady Vanishes*, Angela's ultimate comment was, "So did the film, mercifully."

In 1982, Angela was signed as one of the voices (along with Alan Arkin, Mia Farrow, Jeff Bridges, Tammy Grimes, Robert Klein, Christopher Lee, and Keenan Wynn) in *The Last Unicorn*, a likable animated fantasy that tells of the sole-surviving unicorn who enters a forest in search of others like herself. Angela vividly voices the character of Mommy Fortuna, a mean and ugly witch who captures the unicorn to place her in a carnival. Just when the action heats up, her character is killed off, as the unicorn is rescued and continues on with her adventures.

The following year, Angela appeared in a filmed version of the Gilbert and Sullivan comic operetta *The Pirates of Penzance*, joining the members of the successful Joseph Papp production that had played on Broadway. Angela plays Ruth, who as the somewhat-deaf wet nurse of Frederic (Rex Smith) has mistakenly apprenticed the lad to a band of pirates (his father had said "pilots"). The story focuses on Frederic's attempt to flee the company of the pirates upon his twenty-first birthday.

The Pirates of Penzance is essentially a filmed stage play. The sea on which the pirate ship sails, the sky overhead, and the nearby land are not naturalistic but rather stage sets and backdrops, and the actors give stylized, highly theatrical performances. With heavy mascara and eyeliner making her eyes more pronounced, Angela sings and acts expressively. She first appears with braided buns over each ear; later on, she dresses in flouncy pirate's garb. Angela seems delighted to be playing the role and has a jolly good time as she romps in song with Smith, Kevin Kline, and the rest of the cast.

While filming *The Pirates of Penzance* at London's Shepperton Studios, Angela fulfilled another ambition as she sang opera on a London Records recording of *The Beggar's Opera*. She sent copies of the record to friends back in the United States, along with notes about her fellow performers. "My dear," they read, "Joan Sutherland and Kiri Te Kanawa have absolutely nothing to worry about. I'm in it for the fun, and *Aida* and *Norma* just aren't in my future!"

Angela does well in yet another film that is unworthy of her talents: Neil Jordan's *The Company of Wolves*, a muddled horror-fantasy released in 1984. The film is all atmosphere and special effects; the narrative, which means to be an eerie takeoff on *Little Red Riding Hood*, is often confusing. The film is of interest solely as a precursor in style to Jordan's *Interview With the Vampire*, made a decade later.

Even though she is top-billed, Angela has strictly a supporting role. She plays the grandmother of a little girl named Rosaleen. She looks the part of a fairy-tale granny as she sits by a fireplace knitting and weaving "once-upon-a-time" stories for Rosaleen.

But her look is deceiving because she is no sweet granny. The stories she tells are scary; they are meant to impart a fear of men. Granny meets a sorry fate, as she ends up having her head knocked off—literally—by a man-wolf.

J. Hoberman described Angela's performance as "deliciously clucking." And indeed, she becomes thoroughly immersed in the character, playing the role with just the right tinge of evil.

When John Brabourne and Richard Goodwin, the producers of *Death on the Nile*, were seeking an actress to play Miss Jane Marple, Agatha Christie's fabled septuagenarian spinster-sleuth, they looked no further than Angela. After she finished playing Mrs. Lovett onstage, Angela headed off to England to begin making the film (which was released in 1980).

The Mirror Crack'd would prove to be an intriguing union of Angela's past and future. She was reunited on-screen with Elizabeth Taylor, her old friend and *National Velvet* costar (cast as a fading, pill-addicted movie queen trying for a comeback); Tony Curtis, star of *The Purple Mask* (playing a movie producer); and Kim Novak, star of *The Amorous Adventures of Moll Flanders* (playing a catty rival of Taylor's). Its scenario, set in 1953, was a reminiscence of Hollywood when Harry Cohn was king, Hedda and Louella were queens, and the stars were princes and princesses. Explained director Guy Hamilton, "As such, we wanted to create a feel for the time, for the glamour of the Hollywood stars of the era. What better way to accomplish this than by casting the film with actual stars of the time?"

Angela recalled, of her reunion with Elizabeth Taylor, "Well I was sitting in the lunch tent in costume when I suddenly looked across and there was Elizabeth with a couple of other people. I said, 'Elizabeth, how good to see you.' She looked at me totally blankly and I said, 'It's Angela.' She yelled out, 'Angela—I wouldn't have recognized you in a million years.' Which says something about my makeup. But it's a long time since we worked together. She was eleven and I was eighteen, and I was very conscious of the age gap. Don't forget I'd already played the maid in *Gaslight* and been out on the road doing cabaret, and here I was playing a fifteen-year-old, which I felt was slightly demeaning. But I did see Elizabeth on the MGM lot after that, and I always took an affectionate interest in her."

For this film, Angela was cast in a role that was a forerunner of sorts to her Jessica Fletcher characterization on *Murder, She Wrote.* And, similar to *Murder, She Wrote, The Mirror Crack'd* is a mystery whose plot is dominated by words, rather than action or violence.

As played by Angela, Miss Marple is the essence of a tea-sipping sweet old lady. Garbed in blue cardigan with a modest-length skirt, laced-up shoes (of the sensible variety), and gray hat, with white wig and liver and age spots added to her face, she appeared to be the stereotypical maiden aunt. But she is also a cunning investigator of murder cases, an expert on human nature, and an encyclopedia of poisons and their effects. The scenario of *The Mirror Crack'd* is as much about moviemakers as murder. From among a Hollywood crew shooting a film in a quiet, anonymous English village, Miss Marple must decipher who poisoned Heather Babcock, secretary of the local Women's Institute.

"The problem as an actress," Angela explained while on location in Kent, "is to make Miss Marple's very plainness interesting." The character was described by Agatha Christie as tall and slim with thick white hair piled high atop her head. She has a "pink crinkled face." But many fans identify the character in the manner by which Dame Margaret Rutherford first interpreted the part—dowdy, plump, and dithering. Dame Margaret played Miss Marple in four British films during the 1960s, *Murder, She Said, Murder at the Gallop, Murder Ahoy,* and *Murder Most Foul.* She also appeared as Marple in a cameo in *The Alphabet Murders.* Joan Hickson (who appears in a supporting role in *Murder, She Said*) played Miss Marple in a British television series.

"I never saw Dame Margaret," Angela said, "but I get the impression she played Miss Marple as a tweedy woman in gum boots always falling into duck ponds. I'm trying to get at the woman Agatha Christie created: an Edwardian maiden lady imbued with great humanity and a mind of tremendous breadth. She's very exactly described in the books as tall, pale-complexioned, with twinkling blue eyes and white hair—not a fat galumph of a creature at all. I base my performance on that.

"Also on the fact that she has tremendous alertness and curiosity allied to a great appetite for murder." This last observation about Miss Marple is one that also fits the altogether different sleuth Angela was to go on to play on television, Jessica Fletcher.

"I certainly want to suggest that Miss Marple has a very eager mind and that she has an understanding of humanity based on a detailed knowledge of her own village, St. Mary Mead," Angela said. "I've also made one or two very tiny changes from the book in order to try and heighten the character: for instance, she now does crossword puzzles all the time instead of knitting. But I had to abandon the idea of wearing a whalebone corset for the sake of her posture because you could see it sticking through the costume like some prehistoric animal's rib cage."

All of this offered a glimpse of the manner in which Angela went about developing a character. She added, "I also thought it would be helpful if she did one particular thing while she was thinking so that the audience would always know the old gray cells were ticking over. I felt that, as an Edwardian woman, she would do what my own grandmother did and always smoke a cigarette after dinner. It would be a Turkish cigarette, which she wouldn't inhale but simply use for a period of reflective calm. I did it during tests, but no one liked it. Even Agatha Christie's daughter said, 'I hope you're not going to smoke—Miss Marple would never do that!' I know they're all wrong, [but] I'm desperately searching for some other signal to let everyone know I'm thinking."

Angela also described Miss Marple as "the kind of woman whose big thrill is taking the train up to town and buying some new dishcloths or planting some delphiniums in her garden. I played a cameo part of a drunken novelist in *Death on the Nile*, where I was able to come on and climb up the scenery. But I saw some early rushes here and realized I can't come bustling on as Miss Marple. I have to shut all the doors and shut off. And, after thirteen months of playing *Sweeney Todd* in the Uris Theatre, I promise you that is not easy."

Angela, incidentally, had originally been signed to play Miss

Marple in three films. Following *The Mirror Crack'd*, she was supposed to star in *At Bertram's Hotel*, set in London. However, *The Mirror Crack'd* was the only one produced.

While *Sweeney Todd* was to be Angela's last major Broadway triumph to date, it was far from her last work onstage. In 1982, she opened in *A Little Family Business*, a farce adapted by Jay Presson Allen from a play by Pierre Barillet and Jean-Pierre Gredy, the prolific authors of French boulevard comedy (whose works had previously been adapted into *Cactus Flower* and *Forty Carats* for U.S. audiences).

The play is set in a Boston suburb. Angela starred in a role that had vague similarities to her ill-fated Prettybelle Sweet character: a seemingly shallow housewife wed for three decades to a racist, archconservative (John McMartin), head of a carpet-sweeper factory he took over from her family. The wife becomes head of the company when the husband is felled by a mild heart attack. She comes into her own by promptly going about improving working conditions, thus averting a strike. As a result, the firm earns record profits. By the time her mate returns from a three-month recuperative cruise, our heroine is even pondering a career in politics.

Angela described her character as "a happy woman, who grows even happier. The audience also will leave the theater happier than when they walked in."

Prior to coming to Broadway's Martin Beck Theatre on December 15, *A Little Family Business* played at the Ahmanson Theater in Los Angeles. At that juncture, Angela admitted, "I think we have very, very big production problems. We don't have it all yet." Vivian Matalon was the show's original director. He was replaced after three weeks by Martin Charnin, who worked on it for just three days prior to the Los Angeles opening. Charnin's contributions were not even offered in person; he made them from New York, where he was working on a musical revue. When the play premiered, Matalon was listed as director (although he had been fired). Charnin was credited as "production supervisor." Both men refused to take blame for the show.

A Little Family Business opened to dreadful reviews. The *Variety* critic observed that it "has no business on the stage. . . . [It] is mundane, sordid and stupid. . . . Short of miraculous improvement, it's not a candidate for Broadway." This surprised Angela. "I'm absolutely floored by them [the critics]," she declared. "I didn't expect any critic to love it. But they didn't sit there and listen and watch. The audiences are loving it."

Apparently none of those audiences were of Japanese extraction. Angela's character rescues the family business from "the scourge of Japanese competition"; the Japanese-American community in Los Angeles mounted a protest against what they considered to be "offensive language" in the play.

Despite its problems, *A Little Family Business* did indeed come to Broadway—to no better critical reception. Douglas Watt thought it "a trifling exercise" and a "feeble concoction." Frank Rich called it "the season's worst nonmusical play." Clive Barnes described it as "excessively flimsy" and "thin as a paper parasol in a blizzard."

As usual, Angela emerged unscathed. Wrote Watt, "Lansbury's charm, thrust and almost awesome skill as a comedienne command our respect at all times. . . ." Noted Rich, "Miss Lansbury admirably keeps her wits about her and looks fetching in a wide variety of Theoni V. Aldredge gowns." Added Barnes, "Lansbury . . . is in expansive command of the play. . . . She can even get a terrific, and legitimate, laugh from a line such as: 'I never heard of anything so rude!' "

Despite the failure of *A Little Family Business*, Angela had already enjoyed her share of successes and long runs. In March of 1982, she was honored with a well-earned induction into the Theatre Hall of Fame.

A year later, Angela briefly returned to Broadway once again in a revival of *Mame*. The show opened in July at the Gershwin Theater. All the way down to its dance steps, it was a loving replica of the 1966 production. Also returning from the original were Jane Connell, Sab Shimono, John C. Becher, and Willard Waterman. The only difference for fifty-seven-year-old Angela would be, as she confessed prior to the production, "my figure. It now bunches up in the middle, and that's hard to get rid of."

Mame originally was to come to Broadway in November, after playing for five weeks in Philadelphia and four in Boston. But advance sales in Philadelphia were so bad that the plans were changed, and the show arrived in New York four months earlier. "I just can't believe it," Angela declared. "It's an anathema to find ourselves in this predicament. All I can tell you is, *Mame* is a showstopper. It always was. Believe me, darling, it still is."

However, critic Frank Rich's view that "one doesn't find the present-tense heat that might again weld [the pieces of the show] into a fresh, effortless entertainment" was typical of the majority critical opinion. But as usual, all critics agreed on the quality of the Lansbury performance. Wrote Clive Barnes, "Now only Miss Lansbury remains intact—sensationally intact. . . . The lady is a riot, and an object lesson to everyone over thirty-five or a little something up." Noted Douglas Watt, "I don't think *Mame* is exactly what Broadway has been hungering for. But it can sure use Angela Lansbury . . . looking handsomer and sprightlier than ever." Howard Kissel wrote, "As for Angela Lansbury . . . she makes you question whether years are an accurate term for measurement—if seventeen of them have left her even more elegant and assured, much more energetic than I remember, they cannot be a useful way of gauging time."

After its highly unexpected failure, Angela offered a more thoughtful analysis: "I realized that it's not a show of today. It's a period piece." Certainly, America had changed dramatically in the years since Angela had opened *Mame* on Broadway. Vietnam and Watergate, along with spiraling levels of violence on television sets and movie screens (let alone in everyday life), had made much of the country a darker and more cynical place. With its air of sweet, innocent optimism, *Mame* had become a nostalgia piece. To the cynical listener, such songs as "Open a New Window" and "We Need a Little Christmas" seemed as hopelessly corny and out-of-date as bell-bottoms and beehive hairdos seem today.

But Angela was quick to explain, "The audiences loved it, but it cost a fortune to mount and we couldn't hang on."

20

Committing "Murder"

O ver the years, Angela had been intrigued by the idea of appearing in a weekly television series. Back in 1971, she prophetically observed, "I will save that for my old age." But she was unwilling to forgo starring roles in Broadway musicals and devote herself to the grind of churning out series episode after series episode. "I figured it would burn me out," she explained, "that I would become so familiar it would never enhance my career. The theater had first call on my talents. I genuinely thrill to the excitement of a live audience."

But she also explained, "Quite frankly, I was never offered a leading role commensurate with my experience," adding that "over the years, I was offered series, but the role would always be as a member of some ensemble group in a situation comedy. As I told my agent, I didn't work forty years to come along and support someone I don't even know. If that's what TV was going to mean, I'd have to forget it. If I'm going to do television, I'm going to bring all my experience and specialization to it, plus the expertise one hopes to pick up along the way."

In the property that was to become Angela's debut series, she indeed supported no one. She became the sole star of the smash-hit TV series *Murder, She Wrote*.

Prior to committing to *Murder*, Angela appeared in several made-for-television movies and miniseries, her first TV work since the mid-1960s. She added style and class to her initial project: *Little Gloria . . . Happy at Last*, which aired in 1982. The title refers to Gloria Vanderbilt, and the heart of the film chronicles the custody battle over her between her mother, Gloria Morgan Vanderbilt, and her aunt, Gertrude Vanderbilt Whitney (played by Angela). Playing Alice Claypoole Vanderbilt, Gertrude's mother, was Angela's *Death on the Nile* costar Bette Davis. "I thoroughly enjoyed that [TV film]," Angela said. "[Gertrude] was a fascinating character, and the show was done with great care." Even so, it is one of those "poor little rich girl" stories meant to soothe the middle-class masses by reminding them that the idle rich are venal and petty, unloving and unloved—and thoroughly miserable.

In *The Gift of Love: A Christmas Story*, Angela worked with other former colleagues: costar Lee Remick and director Delbert Mann. It was a Christmas movie that Angela described as "the most unsophisticated thing you can imagine." *The Gift of Love*, which premiered just before Christmas, 1983, is a holiday movie that means to summon to mind *It's a Wonderful Life* and *Our Town*. Janet Broderick (Remick) is depressed. The family business has failed, and she and her husband are experiencing marital woes. Her mother (Angela) has just died. She has a dream in which she joins her mother and relives her life. "Janet feels her marriage and her family slipping away," read the copy on the film's advertising. "To find them again, she must look inside herself and discover the simple secret of happiness."

CBS described the movie as "uplifting." Its preface stresses that it is the "story of a search for simple values." The result, despite typically solid performances by Angela and Remick, may have been a predictable, unabashedly sentimental soaper, but it was extremely popular with audiences.

Angela next was cast opposite an aging, ailing Sir Laurence Olivier (husband of Joan Plowright, with whom Angela had worked decades earlier in *A Taste of Honey*) in the BBC-produced comedy-mystery *A Talent for Murder*, which aired in America on cable television in 1984. The film was based on a Jerome Chodorov–Norman Panama play that opened on Broadway three years earlier with Claudette Colbert and Jean-Pierre Aumont.

Garbed in a Bette Davis–style wig, Angela played Ann Royce Mc-Clain, a wealthy, eccentric, wheelchair-bound mystery writer "second only to the immortal Agatha." Olivier was her attentive, supportive former lover and live-in companion, Dr. Anthony Wainwright, who resides in a cottage on her large estate in Stockbridge, Massachusetts. McClain's greedy family members have convinced themselves that she is senile and are itching to take control of her fortune. She becomes a prime suspect when her daughter-in-law is murdered.

Angela modeled McClain after the legendary Hollywood journalist Adela Rogers St. John. "I liked the character," she said. "In fact, she is so far out over the edge that I remind myself of Miss Piggy in it at times." *A Talent for Murder*, Angela admitted, was a "rush job." But she took the role, she observed, because "I'd always longed to work with Larry," adding the obvious: "He's one of those people we all look up to in this business." Even though Olivier was by that time infirm, he had not lost his acting touch. "He creates that instant of humanity between two characters and you just dissolve," Angela said. "He's a totally original performer."

A far less interesting project was *Lace*, a sudsy, mostly terrible 1984 miniseries based on the popular Shirley Conran novel. *Lace* tells the story of three women who share a secret. While attending a Swiss boarding school way back when, one of them gave birth to an illegitimate daughter. The now-grown-up child, Lili (Phoebe Cates), swears revenge against her birth mother. Only trouble is, the three had sworn never to reveal who had the baby.

"Which one of you bitches is my mother?" Lili demands. "Now it's time to make them suffer," she pronounces. Angela, sporting a thick French accent, knows she is not playing Shakespeare, and so she camps it up in her role as wealthy Aunt Hortense.

Lace was followed that same year by another miniseries, *The First Olympics—Athens 1896*, in which Angela was lost in the crowd as the moneyed mother of an Olympian whose participation in the games serves as his rite of manhood.

All of these projects had bearing upon Angela's career path. "I began to sense that the television audience was very receptive to me," she noted, "and I decided I should stop flirting and shut the door and say to my agents, 'I'm ready to think series.' " So the idea of starring in a television series—the *right* television series—had for Angela become more and more appealing.

There were other reasons for Angela to agree to do a series. For one thing, a lot of money could be made from a successful show. Her initial *Murder, She Wrote* salary was reportedly upward of $1 million per season; even more could be earned if the show became a hit, via reruns and syndication deals. "You're very well paid," observed Angela, "and you pray you'll live long enough to enjoy it."

At the same time, such a venture would allow Angela to reach the widest audience of her career. "A small number of people have seen me on the stage," she said. "This is a chance for me to play to a vast U.S. public, and I think that's a chance you don't pass up." She added, "I'm interested in reaching everybody. I don't want to reach just the people who can pay forty-five or fifty dollars for a [theater] seat." Perhaps out of a long-standing disappointment over her film career, Angela chose not even to consider that she was as familiar to movie audiences as theatergoers.

Additionally, the cost of producing Broadway musicals was becoming increasingly prohibitive. "Every project that came my way for Broadway looked as if it was going to be awfully difficult to finance," Angela noted. One of these was especially fascinating: a Stephen Sondheim–Hal Prince version of *Sunset Boulevard*.

"Hal called me before we closed in *Sweeney Todd*," Angela reported in 1980, "and asked if I'd be interested in *Sunset Boulevard*. I said, 'Wow! No questions asked!' " While on the set of *The Mirror Crack'd*, she explained, "Hugh Wheeler has already written the outline and it seems to me the most perfect subject for a musical."

One only can imagine Angela in the role of Norma Desmond. It might have been a triumph equal to—or perhaps greater than—her Mame Dennis, Rose, or Mrs. Lovett. But this version of *Sunset Boulevard* was not meant to be. The property was not musicalized onstage for another decade, with Andrew Lloyd Webber composing the music and Glenn Close starring.

Angela was also supposed to have starred in *Roza*, a musical with book and lyrics by Julian Moore and score by Gilbert Becaud. The story was based on the Romain Gary novel that had been the basis for the Oscar-winning French film *Madame Rosa*, starring Simone Signoret. Angela would have played the title character, a former prostitute who runs a house for the children of prostitutes. Harold Prince was to direct. But the producers could not raise the money.

"I felt secure enough about my career in the theater that I could safely put it 'on hold' at that particular time of my life," Angela explained. "Not that Broadway wasn't important to me. It got a grip around my ankle in 1957. And thank goodness it did."

The right series came along for Angela in *Murder, She Wrote*. She would play Jessica Beatrice Fletcher, whom Angela described as "an American Miss Marple." What Angela had no way of knowing when she signed on for the series was that she would be doing much more than putting her stage career "on hold."

Actually, two series were proposed to Angela. In addition to *Murder, She Wrote*, she had been approached by Norman Lear to do a situation comedy. Her agents suggested that she accept the sitcom. "But I fell in love with the character of Jessica," Angela recalled. "What appealed to me about Jessica Fletcher is that I could do what I do best and have little chance to play—a sincere, down-to-earth woman." Angela added that "Jessica has extreme sincerity, compassion, extraordinary intuition. I'm not like her. My imagination runs riot. I'm not a pragmatist. Jessica is."

The character was also appealing to Angela because—unlike Miss Marple—Jessica Fletcher is nobody's stereotypical maiden aunt. Nor is she an eccentric. Rather, she is a former substitute English teacher who upon her husband's death began writing mystery novels, which earned her worldwide acclaim. Jessica lives in the picturesque small town of Cabot Cove, on the rocky coast of Maine. Each week, she finds herself at the center of a "real-life" crime, which she is called upon to unravel—or which she insists upon unraveling.

Angela filmed the two-hour television movie that became the pilot of the series. Titled *The Murder of Sherlock Holmes*, it was written by Peter S. Fischer and executive-produced by Fischer, Richard Levinson, and William Link. This trio had previously developed Peter Falk's popular show *Columbo*, another series featuring a crime-solving sleuth.

As the story goes, less than a year before the *Murder, She Wrote* premiere, Levinson (who had met Link in junior high school, resulting in a lifelong friendship and creative partnership) turned on his television set to watch a new made-for-TV movie. The date was October 22, 1983. The show was *Agatha Christie's "A Caribbean Mystery,"* starring Helen Hayes as Miss Marple. He was intrigued by what he saw: an elderly female character carrying an entire movie. Plus, the show did well in the ratings. At the same time, Harvey Shephard, senior vice president, programming, for CBS Entertainment, became interested in developing a weekly mystery series featuring a mature woman in the lead.

(As the show gained strength, the "cozy" mystery-book gossip mill had it that Jessica was modeled after popular mystery writer Charlotte MacLeod. Both are approximately the same age, and both live in Maine. MacLeod's response when asked about this matter is emphatic. "No," she exclaimed. "Everybody asks that. No, no, no, no.")

Despite Angela's relating Jessica to Jane Marple, Levinson, Link, and Fischer had decided not to do Miss Marple but, rather, a combination of the fictional character and her creator, Agatha Christie.

According to Levinson, it was first thought that only one person—Jean Stapleton—could play the role. "CBS loved the idea," he reported. "Jean loved the idea." However, Stapleton was dissatisfied with the *Murder of Sherlock Holmes* script. "She didn't understand the character," added Levinson. "I think after playing Edith Bunker she wanted something more sophisticated than this bicycle-riding widow from Maine."

Stapleton's opinion aside, the trio still saw possibilities for the show. Angela was eventually offered the role and accepted. "She was perfect casting," said William Link. "She had everything we were looking for in Jessica Fletcher."

In its own modest way, *Murder, She Wrote* would prove to be a television landmark. At the time Angela agreed to play Jessica Fletcher, memorable dramatic television series starring a single woman were sparse: Angie Dickinson as *Police Woman;* Anne Francis as *Honey West;* Lindsay Wagner as *The Bionic Woman;* Lynda Carter as *Wonder Woman.* All of these actresses were cast to entice the male libido. Jessica Fletcher was in no way meant to be a sex object. Her brains, rather than her legs, were her main asset. And she was played by an actress who was fifty-nine years old, and who in her other projects was playing grandmothers.

Along with *Cagney & Lacey* (which had premiered in 1982) and *The Golden Girls* (which debuted in 1985), *Murder, She Wrote* was one of a growing trend of successful TV shows centering solely on women, with any males in the cast billed after the title, below the female stars.

Another issue was age. "And let me tell you this," observed Jayne Meadows, a year Angela's junior, as she was guest-starring on the show during the 1985–86 season, "without *Murder, She Wrote* last year, there would be no *Golden Girls* this year. Angela proved to network executives that a lot of us more mature people can help make hit shows too."

Murder, She Wrote was scheduled to air on CBS each Sunday from 8 to 9 P.M. Its lead-in was the solid, widely popular *60 Minutes.* *The Murder of Sherlock Holmes* premiered as a CBS Movie Special on September 30, 1984. In it, the characterization of Jessica differs from what she was to become in the series. Here, she is an unworldly small-towner, a stereotypical Maine downeasterner, with Cabot Cove depicted as provincial to the point of being nineteenth-century. At one point during the first one-hour episode, for no apparent reason, an elderly man is seen manually steering a wooden cart across a street! This depiction segued into the series' first season.

At first, Jessica has authored only one detective novel, *The Corpse Danced at Midnight.* As the series progressed, Jessica became a more sophisticated character. By the series' second season, she had authored a half dozen bestselling novels; her clothes were more chicly tailored, rather than off-the-rack tweedy; and she had lost weight. "People didn't want to see me looking frumpy. Women didn't and neither did men," Angela recalled.

In the *Murder of Sherlock Holmes* scenario, Jessica's nephew

Grady (Michael Horton) brings one of his aunt's manuscripts to the attention of Coventry House, a New York publisher. "I'm not a writer," she tells Grady. "I was just filling time after your uncle died." She adds, "Just because someone wants to publish my book doesn't mean anyone will bother to read it."

However, the book promptly becomes a bestseller. Jessica is invited to New York to promote it and visit her new publisher, Preston Giles. While she's at a costume party at his country estate, a murder is committed. The victim, dressed as Sherlock Holmes, floats dead in the pool. Jessica eventually solves the crime with the help of her nephew (who is falsely accused of the deed), his girlfriend, and the local police chief.

The latter is the first representative of the law to acknowledge Jessica's sleuthing skills. "You know people, ma'am," he tells her. "I can tell that. You see the little things, the inconsistencies."

Assisting Angela was a solid supporting cast of character actors, including Arthur Hill as the publisher (with whom Jessica shares a romantic interlude, before he is uncovered as the killer), Ned Beatty as the police chief, and Brian Keith as a fast-food tycoon who becomes the second murder victim. (In a *Return of . . .* episode that aired seven years later, Hill replayed his character, who had just been released from jail.)

The *Murder, She Wrote* pilot earned numerous favorable reviews. Critic Pat Lowry noted that the series "is just right for mystery lovers." Robert MacKenzie observed, "Jessica is a delightful creation." However, even among those who were not entirely enthralled by *The Murder of Sherlock Holmes*, it was Angela who gained the lion's share of credit for putting the show over. "Stylized, old-fashioned plotting did little to heighten interest nor did obvious goofs about New York (seventy-five cents for bus fare, a railroad terminal with sunlight)," wrote *Variety*, "but Lansbury's surefooted playing and director Corey Allen's use of murky settings effectively save the pilot from falling into the entertainment doldrums." Added John J. O'Connor, "Miss Fletcher's zest occasionally becomes overly cute, but Miss Lansbury keeps the character on a remarkably attractive course."

"When I first heard about *Murder, She Wrote*, I thought it was

a terrible idea," wrote John Leonard. "But Lansbury triumphs in
the two-hour pilot. . . . There [are] . . . cleverly placed clues . . .
and enough snappy dialogue to make you think you might be
watching an MTM sitcom." "With her tall, sturdy frame and
earnest English face, Lansbury can be impressive or amusing to
look at, as she chooses," added Robert MacKenzie. "She knows
how to ride the edge of comedy without going over, and she has
a smile that could toast bread. Television is lucky to get her."

However, Tom Shales, one of the country's highest-profile TV
critics, found serious fault with the character of Jessica Fletcher:
"She's an aggressively adorable little Miss Fixit. She patches up
scrapes and tidies up lives; she even removes stains and cures
corns. Instead of making her feisty and brassy . . . the producers
and writer Peter S. Fischer made her cute and cuddly. She's a
granny Mary Poppins." But what Shales failed to realize was that
some viewers might just prefer cute and cuddly to feisty and
brassy. As Angela noted during the show's first season, "I think it's
the first time a show has really been aimed at the middle-aged audience. I never go shopping without some comfortable lady coming up and saying, 'Thank you for giving us something to watch'."

The Murder of Sherlock Holmes script gently pokes jabs at reviewers and media types. In the show's funniest sequence, Jessica
is interrogated by various television interviewers who are at once
stereotypical and quite recognizable: a snooty elitist, a sensation-
monger, and a pushy feminist, the latter of whom actually reveals
the identity of *The Corpse Danced at Midnight* killer as the "pregnant ballerina."

"I want you to meet some real people, not critics or columnists," Giles tells Jessica as he drives her to his suburban home.
Later on, he alludes to "those self-important media types we live
with because we have to." Jessica responds to his statement with
a question: "Why?" After all, despite her fame, she (at least for the
time being) would choose to remain in quaint old Cabot Cove
rather than move to New York and live among the literati.

The show's writers intended a bias toward simple, small-town
living. Upon first meeting Giles, Jessica tells him that he needs to
eat apples because the pectin would improve his gray complexion.

To a New York cabdriver, Jessica offers a folksy cure for foot calluses.

Meanwhile, life in the big city is at best confrontational and at worst menacing. Jessica sums up her view of New Yorkers when she tells Giles, "Back in Cabot Cove, the only thing we have with claws is lobsters—and we eat them!"

While at a book signing, Jessica asks a customer who has purchased a pile of her books how he would like the copies inscribed. He tells her it doesn't matter, gruffly adding, "If you ever become somebody, they might be worth something." At another juncture, Jessica gets off a bus and walks along a dimly lit Manhattan street. She is promptly mugged by two young men. As one is about to grab her purse and stab her, she is saved by a man who followed her off the bus. He has read her book and says, "Don't you know, Mrs. Fletcher. You're a celebrity."

"We were getting condolences before we even went on the air," observed Richard Levinson. "At best, we hoped that it would be a marginal success." Explained William Link, "The very idea of a series with a mature woman was going against the odds." But *Murder, She Wrote* was an immediate ratings hit. The pilot episode came in first in its time period, with an 18.9 Nielsen rating and twenty-nine share. That season, it was one of five new CBS series; all of the others—*Cover Up*, with Jennifer O'Neill and Jon-Erik Hexum (who a month into the TV season tragically shot himself in the head while loading blanks into a prop gun and died several days later); *E/R*, with Elliott Gould; *Charles in Charge*, with Scott Baio; and *Dreams*, with John Stamos—were short-lived.

Particularly in its first years, *Murder, She Wrote* and *60 Minutes* were CBS's only consistent ratings winners, despite the fact that viewers often had to wait for the shows because CBS football games dragged beyond schedule. Harvey Shephard described the *60 Minutes–Murder, She Wrote* union as "perfect. Both shows appealed to intelligent people and to people over thirty-five. ABC had escapist, youth-oriented programs with *Knight Rider* and *Hardcastle & McCormick* at eight P.M. That maximized our chances of success."

Angela may have been the one *Murder, She Wrote* star, but she was not the show's only regular. During that first season, Jessica shared screen time with Amos Tupper, Cabot Cove's efficient sheriff (Tom Bosley, who had played Angela's husband twenty years earlier in *The World of Henry Orient*). As the series progressed, other characters were added. One of the most popular was Dr. Seth Hazlitt (William Windom), the town's sometimes crusty but always devoted doctor, who is Jessica's best friend. "I love working with him," Angela said of Windom. "We have a terrific chemistry together."

The third primary supporting character has been Mort Metzger (Ron Masak), a replacement sheriff who came on board when Bosley left the series in 1988. Other roles have been sheriff's assistants Deputy Floyd (Will Nye) and Deputy Dave "Andy" Anderson (Louis Herthum); newspaper publisher Ben Devlin (Joe Dorsey); bachelor mayor Sam Booth (Richard Paul); real estate agent Eve Simpson (Julie Adams), Jessica's friend, who often is the first Cabot Cove citizen to meet new residents or visitors; and town gossips Phyllis Grant (Gloria DeHaven) and Ideal Molloy (Kathryn Grayson), who frequent the beauty parlor of Loretta Spiegel (Ruth Roman). In the 1990s, when Jessica began teaching in New York City, she developed a relationship with several of New York's Finest; Barney Martin, Herb Edelman, Jon Polito, Stan Shaw, and Jay Acovone each appeared in several episodes as city cops. George Hearn, who toured with Angela in the *Sweeney Todd* road company, came on board as Sean Culhane, a retired policeman from Ireland who becomes Jessica's teaching colleague.

Angela's other *Sweeney Todd* costar, Len Cariou, appeared in a number of episodes as the enigmatic international agent Michael Hagarty. Keith Michell played Dennis Stanton, jewel thief turned insurance investigator turned cruise ship director. Jerry Orbach appeared as Harry McGraw, a run-down Boston private eye who would work—and conflict—with Jessica. In February 1987, a special ninety-minute *Murder, She Wrote* episode introduced a spin-off show set to premiere the following season: *The Law and Harry McGraw*, featuring Orbach. The show debuted in the fall, but only lasted through February 1988.

While childless herself, Jessica seemed to have endless relatives—all of whom became involved in the show's plots. Grady Fletcher, Jessica's nephew who had such a pivotal role in the series pilot, was most often in evidence. Todd Bryant also appeared as a nephew. Seven actresses—Courteney Cox, Genie Francis, Linda Grovenor, Anne Kerry, Alice Krige, Kristy McNichol, Belinda Montgomery—played nieces.

Jessica had three cousins, played by Dan O'Herlihy, Shirley Jones, and Angela herself, cast as red-haired cousin Emma MacGill. Jackie Cooper appeared as a brother-in-law. Penny Singleton and Peter Bonerz played distant relations.

Over the years, no show the rival networks programmed opposite *Murder, She Wrote* could topple it. In some time zones, the series even drew higher ratings than Sunday-evening World Series games. Even the distinguished Steven Spielberg could not dislodge Angela. In the fall of 1985, Spielberg's half-hour, special-effects-laden anthology series, *Amazing Stories*, broadcast by NBC, was supposed to knock Angela from the Nielsen Top Ten.

Amazing Stories was the TV season's most hyped new show. But on Sunday, September 29, when the two shows bumped heads, *Murder, She Wrote* (with Jessica Fletcher snooping out a killer at a resort hotel) bested the Spielberg entry (which featured a ghost train smashing into a farmhouse). For that week, *Murder* earned the sixth overall spot in the Nielsen ratings, with *Amazing Stories* coming in twelfth place. The following week, *Murder* moved up to fourth place, while its competitor had sunk to the twenty-fourth slot. "I was sure that some of our audience would go to Spielberg out of curiosity," observed Peter S. Fischer. "But, instead, two and a half million more people are watching us each week this year. I didn't believe they wouldn't even be curious."

Spielberg had signed a two-season, forty-four-episode contract with NBC. Some of the shows were directed by Spielberg himself; others were helmed by the likes of Martin Scorsese and Clint Eastwood. But the show neither fulfilled expectations nor found a sizable audience. At the end of the second season, the not so *Amazing Stories* disappeared from the NBC schedule. *Murder, She Wrote* remained ensconced in the CBS Sunday-night lineup years after *Amazing Stories* had become a footnote to Spielberg's career.

The show did on occasion experience dips in the ratings. One such time came during the 1989–90 season, when *Murder, She Wrote* was scheduled against a pair of trendy new series—*America's Funniest Home Videos* on ABC and *The Simpsons* on the Fox network—and Angela cut back on her workload, appearing only to introduce the stories and allow guest sleuths to do the detective work.

Nonetheless, almost ten years after *Amazing Stories, Murder, She Wrote* remained a solid hit. By that time, forty-four series had been programmed opposite it—twenty-one on NBC, thirteen on ABC, and ten on Fox. None had knocked it from the Top Ten. Viewership among younger audiences steadily grew: by 1991, one-third of the show's viewers were under fifty. In January 1995, actor–performance artist John Leguizamo's comedy series, *House of Buggin'*, debuted on Fox opposite *Murder, She Wrote*. His show could not budge Angela in the ratings. A couple of weeks after the *House of Buggin'* premiere, Leguizamo—before making some jokes about *Bedknobs and Broomsticks*—told late-night talk-show host Conan O'Brien, "[Angela's] like an American national treasure. You can't beat her, man."

21

Angela/Jessica

One year into the series, Angela described *Murder, She Wrote* as "a family show, people love it. Best of all, there's no violence. I hate violence." Critic Kay Gardella observed that Jessica solved the crimes "without even using a gun. Now isn't that a change for television!"

Gene F. Jankowski, independent communications consultant and president of the CBS Broadcast Group between 1977 and 1986, was not off-base when he described the show as "possibly the least violent, least sexy show in its class." So what might explain the staying power of *Murder, She Wrote* in an era in which in-your-face shows from *Miami Vice, The A-Team, Hill Street Blues,* and *NYPD Blue* to *Soap, Roseanne,* and *Married . . . With Children* seem the rule rather than the exception?

The show was to become the *Perry Mason* for the 1980s and 1990s, television's equivalent to a cozy mystery novel. The series kept to the formula established in *The Murder of Sherlock Holmes:* a "whodunit" rather than "crime show" formula, which predated television and for that matter radio. On *Murder, She Wrote*, the actual crimes are not seen; instead, the corpse is discovered later on. Despite the fact that violent acts are central to each episode, there is no profanity. There are no bloody corpses. There aren't even car chases, de rigueur for a cops-and-robbers television show.

Rather, the drama is packaged in an inoffensive but highly entertaining manner. Plot and dialogue are the key elements. The drama is more of the drawing room variety, and nothing on the show would offend even the most conservative senior citizen. As with *Perry Mason*, each episode is a puzzle for the mind, with a great part of the fun derived from trying to guess the identity of the culprit and his or her rationale for committing the crime. In the words of Jessica Fletcher, "The unexplained is simply the un-examined"—and during each episode, the unexplained crime is examined and thereby solved.

"People find mysteries extremely satisfying," observed Angela. "There's a beginning, middle, and end. You solve the mystery along with me. Like a crossword puzzle. It's a perfect recipe."

Jessica Fletcher and Perry Mason are also soulmates in that they are perfectly respectable people who are constantly confronted by murder. The accused party is never the guilty party, and it is up to Jessica and Perry to sleuth out the killer.

One *Murder, She Wrote* episode, called "Witness for the Defense," featured a high-powered attorney who challenged Jessica's credibility by pointing out the ungodly number of times she and her family have been involved in murder cases. "I was in the witness box," Angela recalled, "and Patrick McGoohan was saying, 'My dear lady, how is it you have four nephews and three nieces all accused of murder?' 'But they were all innocent!' I answered."

While the show developed a base of younger viewers over the years, its primary appeal has remained among senior citizens. In fact, prior to the show's sale to the USA Cable Network in 1988, this viewership deterred the purchase of syndication rights by independent stations, who feared that advertisers would refuse to pay top dollar for a show with an older audience.

Murder, She Wrote possesses a cordial, familiar ambience, which is partly the result of seeing so many recognizable faces among the guest casts of each episode. Hollywood has been notorious for shrugging off and forgetting faded movie and TV stars. Casting them serves a manifold purpose. First of all, they are fondly welcomed into the living rooms of the older viewers, who remember watching them years earlier on movie and television screens; as the viewers have aged, it is fun to see how these older stars have also aged. Next, those performers are able to earn paychecks and show the world that their acting skills have not eroded.

Because of the tight shooting schedules for a weekly drama series, what Angela came to describe as "instant acting" would have to suffice to get the job done. "You have to know your craft awfully well," Angela observed, to be an effective instant actor. She believed that hiring experienced professionals who came to the set knowing their lines would not only cut down on rehearsal time but also insure that the shoots came off smoothly, since these actors needed little coaching. "But if an actor doesn't know the words well enough to have that emotional drive behind them," Angela said, "he's never going to be really able to play a scene."

By the beginning of the 1994–95 season, more than thirteen hundred guest stars had appeared on the show. Several were in multiple episodes, with an overwhelming number being Angela's old professional colleagues. As early as October 1984—during the series' first month on the air—old MGM cohorts Van Johnson and June Allyson, with whom Angela had appeared in *Remains to Be Seen* over thirty years earlier, filmed an episode called "Hit, Run and Homicide." They played two scientists involved in a murder. Many former MGM contract players followed Johnson and Allyson. Some had appeared with Angela on-screen, while others had not. Among them were Mickey Rooney, Hurd Hatfield, Gloria DeHaven, Kathryn Grayson, Margaret O'Brien, Howard Keel, Cyd Charisse, Jayne Meadows, Ruth Roman, Barry Nelson, Jane Powell, Janet Leigh, Phyllis Thaxter . . .

Still more—Len Cariou, George Hearn, Harry Guardino, Arthur Hill, Michael Connors, John McMartin, Elliott Gould, Mary Wickes, John Saxon, Dan O'Herlihy, Martin Balsam, Richard Johnson, Carroll Baker, Glynis Johns, Mark Stevens, Jean Simmons, Lois Chiles, Shirley Knight, Mildred Natwick, Roddy McDowall, James Coco, Leslie Nielsen, David Warner, Gene Barry, Ernest Borgnine, Olivia Hussey—had appeared with Angela onstage or in her post-MGM films.

While others—the list only begins with Dinah Shore, Yvonne DeCarlo, Vera Miles, Lynn Redgrave, Piper Laurie, Turhan Bey, Robert Culp, Dean Jones, Anne Meara, Dale Robertson, Patrick

Macnee, Eli Wallach, Shirley Jones, Penny Singleton, Janice Rule, Martin Milner, Richard Beymer, Craig Stevens, Jean Peters, Lloyd Nolan (who did his final acting on the show)—were solid veteran movie and television performers with faces familiar to viewers.

One of them, Bradford Dillman, went on to appear in seven different parts. Barbara Babcock and Ken Howard appeared five times. Harry Guardino, Stephen Macht, Norman Lloyd, and Stuart Whitman guest-starred four times. William Lucking appeared as four different cops, in four separate episodes. Hurd Hatfield, Stuart Whitman, Jessica Walter, David Birney, Cliff DeYoung, Steve Forrest, Susan Blakely, and David Soul played both killers and victims.

Jayne Meadows, while filming an episode of the show (in which she appeared as a cosmetics tycoon), observed, "Angela's success with this show has opened the doors to reemployment of, shall we say, seasoned actresses my age."

At the same time, Angela had little tolerance for nonprofessionalism. Once she was kept on the set waiting for a rugged young actor while he pumped up. That was his last appearance on the show. Angela would willingly cater to a less-experienced performer if she sensed he or she had talent. But as she firmly explained, "I do not suffer fools."

Furthermore, Angela insisted on having input on the hiring of directors. During the first *Murder, She Wrote* season, thirteen of them worked on the show. "I enjoy working with [directors]," Angela noted. "But I do object when a director comes in and tries to impose something on the character of Jessica that I feel is out of place and doesn't fit in. I feel like saying to him, 'Look, I've played this role X number of times and I know how to react to this moment.' If they want to say to me, let's sharpen up the moment because it's a story point that I have overlooked, then I'm thrilled and excited. I respond when a director wants to sharpen things and make a moment more acute and interesting because it makes Jessica more interesting in that particular situation."

To ease this problem, the number of directors was reduced to five for the second season. Explained Angela, "I prefer directors with stage experience who know something about actors and acting and who don't make you feel like a piece of furniture to be moved around."

According to producer Fritz Holt, "Any project where Angela is involved, everyone seems to class up. She's very demanding, but of herself first. I know that with *Murder,* she takes home next week's lines to decide if her character would say what's in the script. She brings her great taste to any project, that's why the show is so good." Added Robert Culp, "This show of Angela's is the only dramatic series that stars one no-nonsense, absolutely professional individual. It's a pleasure to work with her. She's a very rare animal in television today."

While the entertainment formula of *Murder, She Wrote* tapped into an audience then being ignored by other television producers, the ultimate success of the show lay with Angela and her characterization of Jessica Fletcher. That success, according to Peter S. Fischer, was "due to [Angela]. She's an absolute delight. Who would have thought that an audience this size would stay week after week to watch a middle-aged lady in sensible shoes?"

In some ways, Jessica Fletcher was born in the character Angela played in *The Mirror Crack'd.* But characters of Miss Marple and Jessica Fletcher are significantly different. Jane Marple is a spinster and an amateur detective, while Jessica is a widow and a writer. Even more important, Jessica is—sensible shoes aside—far more sophisticated and attractive than Christie's sleuth.

If Jane Marple is known to flutter about as she solves crimes, Jessica Fletcher is more grounded. While Marple might be at home in a stuffy Victorian tearoom, Jessica prefers breakfasting at the Cabot Cove diner or keeping fit by bike riding or taking a brisk walk.

In *The Mirror Crack'd,* Angela was made up to look like a dowdy British spinster; in *Murder, She Wrote* she is anything but (despite the manner in which she was depicted during the show's first season). The more "permanent" Jessica Fletcher bespeaks Burberry, while Jane Marple brings to mind Marks and Spencer; it would be simple, classically tailored styling for Jessica.

Angela came to attach much significance to Jessica's wardrobe: "What I have to deal with is keeping the clothes consistent with the character. I have to justify what Jessica is wearing in every scene. I say to myself, well, why did she buy this? Why is she wearing this smart a suit at this point, and why is she in this old shirt here?"

She added, "I've refused to spend my Saturdays putting wardrobe together—I just have that one day to myself. I talk to the costume designer and give him a general idea of what I want, and he also tells me what he feels. I rely on people to help me in these areas."

As Angela explained during the filming of *The Murder of Sherlock Holmes*, "Jessica is an innately sophisticated person, even though she's from a small village in Maine. She's very well educated and fits in everywhere. She becomes a bestselling detective-story novelist, and that takes her all over the world. At first I was going to wear a wig with a lot of gray in it. And my family got around and said, 'No, you go out there and play yourself.' There was no reason to make her dowdy. Women from Maine are terrific-looking dames at fifty-nine or sixty, which is my age."

Angela chose to play Jessica with an animated face. When Angela/Jessica recalls a key clue relating to a murder case, she will crinkle her blue doe eyes. Her bowed mouth gives her a coyness that enables her to convince police to share privileged information. There is a strength to her body. Her shoulders are sturdy and balanced. Often in an affirming gesture, her whole head bobs and rotates on her neck. She turns quickly with an elfish glow. Her way of speaking is distinct, with a respect for words.

Upon the show's premiere, Angela explained, "[Jessica] was the first role I could imagine myself doing. Everything was right there. I could have devised the character of Jessica Beatrice Fletcher myself. I have a feeling she's the kind of person that most people who are familiar with my work will like." Nearing the end of the show's first season, she added, "[Jessica is] not an eccentric, not a busybody or a 'character.' That's just what we didn't want. I think she's a very honest and straightforward person, very ethical, with an open mind. She's a good all-rounder. And she's an American. That's very important, she's very American."

As the years passed, Angela came to see similarities between

Jessica and Auntie Mame. Seven years into the series, she observed, "A lot of little bits of Mame are in Jessica, properties I admire in older women, and did as a child. I had several aunts who let me look in their jewelry boxes and finger their Victorian rings and try on their feathered boas. Young people, particularly, love that in an older relative."

But it is Jessica's ability to solve crimes on paper, as well as in her life, that made her one of the world's most prominent mystery authors—if only within the confines of *Murder, She Wrote*—and such an enduring television creation. To hear the fellow characters she meets in cities across the world tell the story, she is second only to Agatha Christie in the number of loyal readers she has attracted. It ultimately remains a mystery how many mysteries Jessica has actually published. However, the ones cited have such titillating titles as *The Corpse Danced Alone*—a follow-up to *The Corpse Danced at Midnight*—*Murder at Midnight*, and *The Messengers of Midnight*. The latter was even sold to the movies!

Often, plots of the show are set into motion when Jessica visits a locale where she conveniently has a friend or relative who initiates her involvement in the mystery. "It's a device," Angela admitted. "But on the other hand, we're trying to maintain a closed-end mystery, and the only way I can become involved, unless I happen to be out and bump into a crime, is by being brought into it."

Whenever or wherever she is "brought into it," Jessica remains a lovely, friendly woman, one you would like to have as a dinner guest. One imagines she would compliment the antique embroidered tablecloth, be kind to the fine china, and bring a healthy appetite to the table. She is as polite, refined, and friendly as any television character has ever been.

And she remains her own woman. There would be no secondary character who would constantly be at her side as she became immersed in each episode's scenario. Over the years, her good friend Seth Hazlitt might have eased in as a protector of Jessica, who never stops short of danger when on the path to solving a crime. Instead, Jessica remains the sole controller of her life decisions.

In one episode, Jessica moves into a New York apartment whose last tenant has just been murdered, and she is determined to help solve the crime. Seth, who is helping her set up house-keeping, is asleep on the couch early one morning when Jessica tiptoes toward the door in jeans and silk blouse. Seth awakens and questions where she is headed—knowing full well it is into danger. Jessica confronts her friend with no particular anger and only a bit of agitation. "I knew this would happen," she observes. She "will not tolerate" being imprisoned in her own apartment. And off she goes to track the killer.

There is no challenge to her friendship with Seth, no brittle and bothered edge to her voice. While she is a crime solver, there is no need for Jessica to curse like *NYPD Blue*'s Andy Sipowicz or yell at underlings like Theo Kojak.

Angela also resisted network pressures to have Jessica become romantically entangled. "The whole basis of the show is that Jessica is a middle-aged woman alone," Angela noted.

As far back as the show's first season, Angela battled her producers over having Jessica become involved with the owner of a Cabot Cove fishing boat (played by Claude Akins). This character is well-meaning but patronizing and chauvinistic. "There's something wrong with Jessica if she enjoys spending more than fifteen minutes with that man," Angela said. The character was dropped after the show's first season; her subsequent friendship with Seth is far more appropriate to Jessica's temperament.

Angela would also object whenever she felt the show's writers had given Jessica lines or actions that were inconsistent with the character. "I do make suggestions to try and get them to keep Jessica within certain lines and maintain her credibility," she said. "I get upset when her credibility is a little thin at times, because that's when I have to do a lot of eye work to overcome situations where I find myself doing something as that character that I don't buy."

One such example occurred during the filming of an episode set at an archaeological dig. "This is ridiculous," Angela told director Philip Leacock. "Jessica would *know* all about this poison and wouldn't have to ask the doctor." On another occasion, Jessica was supposed to appear at a local library, but instead gets waylaid into going on a television talk show. Angela protested, "Jessica never would be so impolite as to not show up at the library, where fifty people are waiting for her, without at least phoning to apologize." A mention of said phone call was added to the script. In another episode, Jessica appears in a scene garbed in a robe and nightgown while a sheriff (Martin Milner), whose clothes had been drenched in a rainstorm, sits nearby covered by a blanket. "It would be against the character of Jessica to be dressed like that with a man in the room," Angela noted. The scene was changed.

Once she began filming episode upon episode of *Murder, She Wrote*, Angela quickly got in the groove of playing Jessica Fletcher. She noted at the beginning of the show's second season, "[Playing the role] doesn't draw, let's say, on my acting talents beyond knowing how to learn my lines, understand the character, and put myself into the situation." She then added, "It's very enjoyable work in the sense that I don't have to do any, you know, digging down." As the years passed and playing Jessica Fletcher became even more familiar to Angela, she noted, "Series acting is a technique that is quite particular unto itself. There's nothing really required beyond being able to sustain a scene and learn your lines and have attitudes. It's paper-thin, that's what it is. If you try to look behind the eyes of a lot of television actors, there's absolutely nothing going on."

On the tenth anniversary of the show's premiere, Angela observed, "It doesn't represent in any way a stretch, as we call it, to play Jessica Fletcher. But to play Jessica, a role that has such enormous, universal appeal—that was an accomplishment I never expected in my entire life."

Even when *Murder, She Wrote* was just a year old, Jessica Fletcher had come to be a role model for much of its viewership. "I know it's been written that I appeal to the overfifties generation—that's true," Angela said. "I think I've become a role model for a lot of women who are part of unrecognized women of a certain age." Indeed, in an episode broadcast during the show's first season, Jessica arrives in Washington, D.C., to temporarily replace a congressman who has died. A brash publicist attempts to tell her how to conduct herself. "We'll get along," Jessica informs him, "when you recognize I'm not your addlepated old aunt from East Nowhere."

"I know there are some women who are my age, some widows, some who have never married, who relish the fact that I'm there with this character, who really love the fact that Jessica gets out there and messes in with life," Angela noted. "I think it's wonderful to be able to represent that, even to the smallest degree, on television."

On another occasion she observed, "I like to feel that the sky's the limit for women. And just because you're fifty-nine or sixty or sixty-four or eighty-four doesn't mean you can't be a vital, interesting, alive, energetic person. An inquisitive individual who can relate to all kinds of people and have an active interest in many things that aren't necessarily on the menu of the average woman. . . . I'd like Jessica to fall into this category. She takes and gives back all the time. She gives as much as she gets, and there's more to her than being a substitute English teacher or a writer. She's a pretty special piece of feminine goods as far as I'm concerned."

Because of the wide audience a successful television show enjoys, Angela has come to be known more for her performance as Jessica Fletcher than for any Tony Award–winning stage role or Academy Award–nominated screen role. As a result, her most disreputable characters, from the sluttish Nancy in *Gaslight* to Raymond Shaw's loathesome mother in *The Manchurian Candidate* to Nellie Lovett, conspirator with the murderous Demon Barber of Fleet Street in *Sweeney Todd,* have virtually come to seem like footnotes to her career.

"There's nothing like a good villainess," Angela noted when she was preparing to play Jessica Fletcher. "You can go down and chew on great chunks of scenery. But some of the most successful things that I've done have been playing the simplest possible women. The character of Mavis in *The Dark at the Top of the Stairs* was a tiny part and yet remembered to this day by everybody who ever saw that movie. The other part that I got a lovely response from was *Gift of Love* . . . in which I played a grandmother in a Vermont family. The character was so simple and true, and again, the people who saw it absolutely loved it. My sense is that Jessica

Fletcher also embodies many of the qualities which are quintes-
sentially American. She's very open, resilient, and brave, a woman
of very strong moral character. But she's not a bore."

Over the decade-plus in which she has been a television character, Jessica Fletcher has led quite an active—and extraordinary—
life. She has traveled across the United States and the world,
where she would constantly happen upon murder scenes. She has
visited Paris, London, Jamaica, Milan, Mexico City, Moscow,
Monte Carlo. Favorite American locales have been Washington,
D.C., San Francisco, and New Orleans. She has been taken
hostage at a women's prison; temporarily represented her district
in Maine as a congresswoman; helped to halt construction of a
high rise in Cabot Cove; become involved with the U.S. World
Cup ski team; solved a thirty-six-year-old murder, thus clearing
the reputation of her late husband; and even took part in an in-
vestigation of the JFK assassination!

In one of the more intriguing and nostalgic *Murder, She Wrote*
episodes, which aired during the 1985–86 season, Angela appeared
in a dual role: as Jessica and her cousin Emma, a London music-
hall singer whom someone is attempting to kill. The character was
given the surname MacGill in tribute to Moyna. (Indeed, regular
viewers of the show will know that Jessica's maiden name is
MacGill!) At one point in the episode (which was titled "Sing a
Song of Murder"), Emma was supposed to sing; the script described her as that "singular sweetheart of song" and "beauteous
balladeer." Angela called her old colleague Stephen Sondheim for
advice on what to perform. "Do 'Goodbye, Little Yellow Bird,'
which you sang in *The Picture of Dorian Gray*," the composer suggested. Angela did just that, with Emma garbed in a red velvet
dress and false eyelashes.

The name MacGill was seen again on a grave marker in an
episode that aired in 1993. Here, Jessica returns to her ancestral
home in Ireland and visits a graveyard in which her ancestors, the
MacGills, are buried.

In 1986, Jessica united with *Magnum, P.I.*, Tom Selleck's detective series, in an effort to hike the ratings of both shows during November sweeps. The two-part story line began during a

Wednesday-evening *Magnum* and concluded the following Sunday on *Murder, She Wrote*. It had Jessica traveling to Hawaii where she assists Magnum in proving his innocence when he is accused of murder and jailed after being discovered holding a gun over the body of a hired killer. The resulting scenario consisted of multiple murders which both sleuths linked up to solve.

Another unusual episode of *Murder, She Wrote* aired in May 1987. It was the continuation of a story that began in 1949, in a feature film released by RKO entitled *Strange Bargain. Variety* described it in words that might have been used for dozens of *Murder, She Wrote* episodes: a "nifty whodunit for its class. Sharply written and tautly directed, pic rolls with steady momentum, gathering tension right up to the finish line . . . with sufficient number of surprising twists to keep the customers baffled but intrigued all the way."

Strange Bargain is the story of Sam Wilson (Jeffrey Lynn), an underpaid bookkeeper who is the husband of understanding and devoted Georgia Wilson (Martha Scott). Wilson's boss, Malcolm Jarvis (Richard Gaines), offers him $10,000 to help make the latter's projected suicide appear to be a case of murder so that Jarvis's family might receive his life insurance. With a heavy conscience, the bookkeeper handles his end of the deal. However, a crafty police lieutenant, Richard Webb (played by Henry Morgan, who later changed his billing to "Harry Morgan" to differentiate himself from the popular radio comedian-raconteur), senses foul play. Indeed, Jarvis was actually murdered, and Wilson finds himself accused of the crime. At the finale he is exonerated, and the real killer is unmasked.

Lynn, Scott, and Morgan reprised their roles thirty-eight years later on *Murder, She Wrote*. The episode, called "Strangest of Bargains," incorporated black-and-white scenes from the original film. However, the finale of *Strange Bargain* was conveniently ignored. Here, it is noted that Sam Wilson was wrongly found guilty of murder and spent thirty years in jail. The result: Jessica has a mystery to solve.

Another unusual episode that season utilized a gimmick popularized during the 1940s in Lucille Fletcher's twenty-two-minute radio play *Sorry, Wrong Number,* which starred Agnes Moorehead (and was made into a film featuring Barbara Stanwyck). *Sorry, Wrong Number* tells of a bedridden woman who accidently overhears a murder being plotted on the telephone and, at first, does not realize she is the intended victim. The episode features Jessica in a similar situation. The only differences are that the woman in the original is a hypochondriac who dies at the finale, and Jessica is not the killer's target.

Finally, during 1991–92, *Murder, She Wrote* paid homage to Alfred Hitchcock when Jessica solved a murder committed in the famed *Psycho* house, which is located on the Universal Studios lot.

In 1988, the USA Cable Network acquired exclusive syndication rights to 111 episodes of *Murder, She Wrote* for six years. The price: a reported $40 million. The deal was then the largest of its type in the network's eight-year history, as well as the most expensive program to have been acquired by any cable channel.

The show performed as solidly on cable as it did on CBS. Five years after the USA Network deal, Gene Jankowski observed, "The last time I looked, the most popular drama on basic cable was *Murder, She Wrote.* . . . And after eight years, it is still one of the most-watched programs on CBS."

At the time of the cable sale, plans were made for a hardbound book to be "authored" by Jessica Fletcher and real-life mystery writer Donald Bain. *Gin and Daggers,* the first of a series of *Murder, She Wrote* mysteries, reached bookstores in 1989. Set in London, the story places Jessica at a convention of the International Society of Mystery Writers, at which she is scheduled to deliver the keynote address. Before settling into the posh Savoy Hotel, she makes a weekend trip to visit a dear friend, world-renowned octogenarian mystery writer Marjorie Ainsworth. Before long, someone has plunged a dagger into Marjorie's heart, and Jessica finds the body.

Bain attempts to capture the flavor Angela brings to Jessica Fletcher, but the results are disappointing, despite the introduction of a romantic interest in the character of dashing George Sutherland of Scotland Yard. Whether Bain hadn't been a regular viewer, or whether he chose to impart his own creativity onto Jessica's character, things are amiss. Never before have eavesdroppers into Jessica's life had to put up with so much maudlin remembrance of her dear dead husband, Frank. Never before had they looked upon Mort Metzger as such a rube. Also, Mort keeps calling Jessica "Jess" when he usually refers to her as "Mrs. F," and he calls Seth Hazlitt "Seth" instead of "Doc."

The biggest faux pas involves Jessica getting into the driver's seat of a car and proceeding to motor off from the Savoy through London traffic. As any *Murder, She Wrote* devotee knows, Jessica Fletcher is strictly a bicycle rider. She does not know how to drive.

It was five years before the second book in the series arrived. Entitled *Manhattans and Murder*, it was also "authored" by Fletcher and Bain. In a story set only a year after the one told in *Gin and Daggers*, Jessica is on a publicity jaunt to New York City during the Christmas holidays. She recognizes a sidewalk Santa as a Cabot Cove native who had been involved in drug smuggling and had disappeared years earlier. He becomes the first in a string of murder victims.

In this book, the character inconsistencies remain uncorrected, but at least Jessica does not drive.

Book number three is *Rum and Razors*, an entertaining tale of Jessica's scuttled attempt to enjoy a relaxing vacation at the luxurious St. Thomas resort owned by a couple formerly of Cabot Cove. However, here, Bain's mea culpa attitude toward his error of Jessica driving is made plain. As her passport is being stamped, she notes, "A valid driver's license would have sufficed, but I don't drive." Later in the story, Jessica wants to rent a boat from a local man. He asks her, "You know how to run a boat?" to which her response is, "I don't even know how to drive a car."

At one point, Jessica describes her attempt to appear to the police as though she has been awake for hours, rather than having just awakened. "I failed. Another lost Oscar nomination," she muses. Considering that Jessica was never an actress, and that Angela has actually been nominated for three Oscars but came home statueless each time, this remark would seem to erase the line of demarcation between the fictional mystery writer and the actress who plays her.

After placing Jessica in different locales, the fourth book in the series, *Brandy and Blood*, brings the action back to Cabot Cove. The mystery centers around the conversion of a local mansion into a fancy artists' retreat, the Worrell Institute for Creativity. At a town meeting, the locals voice prejudices against artists comparable to the elders of Salem decrying witches. To television viewers of *Murder, She Wrote*, such a group of small-minded rubes populating Cabot Cove seems unimaginable.

In what appears to be a leitmotif in this series of cozies, Bain continues to expound upon Jessica's inability to drive. On four occasions he telegraphs this fact to the readership, including a scene in a Boston nightclub where Jessica, having been placed in a trance by a show-biz hypnotist, panics when she is told she is "driving down a beautiful coastline."

In this book and the following one, a San Francisco–based yarn entitled *Martinis and Mayhem*, Jessica is placed in pulse-pounding, life-threatening predicaments that certainly keep the readers turning pages. But Bain does not capture the *Murder, She Wrote* characters in their true spirit. He has yet to learn the details of Jessica and her life in Cabot Cove.

22

Stress on the Set

Despite the tremendous success of *Murder, She Wrote*, not all was sweetness on the set. When Angela signed on, she quite frankly did not realize what being the sole star of an hour-long weekly television series entailed. For a veteran actress who had come to value attention to detail in her work, the speed in which the series was produced proved daunting.

Is the script high quality? Angela would ask. Have the right actors been cast? Will the director be supportive? These concerns forced Angela to become increasingly involved behind the scenes.

The toughest issue of all for Angela was the grind of a tight shooting schedule with long, concentrated hours. Prior to retiring on the night before a typical workday, Angela would rehearse her lines. The following morning, she would arise at five-thirty. She would have breakfast and be on her way to the studio by six-fifteen. While being driven to work, she would review her lines.

Upon arriving at the studio, Angela would retire to the privacy of her trailer. There, she would put on her makeup base by herself, rather than depend upon the makeup artists in the crowded, smoky makeup trailer. Fifteen minutes into this, a hairdresser would come to her trailer and begin curling her hair. Getting her hair done, putting on makeup, and dressing for her first scene would take an hour and a quarter. During this, Angela might also be conferring with the costume designer over wardrobe for the following episode.

The first rehearsal would begin at seven forty-five, when Angela would meet the actors on the set. The director would discuss his ideas on how the scenes should be played and where the camera should be set. The show was rarely filmed in sequence; once rehearsal began, and the essence of the scene and how it fit into the greater whole became clear, Angela would offer input. Here, she would try to insure that Jessica was not in any way acting out of character—a special concern if the director was new to the show.

After rehearsals and lighting tests, filming would begin at about eight-thirty and continue until 1 P.M. After a forty-five-minute lunch break, and fifteen minutes for retouching hair and makeup, shooting would resume. During the show's first season, this would continue until the day's allotted scenes were completed, which would be at 8 or 9 P.M., or even later.

Angela would then return home. At her arrival, Peter would hand her a Perrier with lime. After a light dinner, she would check over the following day's script and then retire for the night.

Almost from its outset, rumors abounded that Angela would be leaving the series. Several months into its first season, she even admitted, "I'm not going to work this hard forever. It's almost forced labor." During the fall of 1988—the beginning of the show's fifth season—Angela reiterated these concerns when she declared, "I think at my time of life I need more time for myself," adding, "I have a lot of projects and things I can do. We had a long season last year."

Around that time, Angela was planning to depart the show but still play Jessica in three or four television movies per season—a format similar to the one in which Raymond Burr's Perry Mason had been resurrected. She also expressed interest in doing a television situation comedy. "A sitcom is a piece of cake compared to dramatic television," she observed. "They rehearse all week and do the show rather like a live performance on Friday night. It's concentrated work, but it's fun and bright and alive. It sounds as if I'm interested in it, quite frankly."

As the years passed, Angela tired somewhat both of the grind of playing Jessica and of the character herself. "I'm a woman of the theater and of movies, and a television series becomes a habitual involvement over five seasons. It's not real life," she explained in 1988. "Jessica is a listener, a questioner. She's a cerebral soul. She's seldom emotionally involved in the plots. That's up to the guests. They get to play the dramatic roles. I don't mind. It's fun. But, you know, someone likened my job on *Murder, She Wrote* to my being a horse pulling a milk wagon, while I'm ready to run the Grand National." She described acting on a weekly television show as "a production-line process, like making slices of cheese. They have to be uniform and cut to size."

Additionally, Angela had become dismayed by the lack of concern among Hollywood honchos for the viewership that preferred *Murder, She Wrote* to a far more glitzy show. Even more specifically, she had wearied of the attitude among CBS executives toward Jessica Fletcher. "People in this town are so cut off from their audience," she observed as the show was into its eighth season. "I never felt they gave the show its due. They don't watch it. They don't understand what this show means in the scheme of things for viewers."

But Angela stayed with the show, year after year. Her incentives were her salary, plus the opportunity to entertain millions of viewers each Sunday night, plus the realization that she was a role model to older women. Over time, Angela was to become her era's highest-paid television actress and one of the most notable and successful people in her profession.

There also were reports of contention among Angela, CBS, and Universal Television, the show's coproducer. The network had allegedly been ignoring her complaints of being overworked. When *Murder, She Wrote* began, Angela—who was in most every scene—toiled fourteen or more hours each day. Living a sedentary lifestyle, she gained fifteen pounds. "It was ridiculous," she noted. "I became emotionally weak and physically ill. I went to chiropractors because I developed pains in my legs and hips and had difficulty walking." Once the show went on hiatus, Angela lost the extra weight in four months through a modified diet and increased physical activity.

During the show's second season, the network had no choice but to extend the shooting schedule of each episode from seven to eight days and permit Angela to work no more than twelve hours a day. Now, she would stop working promptly at 6 P.M. "If I make an exception for one scene," she explained, "they'll say, 'You did it last week so why can't you stay over now?' I have to be bull-headed—which is very much against my grain."

What's more, CBS had objected to her purchase of a $6,000 Bob Mackie gown she wore as hostess of the 1988 Tony Awards. Considering the show aired on CBS, the network finally agreed to pay the bill.

At this time, CBS was trailing rival networks ABC and NBC in the prime-time ratings wars, with *Murder, She Wrote* one of the network's few solid hits. Furthermore, prior to the 1989–90 season, ABC was reportedly attempting to negotiate a deal for *Murder, She Wrote* to switch networks and fit in as a rotating segment of its *Saturday Mystery Movie*.

All of this allowed Angela leverage with CBS. In 1989, Angela and her production company, Corymore—named for a favored vacation spot in Ireland—became the show's coproducer with Universal. In February of that year, Angela and Corymore signed an exclusive pact with CBS insuring the network her services on *Murder, She Wrote* for the 1989–90 television season—the sixth and "last" for the show. Part of the deal gave Angela a reduced workload. For certain episodes, she would simply sit in an armchair and introduce guest sleuths. At the show's end, she would reappear. *Murder, She Wrote*, of course, continued the following season, during which Angela introduced five more episodes.

Earlier, the network contracted with Corymore to produce thirteen episodes of a new half-hour series starring Angela, for broadcast beginning in the fall of 1990. Nothing came of this plan. However, in May 1990, Angela referred to the possibility of a new series, this time slated for the fall of 1991. With quite a measure of sarcasm, she announced that those involved in the series would be husband Peter, sons Anthony and David, and "all the creative geniuses at CBS—and a lot of others, I'm afraid, who want in on our deal." Neither did this plan come to fruition.

In September 1990, it was reported that the 1990–91 season would definitely be the *Murder, She Wrote* finale. "It is the last season," Angela stated. "I don't want to continue with a weekly show."

The 1990–91 season came and went. *Murder, She Wrote* endured. In March 1991, it was announced that Angela planned to return to the series the following season—and work a complete schedule. "She had previously told the network that this would be her last season," observed a CBS spokesperson. The show was then in its seventh year. Angela's contract called for her to work a maximum of twelve hours per day, on a four-day workweek. Three months later, Angela told the press, "I'll have to work more weeks in the year, but if I weren't enjoying it, I wouldn't be doing it."

At that juncture, the creative forces behind the show felt it beneficial to ratings to relocate Jessica to New York City, where she would take an apartment on Manhattan's Upper West Side. She would commute there each week from Cabot Cove and resume teaching as an instructor of creative writing and criminology at fictional Manhattan University. The goal was to increase the show's appeal to younger viewers. Indeed, during this season Jessica joined the high-tech age, finally replacing her manual typewriter with a personal computer.

Angela, who was then sixty-five years old, described Jessica as being "vitally involved with a young group of people who are her students there. . . . She's teaching a class in criminology, using all the arts she has utilized for solving her crimes and writing her books and putting it all back into this young group."

Later on, she said, "What really brought me back was the realization that *Murder, She Wrote* had really become a national habit." As the 1991–92 season started, the show had become television's second-longest-running drama, trailing only *Knots Landing*.

Soon afterward, however, the hype was that Angela would be leaving the show to star in a television series based on the Academy Award–winning film *Driving Miss Daisy*. Angela was to have been cast in the weekly half-hour show as an elderly Southern Jewish woman. Peter Tortorici, CBS executive vice president for programming, noted, "It's going to be a very difficult decision. But we are committed to doing whatever Angela wants." The show would have run in the same Sunday time slot as *Murder, She*

Wrote. "We'd be crazy not to put her there where audiences know where to find her," added Tortorici. But nothing came of Angela and *Driving Miss Daisy.* In 1992, a pilot aired on CBS for a prospective *Driving Miss Daisy* series, starring Joan Plowright— Angela's onstage daughter over thirty years earlier in *A Taste of Honey. Murder, She Wrote* continued on the network.

Another reason for Angela's staying with the series was that she was able to surround herself with her family while on the job. By that time, Angela and Peter had long been ensconced in "a typical California house" in Brentwood. Their children and grandchildren lived nearby. They also maintained a small apartment in Manhattan; they had sold their house in Ireland more than a decade earlier, but still made short trips there, residing in hotels.

Peter had become heavily involved in *Murder, She Wrote* as Angela's unofficial consultant and adviser, a role that evolved into what she described as "the watchdog over everything." Eventually, he became chairman of Corymore Productions. During the show's first season, son Anthony was Angela's dialogue coach. He later became one of the show's directors, eventually helming every third episode. Stepson David became Corymore's president. Brother Bruce became a supervising producer and an occasional writer on the show; during the 1992–93 season, he and Anthony coauthored an episode, entitled "A Christmas Secret," which was a *Murder, She Wrote* first: it had no murder! "I don't believe that I would have remained with the series if I hadn't had my family around," Angela said.

And by the 1992–93 season, Angela had risen through the show's behind-the-scenes ranks, becoming its executive producer. As old friend Hurd Hatfield explained, "Angela's got the whole show on her neck now." A year earlier, Peter S. Fischer allegedly wearied of the series. Angela pressed and was rewarded with what she had rightfully earned. "It means," she explained, "I have a tremendous amount to say now about what we do and how we do it." That season she was busier than ever, not just with playing Jessica Fletcher but with her responsibilities in finding fresh story lines, casting the right actors, and creating the proper ambience.

Angela would play her scene, then she would sit in a chair and nod to the director that all had gone well. With that, he would yell, "Cut."

Yet Angela would not allow her executive position to jeopardize the quality of her performance. "I think the last time I did the show was her first year as executive producer," noted Len Cariou. "She was fine. She was never split in the sense that she wasn't there to work [as an actress]. She's a very professional lady and never let the fact of her being executive producer compromise her work as an actress."

By all accounts, CBS—for the time being, at least—knew it had a winning formula with *Murder, She Wrote*. The show had slumped a bit in the ratings when Angela made fewer appearances. But now Angela was back in full force, starring in every episode, and *Murder, She Wrote* was firmly ensconced as a Top Five show. Observed then CBS president Jeff Sagansky, "This show was tracking downwards. This never happens; shows that are a decade old don't get stronger like this one has."

And so *Murder, She Wrote* kept on rolling. It had long ago become a Sunday-night institution; it and *60 Minutes* were end-of-the-weekend staples to rival the popularity of that old CBS Sunday-night standard-bearer *The Ed Sullivan Show* during the 1950s and 1960s.

On September 12, 1993, Angela began her tenth season as Jessica Fletcher. Early on, the show's two hundredth episode was aired. That landmark program featured a guest appearance by Mickey Rooney. At the end of the 1993–94 season, 219 episodes had been broadcast. There had been 233 murder victims. Only 49—or 21 percent—had gasped their last breaths in Cabot Cove.

By then, the show had become the longest-running detective drama in television history. It held the record for most consecutive seasons as the highest-rated dramatic series and had been seen by over 10 billion viewers. In September 1994, on the tenth anniversary of the *Murder, She Wrote* premiere (and at the beginning of its eleventh season), Larry King asked Angela if she was planning to give up the show. "That's the $64,000 question," she said. "When I became executive producer, I got a whole new lease on life. Suddenly, I'm a businesswoman as well as an actress. Balancing those two aspects of the job has made it far more interesting to me." In the middle of the 1994–95 season, it was announced that Angela had signed for yet another season.

However, Angela's problems with CBS were not all past history. In June 1995, after concluding yet another in a string of disappointing prime-time seasons, the network announced its new fall lineup. In what can only be described as an act of desperation on the part of CBS, *Murder, She Wrote* was yanked from its Sunday slot and switched to Thursday at 8 P.M.

Why tinker with one of the networks' few successes? After all, just a few years earlier, Peter Tortorici had declared that CBS would be "crazy" to move Angela out of her Sunday slot, "where audiences know where to find her." *TV Guide* described the move as "a possible burial" of the show, placing it opposite NBC's hot new youth-oriented sitcom *Friends*, a high ratings earner. "We think Thursday is a good spot for the show," David Poltrack, CBS's scheduling executive, told the press. "The fifty-plus audience hasn't been served there."

Rumors circulated throughout the industry that Angela was livid. "We're very disappointed and in shock," admitted David Shaw. "We just hope the audience will find us."

"But we'll do our best to win here too," Angela declared.

In all fairness, it must be noted that the other networks also fiddled with their schedules. NBC moved its hit comedy *Mad About You* from Thursday to Sunday, with the original intent to have it compete with *Murder, She Wrote*. The switch was that show's fourth time change, angering star Paul Reiser so much that he did not attend NBC's presentation to its advertisers.

Still, by the mid-1990s, CBS—once the Tiffany of networks—had become solidly entrenched in third place in the Nielsen ratings, behind ABC and NBC. Fooling with one of its few hits seemed to be outright lunacy.

Over the years Angela won Emmy Award nomination after Emmy Award nomination for playing Jessica Fletcher. "I vowed I wouldn't [attend]," she said beforehand, of the September 22,

1985, show, "after recalling what it was like to sit in the auditorium the three times I was nominated for Oscars—and lost. It was the most humiliating thing in the world. One gets more philosophical about such things when one gets older. Still, I can't forget how nice it was with the Tonys." By this time, Angela was becoming a happy fixture as a Tony Award hostess-presenter, where each year she would return to Broadway and model beautiful Bob Mackie gowns. "I take full advantage of the occasion to put on something glamorous," she declared.

But with television, Angela was destined to become the prime-time version of Susan Lucci. Not all of her nominations were for Jessica Fletcher. In 1982, she was up for an Emmy as Outstanding Lead Actress in a Limited Series for her role in *Little Gloria . . . Happy at Last*, but lost to Barbara Stanwyck, for *The Thorn Birds*. That first *Murder, She Wrote* season, she was nominated twice, for playing Jessica Fletcher and for the Outstanding Individual Performance in a Variety or Musical Program in her role as Mrs. Lovett in the televised *Sweeney Todd*. For the latter, she lost to her costar, George Hearn, in a category that does not segregate the sexes. For the 1986–87 season, she was again nominated in that category, for hosting the 1987 Tony Awards; the winner was Robin Williams, for his appearance on "A Carol Burnett Special." For 1989–90, Angela was nominated yet again for hosting the Tony Awards. This time around, the victor was Tracey Ullman, star of *The Tracey Ullman Show*.

Each season from 1984–85 on, Angela received nominations for Outstanding Lead Actress in a Drama Series. She lost, year after year, to Tyne Daly *(Cagney & Lacey)*; Sharon Gless *(Cagney & Lacey)*; Gless again; Daly again; Dana Delany *(China Beach)*; Patricia Wettig *(thirtysomething)*; Wettig again . . . "It just makes me laugh now," Angela told Larry King in 1994. "I think it's very funny, to be neglected like that so often. I just have to take it with a grain of salt."

Angela may have gone home year after year without a statuette, but this gaffe did not dim her approval rating in the eyes of the press or her fans. In May 1991, she was presented with a lifetime achievement award from the British Academy of Film &

Television during a luncheon for Queen Elizabeth at the Library of Congress in Washington, D.C. A year later, columnist Liz Smith wrote that Angela deserved a special Emmy citation for her years of service on *Murder, She Wrote*.

When Angela was a hostess of the 1993 Emmy Awards show, *TV Guide* saluted her with a hearty "Cheers to Angela Lansbury, host with the most and, though Emmy-less again, the evening's most winning star."

Reported Liz Smith, "Loved the comment by a TV producer on the big-time temperament of small-screen stars. 'There should be a sign on the L.A. city limits. It should read, 'Look! They Can't All Be Angela Lansbury!' "

23

Movies for the Small Screen

Despite all of the time she was devoting to *Murder, She Wrote*, Angela continued appearing in made-for-television movies and miniseries. While she had her choice of roles, allowing her the artistic challenge of playing characters other than Jessica Fletcher, her dream of finding true stardom on the big screen was not realized.

Her first telefilm during the *Murder, She Wrote* years was not her best: *Rage of Angels: The Story Continues*, based on a Sidney Sheldon novel and broadcast in 1986. The main character was beautiful, brilliant New York trial lawyer Jennifer Parker (Jaclyn Smith). Angela played Parker's dipsomaniacal, long-lost mother, Marchesa Allabrandi. The result was at best trite, with Angela doing what she could to brighten the proceedings.

Two years later, she made *Shootdown*, about the infamous 1983 downing of Korean Airlines Flight 007 by a Russian fighter plane after it strayed into Soviet territory. All 269 persons on board, including 63 Americans, were killed. Angela played Nan Moore, a government clerk and fiesty mother of one of the casualties, a twenty-seven-year-old American on his way to China. Moore battles government bureaucracy to determine the facts behind the catastrophe.

"I did the film because I felt it was a story that should be told," Angela said. "It had tremendous dramatic qualities, although it's a terribly sad story. Still, I thoroughly enjoyed doing an about-face [from playing Jessica Fletcher]. However, for the long haul I don't relish this kind of drama."

Nan Moore was the polar opposite of Angela's characters in *The Manchurian Candidate* and *All Fall Down* and *Gypsy:* a mother who was caring and decidedly not neurotic. Playing Nan struck a personal chord with Angela. "One can't help but put oneself in her position playing this role," she said. "One had to realize that it could happen to any mother, you know? And being a mother myself, I was enormously touched by the incident and the episode in that woman's life—how she dealt with it and how I might have."

The subject matter of *Shootdown* was indeed controversial. From the time Flight 007 was shot down, the specifics of the events leading to the tragedy were a subject of contention. Did the Soviets shoot down the plane on purpose, or was it all just a horrible mistake? Was the pilot on a secret mission for the CIA? Even at the time the film aired—five years after the event took place— hundreds of documents relating to it remained classified by the U.S. government.

While the movie was in production, problems arose between its producers and the Broadcast Standards Department of NBC, the network on which it was to air. The discord resulted from the producers' desire to make a film with a political point of view, and the network's concerns over telling a "balanced"—translate: inoffensive—story. The producers, Leonard Hill and Joel Fields, had come to believe that the government was covering up its role in the affair. NBC's view was that no one really knew the facts behind the case, and that the various theories surrounding it should be put forth. After negotiations, the script was tempered. For example, a sequence in which Nan Moore appears on a radio show was rewritten to include a fictional airline pilot who contests her allegations of a cover-up. While certain criticisms of government policy during the administration of President Ronald Reagan remained, others were lessened.

Both artistically and politically, the result was a film less pointed and personal and more wishy-washy. At first, the impression is that Nan Moore was justified in her suspicion of a cover-up. By the finale, the feeling is that she might be wrong—even though in reality much of the evidence had not been made public.

As usual, Angela emerged unscathed. It is a treat to watch her in *Shootdown*, even though the pain her character experiences is so pervasive. Television critic John J. O'Connor noted that she "convincingly demonstrates that several seasons of playing [Jessica Fletcher] haven't dulled her versatility."

Angela next starred in *The Shell Seekers*, a 1989 Hallmark Hall of Fame presentation based on Rosamunde Pilcher's bestselling novel and filmed on location in London, the Cotswolds, Cornwall, and Ibiza. Angela played Penelope Keeling, a sixty-three-year-old Englishwoman recovering from a heart attack. She is fiercely intent on maintaining her independence; Angela must have relished her character's determination to "make my garden into something special."

Penelope has to examine her place in the lives of her three children and acknowledge their failures in finding happiness. "To see my children so lost is unendurable," she observes. "They have none of that joy in their lives." She loves them all equally, but her relationship with each is quite different. Also, as she ponders her past, Penelope admits that she is searching for something in the present. She does not know what. She does not know where.

The Shell Seekers is an absorbing, deeply personal story of how one deals with loss and deep disappointment, and how one must make life decisions that are both constructive and fulfilling. John Leonard wrote that Angela "is as fragile here as she's spry on *Murder, She Wrote*—as she was bloodthirsty in *Sweeney Todd*. What a pleasure."

In 1990, Angela got to work in her beloved Ireland when she starred in *The Love She Sought*, filmed in and around Dublin and Dun Laoghaire. She starred as Agatha McGee, a spinster school-teacher from the small town of Staggerford, Minnesota. On one level, Agatha is predictable: a stern, conservative, devoutly religious woman who enjoys peace and order in her life. Yet, her generosity allows her to take into her home a young, unwed mother

(Cynthia Nixon). Agatha has also developed a special pen-pal relationship with an Irishman, James O'Hannon (Denholm Elliott). As she nears retirement, Agatha's school rewards her with a trip to Ireland. There she meets James. Perhaps they will fall in love. Only problem is, James has been withholding from Agatha that he is a priest.

Angela was on target when she described *The Love She Sought* as "a marvelous woman's story." The film is a literate, deeply moving drama of love and loneliness that intelligently probes its characters and their relationships. John J. O'Connor noted, "And the performances are just about perfect, which is what you would expect from three wily veterans on the accomplished levels of Ms. Lansbury, Mr. Elliott and Mr. [Robert] Prosky [playing a bishop with whom Agatha conflicts]."

Angela's most significant nontelevision work in years came in 1991, when she voiced the role of Mrs. Potts, the talking teapot, in the smash-hit Disney animated feature *Beauty and the Beast*. It was her second Disney film, her first being *Bedknobs and Broomsticks* twenty years earlier. The film's success made her famous to a new generation who might not know of Angela's stage work or be interested in watching *Murder, She Wrote* or renting her films on video. *Beauty and the Beast*, interestingly, was Angela's highest-profile screen role since *The Manchurian Candidate*.

"It's a voice, yessssss, but I don't think you could call it a part," Angela modestly said around the time of the film's release. In *Beauty and the Beast*, Mrs. Potts rattles around the Beast's castle admonishing her sweetly mischievous son, a cup called Chip. Angela modeled the voice of her character after Mrs. Bridges, the brusque but kindhearted *Upstairs Downstairs* cook.

She sang the title song, a warm ballad penned by Alan Menken and Howard Ashman, which went on to win an Academy Award. "My decision to do it revolved around the song 'Beauty and the Beast,'" Angela explained. Ashman and Menken had sent her a copy of it, with a request that she sing it. "I wasn't sure that I *could* sing it," she added. "But as it turned out, they were right. For me, one of the great rewards of the film is that it has served as a passport to a whole new generation of five-year-olds, who only know me as Mrs. Potts." Indeed, beyond the simple sentimental beauty of the song, Angela chose to make the film primarily as a gift for her three grandchildren.

Film historian Leonard Maltin noted, "Her performance is just charming. It has such warmth. To convey that with just your voice ... there's something tremendously appealing about the character and the way she plays it."

A year later, Angela starred in the television movie *Mrs. 'Arris Goes to Paris*, based on Paul Gallico's novel. The film was a family affair: it was directed by son Anthony and executive-produced by stepson David.

The time is the early 1950s, and Angela plays Mrs. Harris (or 'Arris, as she would say), an aged cockney charwoman determined to realize a fantasy: to travel to Paris and purchase a Christian Dior dress. She saves her shillings and does just that, along the way befriending a government minister (who also happens to be a marquis) and instigating his reunion with his estranged daughter, initiating recognition of a forgotten war hero, and playing cupid for a beautiful model and shy accountant.

The film is slight but engaging, essentially a fairy tale. But Angela's character is lovable, and she offers a performance to match. John J. O'Connor wrote, "Ms. Lansbury accomplishes the incredible feat of making this totally unbelievable journey quite charming."

Still, work in feature films had not completely disappeared from Angela's mind. She observed in 1992, "Maybe Hollywood will finally offer me that leading role that will win me an Academy Award!"

24

Positive Moves

For most of her career, Angela avoided celebrity endorsements and commercial associations. Then, in June 1976, she high-kicked her way through the "Milliken Breakfast Show," a trade show presented in New York at the Waldorf-Astoria. She appeared with Robert Morse, Georgia Engel, and a male chorus exalting fabrics and yarns to buyers and retailers from around the country.

Next, she joined the likes of Myrna Loy, Bette Davis, and Lillian Hellman in the upscale "What becomes a legend most" ad campaign for Blackglama furs.

With the success of *Murder, She Wrote*, Angela became a cottage industry. Bristol-Myers hired her to pitch Bufferin. Master-Card hired her to convince consumers that "anything is possible" with a credit card. The Beatrix Potter children's book people cashed in on her popularity with a half-hour infomercial.

Oddly enough, and perhaps with tongue in cheek, a 1994 episode of *Murder, She Wrote* lampoons the infomercial phenomenon. A group of mystery writers come together to create an infomercial for the Murder of the Month book club. The program's producer defines the format as "one of those beauties you see listed in the TV pages as paid programming." A writer responds, "Figures, doesn't it, Jessica, it was only a matter of time before they started peddling books along with Ginsu knives and teeth whitener." Jessica responds, "If that replaces those long cross-country promotional tours, you won't hear any argument from me."

The two detectives in the episode are Lieutenant Fogel and Detective Henderson. Fogel takes swipe after swipe at infomercials, "those pretend TV shows," which have turned Henderson into a distracted television-shopping addict. He tells Jessica that his partner "buys this stuff like it's going out of style. All they got to do is tell him how wonderful it's gonna make his life." Henderson then displays a bandaged thumb, the result of creating a salad with the TV-touted "veginator." Later in the program, Fogel suggests, "They ought to make an infomercial pushing a cure for people who order stuff from infomericals."

One wonders how this episode of *Murder, She Wrote* affected those who chose Angela for the Beatrix Potter infomercial.

In 1988, Angela starred in a fifty-minute video, *Angela Lansbury's Positive Moves: A Personal Plan for Fitness and Well-Being at Any Age.* In it, she stresses the need for a woman to have "a realistic attitude and a positive state of mind." She graciously takes viewers into her home and illustrates her personal exercise regimen, including "gentle morning stretches" and "rhythmic dance movements." While watching the video, one can imagine Angela as a little girl performing similar movements with her mother in Regent's Park, where Moyna exercised with other progressive-thinking women. Angela stresses the importance of activities she herself enjoys—swimming, bike riding, walking, sewing, catnapping, and gardening—and notes how such simple acts as taking afternoon tea and luxuriating in the bathtub release her mind from the tensions of the day.

She discusses the importance of maintaining a low-fat, high-fiber diet—a regimen that helped her to lose the weight she gained when she began starring on *Murder, She Wrote*, and to maintain a 147-pound weight on her five-foot-seven-inch frame. While kneading what she calls "Angie's Power Loaf," a yeast bread filled with whole grains, she is garbed in a white "Mrs. Lovett's Meat Pies" apron. Angela also offers her views on sexuality and feminine expression for the postmenopausal woman.

At that time, Angela was maintaining a busy *Murder, She Wrote* shooting schedule. "That's why on my tape I point out you can do [the exercises] anytime during the day," she explained. "Even thinking of stretching is helpful, or just wiggling your ankles. The whole point of the tape is to deliver this message. For busy women, setting aside a half hour in the morning can be stressful. It's intimidating. So my exercises can be done anywhere, anytime."

This was followed two years later by a book, *Angela Lansbury's Positive Moves*, written with Mimi Avins. "Strenuous exercise is something I avoid at all costs," she explained while promoting the video. "The moves and stretches that I demonstrate on the tape are not excruciatingly difficult. But I wanted to stress that it's okay to care about your body and look after it, to care about how you look to yourself in the mirror and to your husband. It's okay at any age, but as you grow older, caring about fitness can be a battle."

She added, "My career aside, I consider myself a very average woman, really. I have a wonderful marriage, three children, three grandchildren. As I said in my video, I was never considered a beauty. But theatrically I can project an illusion of great glamour. I think a woman who isn't an actress can also project herself as a woman of dignity and liveliness, a woman who feels good and knows she looks good. A woman should maintain a certain sense of mystery about herself, and I think that can continue to any age."

Angela also explained that she had had plastic surgery. While in her third season on *Murder, She Wrote*, she declared, "It's rough to see yourself at this stage on television, particularly on tape, which is the worst. I have a wonderful cameraman, who photographs me very carefully, using diffused lighting to take out the shadows in my face. In the old movie days, we used to joke that we wanted to be filmed through linoleum."

As Angela aged, her neck broadened; this made her appear to be heavier on-camera, and older than her years. In 1976 and again in 1987, she had cosmetic surgery on her neck. "It's one of the most helpful things we can do to fight aging," she said. "If you need it, have it. I had my neck nipped and tucked, and it made a tremendous difference. I haven't had anything done to my face, though, because I fear changing my expression." Three years earlier—before the second nip-and-tuck—Angela noted, "My neck tends to be a little heavy, and I worry about that. I won't be encumbered by turtlenecks all the time.... An audience doesn't want to look at an ugly picture. I don't plan to break the mirror with beauty; I just want to look pleasant."

Over the years, Angela had developed arthritis, which sometimes made walking painful. She had replacement surgery in her left hip in May 1994, two days after completing the final segment of that season's *Murder, She Wrote* filming. However, two days after the operation, the sixty-eight-year-old actress was conferring on the telephone with her *Murder, She Wrote* staff. Three days later, she was recuperating at home—two days before her doctors anticipated her leaving the hospital. The painful surgery, plus a flare-up of arthritis in her right hip, did not interfere with her continuing to play Jessica Fletcher.

"Who knows? I might be around for another ten years," Angela quipped. Noted husband Peter Shaw (who himself was to undergo heart bypass and valve-replacement surgery within the following months), "My wife is feeling terrific. She was very happy to come home and rest after the surgery." He added, "The doctors say she will be ready for our vacation to Ireland in six weeks. We can't wait to see the countryside. It will be wonderful."

25

"I Can Go Full Throttle
Until I'm Eighty-Five"

In 1993, Madlyn Rhue became a regular on *Murder, She Wrote* in the role of a reclusive, wheelchair-bound widow who is a friend of Jessica Fletcher's. Rhue had played the character several years before in a guest spot on the show. In 1975, the actress was diagnosed with multiple sclerosis, a condition she did not reveal to casting directors. Even so, over the years she was unable to work enough to be entitled to adequate health insurance coverage as provided by the Screen Actors Guild. Rhue's medical bills would be covered if she could find full-time employment—so Angela had her character written into the series. Guard rails and ramps were added to the *Murder, She Wrote* set to make it user-friendly for Rhue.

Angela could not forget or erase her mistakes in raising her children. But even before she was aware of their problems, she was concerned with the plight of all children. Thus, she devoted whatever spare time she could to groups that battle child and spousal abuse and domestic violence, especially Abused Wives in Crisis (AWIC).

Back in the 1960s, Angela helped raise money for the United Nations Children's Fund (UNICEF). In 1967, she was crowned queen of the Peacock Ball at a benefit for the Lila Motley Cancer Foundation; a month later, she was guest of honor at the March of Dimes annual benefit luncheon. She was chairperson of the 1968–69 Bread Basket Drive, the annual fund-raising campaign of the Actors Fund of America. She also taped a public service announcement for the New York Association for the Blind, stressing that businesspeople should employ visually impaired workers.

In 1993, Angela was presented with the American Ireland Fund Heritage Award in a gala at the Beverly Hilton hotel. That same year, she arranged for CBS and Universal Television to each contribute $50,000 to the American Foundation for AIDS Research, a charity dear to the heart of Elizabeth Taylor, in lieu of a party celebrating the two hundredth *Murder, She Wrote* episode. In March of the following year, she took over for an ailing Taylor as hostess at an AIDS research fund-raiser in Houston. Taylor had undergone the same surgery that Angela was to have three months later. In May 1995, Angela came to New York to christen the Crystal Symphony, a $250-million luxury liner. She agreed to participate in the ceremony in return for a $1-million donation to the American Foundation for AIDS Research. Rex Reed described her as a "general in the war against AIDS."

In June 1994, *TV Guide* cited Angela in a survey determining the "lovability index" of Hollywood personalities. She earned a perfect 100 percent rating, with a special mention made of her efforts to telephone coworkers and friends hit hard by the January 1994 Los Angeles earthquake.

As the years passed, Angela earned more honors, to add to her Tony Awards, Oscar and Emmy nominations, and induction into the Theatre Hall of Fame. In 1992, she received the Silver Mask for Lifetime Achievement from the British Academy of Films and Television Arts. In 1994, she was named a Commander of the British Empire by Queen Elizabeth II.

In 1987, a reporter asked Angela if she wished her life had been any way different. "If I had to do it over . . . oh . . . maybe . . . I'd change some personal relationships," was her lingering, thoughtful response. "I haven't had it easy by any means, but I've had a good, varied life.

"There were times my career just coasted and I didn't get offered things. Luckily, something always came along and sent me on my way to the next step. They weren't always the best things. Sometimes the films didn't pay much money. Sometimes they were shot in supermarkets. But in most cases, I've had such damn good luck."

In 1991, Angela and Peter purchased land in Ireland and began building what Angela described as "a small holiday farmhouse" in County Cork. It would be located on thirty isolated acres above a cliff overlooking Ballycotton Bay and the Irish Sea in the village of Churchtown, about twenty-five miles east of Cork City. Construction was completed two years later on the whitewashed, six-bedroom abode, nicknamed Bally William, which Peter and Angela designed. Of course, it was not without a garden for Angela to cultivate.

"It's a very practical house," explained Angela's friend Maggie Williams. "It has a whole wing for the grandchildren. The kitchen is right in the living room, because Angie's always cooking. This way, she doesn't miss anything, the way you always do when the kitchen is off to the side and the people always are in the living room.

"It reminds me of a Mediterranean house, which is very unusual in Ireland."

Here, Angela and Peter could savor their privacy. In fact, they would go for days without seeing a soul. They employed no servants. Angela, sometimes accompanied by Peter, would drive their rented Nissan to nearby Midleton to patronize the local stores. Here, she would prefer to be looked upon as just another shopper and would not seek special treatment. Or Angela and Peter would partake in village life in Churchtown, chitchatting with the town postmaster to catch up on the local comings and goings.

Angela had no immediate intention of retiring to Ireland, or even slowing down her career. When Bally William was built, she was edging into her upper sixties. But its primary purpose was to serve as a getaway spot when *Murder, She Wrote* was on hiatus.

In September 1994, Larry King asked Angela if she was bothered by aging. "No, not at all," she responded, "because it simply opens up new pages of possibilities."

Earlier that year, it was announced that Jerry Herman and

writer Mark Saltzman were collaborating on a Christmas-themed musical project for Angela. Titled *Mrs. Santa Claus,* the program was being prepared by Corymore Productions for airing on CBS during Christmas, 1995. Other Corymore projects included another hour-long television series, two half-hour series, and a sequel to *Mrs. 'Arris Goes to Paris.*

Len Cariou spoke for the vast majority of Angela's colleagues when he declared, "She's just a terrific person. She's had a remarkable career, and she's still going strong."

As she neared her seventieth year, Angela explained, "I can go full throttle until I'm eighty-five. And that is precisely what I intend to do."

Film, Television, Video, and Theater Credits

FILM

Gaslight   1944, MGM. *Director:* George Cukor. *Cast:* Charles Boyer, Ingrid Bergman, Joseph Cotten, Dame May Whitty, Angela Lansbury, Barbara Everest, Emil Rameau, Edmund Breon, Halliwell Hobbes, Terry Moore. AL plays Nancy.

National Velvet   1944, MGM. *Director:* Clarence Brown. *Cast:* Mickey Rooney, Donald Crisp, Elizabeth Taylor, Anne Revere, Angela Lansbury, Jackie "Butch" Jenkins, Juanita Quigley, Arthur Treacher, Reginald Owen, Terry Kilburn, Alec Craig, Norma Varden, Arthur Shields, Dennis Hoey, Eugene Loring, Aubrey Mather, Frederick Worlock. AL plays Edwina Brown.

The Picture of Dorian Gray   1945, MGM. *Director:* Albert Lewin. *Cast:* George Sanders, Hurd Hatfield, Donna Reed, Angela Lansbury, Peter Lawford, Lowell Gilmore, Richard Fraser, Reginald Owen, Sir Cedric Hardwicke (narrator), Moyna MacGill. AL plays Sybil Vane.

The Harvey Girls   1946, MGM. *Director:* George Sidney. *Cast:* Judy Garland, John Hodiak, Ray Bolger, Preston Foster, Virginia O'Brien, Angela Lansbury, Marjorie Main, Chill Wills, Kenny Baker, Selena Royle, Cyd Charisse, Ruth Brady, Catherine McLeod, Jack Lambert, Edward Earle, Virginia Hunter, William "Bill" Phillips, Norman Leavitt, Morris Ankrum, Ben Carter, Mitchell Lewis, Stephen McNally. AL plays Em.

The Hoodlum Saint   1946, MGM. *Director:* Norman Taurog. *Cast:* William Powell, Esther Williams, Angela Lansbury, James Gleason, Lewis Stone, Rags Ragland, Frank McHugh, Slim Summerville, Roman Bohnen, Charles Arnt, Louis Jean Heydt, Charles Trowbridge, Henry O'Neill, Matt Moore, Trevor Bardette, Addison Richards, Tom Dugan, Emma Dunn, Mary Gordon, Ernest Anderson. AL plays Dusty Millard.

Till the Clouds Roll By   1946, MGM. *Director:* Richard Whorf. *Cast:* Robert Walker, Judy Garland, Lucille Bremer, Van Heflin, Paul Langton, Dorothy Patrick, Mary Nash, Harry Hayden, Paul Maxey, Rex Evans, William "Bill" Phillips, Dinah Shore, Van Johnson, June Allyson, Angela Lansbury, Ray McDonald, Kathryn Grayson, Frank Sinatra, Virginia

O'Brien, Lena Horne, Tony Martin, Johnny Johnston, Maurice Kelly, Cyd Charisse, Gower Champion. AL appears as a Guest Star.

The Private Affairs of Bel Ami   1947, United Artists. *Director:* Albert Lewin. *Cast:* George Sanders, Ann Dvorak, Angela Lansbury, Frances Dee, John Carradine, Susan Douglas, Hugo Haas, Marie Wilson, Albert Basserman, Warren William, Katherine Emery, Richard Fraser. AL plays Clotilde de Marelle.

Tenth Avenue Angel   1948, MGM. *Director:* Roy Rowland. *Cast:* Margaret O'Brien, Angela Lansbury, George Murphy, Phyllis Thaxter, Warner Anderson, Rhys Williams, Barry Nelson, Connie Gilchrist, Tom Trout, Dickie Tyler. AL plays Susan Bratten.

If Winter Comes   1948, MGM. *Director:* Victor Saville. *Cast:* Walter Pidgeon, Deborah Kerr, Angela Lansbury, Binnie Barnes, Janet Leigh, Dame May Whitty, Rene Ray, Virginia Keiley, Reginald Owen, John Abbott, Rhys Williams, Dennis Hoey, Hugh French, Nicholas Joy, Halliwell Hobbes. AL plays Mabel Sabre.

State of the Union   1948, MGM. *Director:* Frank Capra. *Cast:* Spencer Tracy, Katharine Hepburn, Van Johnson, Angela Lansbury, Adolphe Menjou, Lewis Stone, Howard Smith, Charles Dingle, Maidel Turner, Raymond Walburn, Florence Auer, Pierre Watkin, Margaret Hamilton, Irving Bacon, Patti Brady, George Nokes, Carl "Alfalfa" Switzer, Tom Pedi, Tom Fadden, Charles Lane, Art Baker, Rhea Mitchell, Arthur O'Connell, Marion Martin, Tor Johnson, Stanley Andrews, Dave Willock. AL plays Kay Thorndyke.

The Three Musketeers   1948, MGM. *Director:* George Sidney. *Cast:* Lana Turner, Gene Kelly, June Allyson, Van Heflin, Angela Lansbury, Frank Morgan, Vincent Price, Keenan Wynn, John Sutton, Gig Young, Robert Coote, Reginald Owen, Ian Keith, Patricia Medina, Richard Stapley. AL plays Queen Anne.

The Red Danube   1949, MGM. *Director:* George Sidney. *Cast:* Walter Pidgeon, Ethel Barrymore, Peter Lawford, Angela Lansbury, Janet Leigh, Louis Calhern, Francis L. Sullivan, Melville Cooper, Robert Coote, Alan Napier. AL plays Audrey Quail.

Samson and Delilah   1949, Paramount. *Director:* Cecil B. DeMille. *Cast:* Hedy Lamarr, Victor Mature, George Sanders, Angela Lansbury, Henry Wilcoxon, Olive Deering, Fay Holden, Julia Faye, Rusty Tamblyn, William Farnum, Lane Chandler, Moroni Olsen, Francis J. McDonald, William "Wee Willie" Davis, John Miljan, Arthur Q. Bryan, Laura Elliott, Victor Varconi, John Parrish, Frank Wilcox, Russell Hicks, Fritz Leiber, Mike Mazurki, Davison Clark, George Reeves, Pedro de Cordoba, Frank Reicher. AL plays Semadar.

Kind Lady   1951, MGM. *Director:* John Sturges. *Cast:* Ethel Barrymore, Maurice Evans, Angela Lansbury, Keenan Wynn, Betsy Blair, John Williams, Doris Lloyd, John O'Malley, Moyna MacGill. AL plays Mrs. Edwards.

Mutiny   1952, United Artists. *Director:* Edward Dmytryk. *Cast:* Mark Stevens, Angela Lansbury, Patric Knowles, Gene Evans, Rhys Williams, Robert Osterloh, Peter Brocco, Norman Leavitt, Gene Roth, Walter Sande, Clayton Moore, Morris Ankrum, Todd Karnes, Louis Jean Heydt. AL plays Leslie.

Remains to be Seen   1953, MGM. *Director:* Don Weis. *Cast:* June Allyson, Van Johnson, Louis Calhern, Angela Lansbury, John Beal, Dorothy Dandridge, Barry Kelley, Sammy White, Kathryn Card, Paul Harvey. AL plays Valeska Chauvel.

A Life at Stake   1955, Filmakers. *Director:* Paul Guilfoyle. *Cast:* Angela Lansbury, Keith Andes, Douglass Dumbrille, Claudia Barrett, Jane Darwell, Gavin Gordon, Bill Henry. AL plays Doris Hillman.

A Lawless Street   1955, Columbia. *Director:* Joseph H. Lewis. *Cast:* Randolph Scott, Angela Lansbury, Warner Anderson, Jean Parker, Wallace Ford, John Emery, James Bell, Ruth Donnelly, Michael Pate, Don Megowan, Jeanette Nolan, Peter Ortiz, Frank Ferguson. AL plays Tally Dickinson.

The Purple Mask   1955, Universal. *Director:* H. Bruce Humberstone. *Cast:* Tony Curtis, Colleen Miller, Gene Barry, Dan O'Herlihy, Angela Lansbury, George Dolenz, John Hoyt, Donald Randolph, Robert Cornthwaite, Stephen Bekassy, Paul Cavanagh, Myrna Hansen, Allison Hayes. AL plays Madame Valentine.

Please Murder Me   1956, Distributors Corp. of America. *Director:* Peter Godfrey. *Cast:* Angela Lansbury, Raymond Burr, Dick Foran, John Dehner, Lamont Johnson, Robert Griffin, Denver Pyle, Madge Blake. AL plays Myra Leeds.

The Court Jester   1956, Paramount. Directors: Norman Panama, Melvin Frank. *Cast:* Danny Kaye, Glynis Johns, Basil Rathbone, Angela Lansbury, Cecil Parker, Mildred Natwick, Robert Middleton, Michael Pate, Herbert Rudley, Noel Drayton, Edward Ashley, John Carradine, Alan Napier, Lewis Martin, Patrick Aherne, Richard Kean, Larry Pennell. AL plays Princess Gwendolyn.

The Long Hot Summer   1958, Twentieth Century–Fox. *Director:* Martin Ritt. *Cast:* Paul Newman, Joanne Woodward, Anthony Franciosa, Orson Welles, Lee Remick, Angela Lansbury, Richard Anderson, Sarah Marshall, Mabel Albertson, J. Pat O'Malley, William Walker, George Dunn, Jess Kirkpatrick, Val Avery. AL plays Minnie Littlejohn.

The Reluctant Debutante   1958, MGM. *Director:* Vincente Minnelli. *Cast:* Rex Harrison, Kay Kendall, John Saxon, Sandra Dee, Angela Lansbury, Peter Myers, Diane Clare. AL plays Mabel Claremont.

Season of Passion (Summer of the 17th Doll)   1959, United Artists. *Director:* Leslie Norman. *Cast:* Ernest Borgnine, Anne Baxter, John Mills, Angela Lansbury, Vincent Ball, Ethel Gabriel, Janette Craig. AL plays Pearl.

The Dark at the Top of the Stairs   1960, Warner Bros. *Director:* Delbert Mann. *Cast:* Robert Preston, Dorothy McGuire, Shirley Knight, Robert Eyer, Eve Arden, Angela Lansbury, Lee Kinsolving, Frank Overton, Penney Parker, Ken Lynch, Dennis Whitcomb, Nelson Leigh. AL plays Mavis.

A Breath of Scandal   1960, Paramount. *Director:* Michael Curtiz. *Cast:* Sophia Loren, John Gavin, Maurice Chevalier, Isabel Jeans, Angela Lansbury, Tullio Carminati, Roberto Risso, Milly Vitale. AL plays Countess Lina.

Blue Hawaii   1961, Paramount. *Director:* Norman Taurog. *Cast:* Elvis Presley, Joan Blackman, Nancy Walters, Roland Winters, Angela Lansbury, John Archer, Howard McNear, Flora Hayes, Gregory Gay, Steve Brodie, Iris Adrian. AL plays Mrs. Gates.

All Fall Down   1962, MGM. *Director:* John Frankenheimer. *Cast:* Eva Marie Saint, Warren Beatty, Karl Malden, Angela Lansbury, Brandon De Wilde, Constance Ford, Barbara Baxley, Evan Evans, Madame Spivy, Albert Paulsen. AL plays Annabel Willart.

The Manchurian Candidate   1962, United Artists. *Director:* John Frankenheimer. *Cast:* Frank Sinatra, Laurence Harvey, Janet Leigh, Angela Lansbury, Henry Silva, James Gregory, Leslie Parrish, John McGiver, Khigh Deigh, James Edwards, Albert Paulsen, Douglas Henderson, Barry Kelley, Lloyd Corrigan, Madame Spivey. AL plays Raymond's Mother.

In the Cool of the Day   1963, MGM. *Director:* Robert Stevens. *Cast:* Peter Finch, Jane Fonda, Angela Lansbury, Arthur Hill, Constance Cummings, Alexander Knox, Nigel Davenport, John Le Mesurier, Alec McCowen. AL plays Sybil Logan.

The World of Henry Orient   1964, United Artists. *Director:* George Roy Hill. *Cast:* Peter Sellers, Paula Prentiss, Tippy Walker, Merrie Spaeth, Angela Lansbury, Tom Bosley, Phyllis Thaxter, Bibi Osterwald, Peter Duchin, John Fiedler, Al Lewis. AL plays Isabel Boyd.

Dear Heart   1965, Warner Bros. *Director:* Delbert Mann. *Cast:* Glenn Ford, Geraldine Page, Angela Lansbury, Michael Anderson Jr., Barbara Nichols, Patricia Barry, Charles Drake, Ruth McDevitt, Neva Patterson, Alice Pearce, Richard Deacon, Mary Wickes, Ken Lynch. AL plays Phyllis.

The Greatest Story Ever Told   1965, United Artists. *Director:* George

Stevens. *Cast:* Max von Sydow, Charlton Heston, Dorothy McGuire, Michael Anderson Jr., Pat Boone, Jose Ferrer, Richard Conte, Victor Buono, David Hedison, Martin Landau, Angela Lansbury, Robert Loggia, Van Heflin, Janet Margolin, David McCallum, Roddy McDowall, Sal Mineo, Claude Rains, Ed Wynn, Shelley Winters, Telly Savalas, Sidney Poitier, Nehemiah Persoff, Donald Pleasance, John Wayne, Carroll Baker, Robert Blake, Burt Brinckerhoff, John Considine, Jamie Farr, Peter Mann, Gary Raymond, Tom Reese, Ina Balin, Joseph Schildkraut. AL plays Claudia.

The Amorous Adventures of Moll Flanders   1965, Paramount. *Director:* Terence Young. *Cast:* Kim Novak, Richard Johnson, Angela Lansbury, Lilli Palmer, George Sanders, Leo McKern, Vittorio De Sica, Daniel Massey, Derren Nesbitt, Cecil Parker, Daniel Massey, Roger Livesey, Hugh Griffith, Richard Wattis, Reginald Beckwith. AL plays Lady Blystone.

Harlow   1965, Paramount. *Director:* Gordon Douglas. *Cast:* Carroll Baker, Red Buttons, Michael Connors, Peter Lawford, Martin Balsam, Angela Lansbury, Raf Vallone, Leslie Nielsen, Peter Hansen, Mary Murphy, Peter Leeds. AL plays Mama Jean Bello.

Mister Buddwing   1966, MGM. *Director:* Delbert Mann. *Cast:* James Garner, Jean Simmons, Suzanne Pleshette, Katharine Ross, Angela Lansbury, George Voskovec, Jack Gilford, Joe Mantell, Raymond St. Jacques, Ken Lynch, Beeson Carroll, Billy Halop. AL plays Gloria.

Something for Everyone   1970, National General Pictures. *Director:* Harold Prince. *Cast:* Angela Lansbury, Michael York, Anthony Corlan, Heidelinde Weis, Eva-Marie Meineke, John Gill, Jane Carr. AL plays Countess Herthe von Ornstein.

Bedknobs and Broomsticks   1971, Buena Vista. *Director:* Robert Stevenson. *Cast:* Angela Lansbury, David Tomlinson, Roddy MacDowall, Sam Jaffe, Cindy O'Callaghan, Roy Snart, John Ericson, Reginald Owen, Tessie O'Shea, Bruce Forsyth. AL plays Miss Price.

Death on the Nile   1978, EMI/Paramount. *Director:* John Guillermin. *Cast:* Peter Ustinov, Jane Birkin, Lois Chiles, Bette Davis, Mia Farrow, Jon Finch, Olivia Hussey, I. S. Johar, George Kennedy, Angela Lansbury, Simon MacCorkindale, David Niven, Maggie Smith, Jack Warden, Harry Andrews, Sam Wanamaker. AL plays Mrs. Salome Otterbourne.

The Lady Vanishes   1979, Hammer/Rank. *Director:* Anthony Page. *Cast:* Elliott Gould, Cybill Shepherd, Angela Lansbury, Herbert Lom, Arthur Lowe, Ian Carmichael, Gerald Harper, Jean Anderson, Jenny Runacre. AL plays Miss Froy.

The Mirror Crack'd   1980, EMI/Associated Film Distribution. *Director:* Guy Hamilton. *Cast:* Angela Lansbury, Elizabeth Taylor, Kim Novak,

Rock Hudson, Tony Curtis, Geraldine Chaplin, Edward Fox, Charles Gray, Wendy Morgan, Maureen Bennett, Carolyn Pickles, Anthony Steel, Dinah Sheridan, Hildegard Neil, Allan Cuthbertson, Nigel Stock. AL plays Miss Marple.

The Last Unicorn   1982, ITC. *Directors:* Arthur Rankin Jr., Jules Bass. Voices: Alan Arkin, Jeff Bridges, Mia Farrow, Tammy Grimes, Robert Klein, Angela Lansbury, Christopher Lee, Keenan Wynn, Paul Frees, Rene Auberjonois. AL speaks the voice of Mommy Fortuna.

The Pirates of Penzance   1983, Universal. *Director:* Wilford Leach. *Cast:* Kevin Kline, Angela Lansbury, Linda Ronstadt, George Rose, Rex Smith, Tony Azito. AL plays Ruth.

The Company of Wolves   1984, Cannon. *Director:* Neil Jordan. *Cast:* Angela Lansbury, David Warner, Graham Crowden, Brian Glover, Kathryn Pogson, Stephen Rea, Sarah Patterson, Terence Stamp. AL plays Granny.

Beauty and the Beast   1991, Buena Vista. *Directors:* Gary Trousdale, Kirk Wise. *Voices:* Paige O'Hara, Robby Benson, Jerry Orbach, Angela Lansbury, Richard White, David Ogden Stiers, Jesse Corti, Rex Everhart, Bradley Michael Pierce, Jo Anne Worley, Kimmy Robertson. AL speaks the voice of Mrs. Potts.

Angela Lansbury dubbed Ingrid Thulin's dialogue in *The Four Horsemen of the Apocalypse* (1962).

Television

"The Citadel," *Robert Montgomery Presents*, June 19, 1950, NBC.

"The Wonderful Night," *Lux Video Theatre*, November 6, 1950, CBS.

"Operation Weekend," *Lux Video Theatre*, April 21, 1952, CBS.

"Stone's Throw," *Lux Video Theatre*, September 15, 1952, CBS.

"Cakes and Ale," *Robert Montgomery Presents*, October 26, 1953, NBC.

"Dreams Never Lie," *Revlon Mirror Theatre*, October 31, 1953, CBS.

"The Ming Lama," *Ford Theatre*, November 12, 1953, NBC.

"Storm Swept," *Schlitz Playhouse of Stars*, December 4, 1953, CBS.

"A String of Beads," *Four Star Playhouse*, January 21, 1954. CBS.

"The Crime of Daphne Rutledge," *G.E. Theatre*, June 13, 1954, CBS.

"The George Gobel Show," October 9, 1954, NBC.

"The Indiscreet Mrs. Jarvis," *Fireside Theatre*, January 4, 1955, NBC.

"Madeira, Madeira," *Four Star Playhouse*, April 14, 1955, CBS.

"Billy and the Bride," *Stage 7*, May 8, 1955, CBS.

"The Treasure," *Rheingold Theatre (The Star and the Story)*, May 28, 1955, NBC.

"The Rarest Stamp," *Studio 57*, March 11, 1956, syndicated.

"The Force of Circumstance," *Rhinegold Theater (The Star and the Story)*, March 24, 1956, NBC.

"Instant of Truth," *Front Row Center*, April 8, 1956, CBS.

"Claire," *Screen Directors Playhouse*, April 25, 1956, NBC.

"The Brown Leather Case," *Studio 57*, June 10, 1956, syndicated

"The Devil's Brood," *Climax*, December 5, 1957, CBS.

"Verdict of Three," *Playhouse 90*, April 24, 1958, CBS.

"The Grey Nurse Said Nothing," *Playhouse 90*, November 26, 1959, CBS.

"Something Crazy's Going On in the Back Room," *Eleventh Hour*, April 3, 1963, NBC.

"The Perry Como Christmas Show," December 21, 1964, NBC.

"The Deadly Toys Affair," *The Man From U.N.C.L.E.*, November 12, 1965, NBC.

"Leave It to Me," *Trials of O'Brien*, December 17, 1965, CBS.

"The Perry Como Thanksgiving Show," November 21, 1966, NBC.

"The Julie Andrews Hour," February 10, 1973, ABC.

The Story of the First Christmas Snow/First Christmas (voice only), December 19, 1975, NBC.

Sweeney Todd, September 12, 1982, Entertainment Channel.

The Spencer Tracy Legacy, March 10, 1986, PBS.

"Novel Connection," *Magnum, P.I.*, November 19, 1986, CBS.

During the 1950s, Lansbury appeared as a member of a celebrity team on *Pantomime Quiz*. She has also appeared many times as hostess, presenter, guest, nominee, and/or musical performer on the Academy Awards, Tony Awards, Emmy Awards, Kennedy Center honors, *What's My Line*, etc. She has been interviewed on shows hosted by Larry King, David Letterman, David Frost, Barbara Walters, Richard Brown, etc.

Television Series

Murder, She Wrote, CBS. Created by Richard Levinson, William Link, Peter S. Fischer. Pilot, *The Murder of Sherlock Holmes*, aired September 30, 1984. AL plays Jessica Beatrice Fletcher.

Made-for-TV Movies/Miniseries

Little Gloria . . . Happy at Last   October 24–25, 1982, NBC. *Director:* Waris Hussein. *Cast:* Martin Balsam, Bette Davis, Angela Lansbury,

Michael Gross, Lucy Gutteridge, John Hillerman, Barnard Hughes, Glynis Johns, Rosalyn Landor, Joseph Maher, Christopher Plummer, Maureen Stapleton, Jennifer Dundas. AL plays Gertrude Vanderbilt Whitney.

The Gift of Love: A Christmas Story   December 20, 1983, CBS. *Director:* Delbert Mann. *Cast:* Lee Remick, Angela Lansbury, Polly Holliday, Joseph Warren, Mart Hulswit, Michael Pearlman, Samantha Atkins, Alexander Harrington, Michael Higgins. AL plays Amanda Fenwick.

A Talent for Murder   January 13, 1984, Showtime. *Director:* Alvin Rakoff. *Cast:* Laurence Olivier, Angela Lansbury, Charles Keating, Hildegard Neil, Garrick Hagon, Tracey Childs, Tariq Yunus. AL plays Ann Royce McClain.

Lace   February 26–27, 1984, ABC. *Director:* Billy Hale. *Cast:* Bess Armstrong, Brooke Adams, Arielle Dombasle, Phoebe Cates, Anthony Higgins, Angela Lansbury, Herbert Lom, Anthony Quayle, Honor Blackman, Nickolas Grace, Leigh Lawson, Simon Chandler, Trevor Eve. AL plays Aunt Hortense Boutin.

The First Olympics—Athens 1896   May 20–21, 1984, NBC. *Director:* Alvin Rakoff. *Cast:* David Ogden Stiers, Hunt Block, David Caruso, Alex Hyde-White, Benedict Taylor, Edward Wiley, Nikos Ziagos, Honor Blackman, Gayle Hunnicutt, Virginia McKenna, Bill Travers, Louis Jourdan, Angela Lansbury, Jason Connery, Matt Frewer. AL plays Alice Garrett.

Rage of Angels: The Story Continues   November 2–3, 1986, NBC. *Director:* Paul Wendkos. *Cast:* Jaclyn Smith, Ken Howard, Michael Nouri, Susan Sullivan, Brad Dourif, Angela Lansbury, Mason Adams. AL plays Marchesa Allabrandi.

Shootdown   November 28, 1988, NBC. *Director:* Michael Pressman. *Cast:* Angela Lansbury, George Coe, Kyle Secor, Molly Hagan, Jennifer Savidge, John Cullum. AL plays Nan Moore.

The Shell Seekers   December 3, 1989, ABC. *Director:* Waris Hussein. *Cast:* Angela Lansbury, Sam Wanamaker, Christopher Bowen, Michael Gough, Patricia Hodge, Sophie Ward, Denis Quilley, Irene Worth, Anna Carteret. AL plays Penelope Keeling.

The Love She Sought   October 21, 1990, NBC. *Director:* Joseph Sargent. *Cast:* Angela Lansbury, Denholm Elliott, Robert Prosky, Cynthia Nixon, Gary Hershberger, Doreen Hepburn, Kate Flynn, Breffni McKenna, Niall Toibin. AL plays Agatha McGee.

Mrs. 'Arris Goes to Paris   December 27, 1992, CBS. *Director:* Anthony Shaw. *Cast:* Angela Lansbury, Omar Sharif, Diana Rigg, John Savident, Tamara Gorski, Lothaire Bluteau. AL plays Mrs. Harris.

Video

Angela Lansbury's Positive Moves: A Personal Plan for Fitness and Well-Being at Any Age   1988, Wood Knapp Video. An exercise and lifestyle videotape, followed by a similarly named book published by Delacort Press in 1990.

Theater

Hotel Paradiso   Adapted by Peter Glenville from the French farce by Georges Feydeau and Maurice Desvallieres. Staged by Peter Glenville. Opened at the Henry Miller Theatre, New York City, April 12, 1957. *Cast:* Bert Lahr, Vera Pearce, Angela Lansbury, John Emery, Carlton Carpenter, Sondra Lee, Douglas Byng, James Coco, George Tyne. AL plays Marcelle.

A Taste of Honey   A drama by Shelagh Delaney. *Directors:* Tony Richardson, George Devine. Opened at the Lyceum Theatre, New York City, October 4, 1960. *Cast:* Angela Lansbury, Joan Plowright, Nigel Davenport, Billy Dee Williams, Andrew Ray. AL plays Helen.

Anyone Can Whistle   A musical with book by Arthur Laurents, music and lyrics by Stephen Sondheim. Staged by Laurents. Opened at the Majestic Theatre, New York City, April 4, 1964. *Cast:* Angela Lansbury, Gabriel Dell, Lee Remick, Harry Guardino, Arnold Soboloff, James Frawley, Peg Murray, Don Doherty. AL plays Cora Hoover Hooper.

Mame   A musical with book by Jerome Lawrence and Robert E. Lee, based on the novel by Patrick Dennis and the play *Auntie Mame* by Lawrence and Lee. Music and lyrics by Jerry Herman. Directed by Gene Saks. Opened at the Winter Garden Theatre, New York City, May 24, 1966. *Cast:* Angela Lansbury, Beatrice Arthur, Jane Connell, Willard Waterman, Frankie Michaels, Sab Shimono, Charles Braswell, Jerry Lanning, George Coe, Diana Walker, John C. Becher, Johanna Douglas, Diana Coupe. AL plays Mame Dennis.

Dear World   A musical adapted by Maurice Valency, based on *The Madwoman of Chaillot* by Jean Giraudoux. Book by Jerome Lawrence and Robert E. Lee. Music and lyrics by Jerry Herman. Staged by Joe Layton. Opened at the Mark Hellinger Theatre, New York City, February 6, 1969. *Cast:* Angela Lansbury, Milo O'Shea, Joe Masiell, Jane Connell, Carmen Matthews. AL plays Countess Aurelia, the Madwoman of Chaillot.

Prettybelle   A musical with book and lyrics by Bob Merrill, music by Jule Styne, based on the novel of the same name by Jean Arnold. Staged by Gower Champion. Opened at the Shubert Theatre, Boston, February 1, 1971. *Cast:* Angela Lansbury, Jon Cypher, Joe Morton, Charlotte Rae,

Mark Dawson, Renee Lippin, Peter Lombard, Bert Michaels, Michael Jason. AL plays Prettybelle Sweet.

All Over   A play by Edward Albee. Directed by Peter Hall. Opened at the Aldwych Theatre, London, January 31, 1972. *Cast:* Peggy Ashcroft, Angela Lansbury, David Waller, Sheila Hancock, Sebastian Shaw, David Markham, Patience Collier, Graham Leaman, Colin Edwynn, Vernon Smythe, Godfrey Jackman. AL plays the Mistress.

Sondheim: A Musical Tribute   A musical revue presented for one performance on behalf of the American Musical and Dramatic Academy and the National Hemophilia Foundation, and consisting of the lyrics and music of Stephen Sondheim. Directed by Burt Shevelove. Presented at the Shubert Theatre, New York City, March 11, 1973. *Cast:* Stephen Sondheim, Jack Cassidy, Hermione Gingold, Donna McKechnie, Alexis Smith, Larry Blyden, Len Cariou, Dorothy Collins, Ron Holgate, Glynis Johns, Larry Kert, Angela Lansbury, Mary McCarty, John McMartin, Anthony Perkins, Chita Rivera, Ethel Shutta, Nancy Walker.

Gypsy   A musical fable suggested by the memoirs of Gypsy Rose Lee, with book by Arthur Laurents, music by Jule Styne, and lyrics by Stephen Sondheim. Directed by Laurents. Opened at the Piccadilly Theatre, London, May 29, 1973. *Cast:* Angela Lansbury, Zan Charisse, Debbie Bowen, Barrie Ingham, Andrew Norman, Helen Raye, Bonnie Langford. AL plays Rose.

Gypsy   A musical fable suggested by the memoirs of Gypsy Rose Lee, with book by Arthur Laurents, music by Jule Styne, and lyrics by Stephen Sondheim. Directed by Laurents. Opened at the Winter Garden Theatre, New York City, September 24, 1974. *Cast:* Angela Lansbury, Zan Charisse, Maureen Moore, Rex Robbins, John Sheridan, Lisa Peluso, Bonnie Langford, John C. Becher, Denny Dillon, Mary Louise Wilson. AL plays Rose.

Hamlet   A play by William Shakespeare. Directed by Peter Hall. Opened at the Old Vic, London, December 9, 1975. *Cast:* Albert Finney, Angela Lansbury, Susan Fleetwood, Denis Quilley, Roland Culver, Simon Ward, Oliver Cotton, Gareth Hunt, David Yelland. AL plays Gertrude.

Counting the Ways and **Listening**   Two one-act plays by Edward Albee. Directed by Albee. Presented in repertory at the Hartford Stage Company, beginning January 28, 1977. *Cast:* William Prince, Angela Lansbury, Maureen Anderman. AL plays She in *Counting the Ways* and the Woman in *Listening*.

Sweeney Todd   A musical with book by Hugh Wheeler, music and lyrics by Stephen Sondheim, based on *Sweeney Todd* by Christopher Bond. Directed by Harold Prince. Opened at the Uris Theatre, New York City, March 1, 1979. *Cast:* Angela Lansbury, Len Cariou, Victor Garber, Sara Rice, Edmund Lyndeck, Jack Eric Williams, Robert Ousley, Joaquin Romaguera, Ken Jennings, Merle Louise. AL plays Mrs. Lovett.

A Little Family Business   Adapted by Jay Presson Allen from a play by Barillet and Gredy. Directed by Martin Charnin. Opened at the Martin Beck Theatre, New York City, December 15, 1982. *Cast:* Angela Lansbury, John McMartin, Sally Stark, Anthony Shaw, Tracy Brooks Swope, Theodore Sorel, Tony Cummings, Hallie Foote, Gordon Rigsby, Donald E. Fischer. AL plays Lillian.

Mame   A musical with book and lyrics by Jerome Lawrence and Robert E. Lee, based on the novel by Patrick Dennis and the play *Auntie Mame* by Lawrence and Lee. Music and lyrics by Jerry Herman. Directed by John Bowab. Opened at the Gershwin Theater, New York City, July 24, 1983. *Cast:* Angela Lansbury, Jane Connell, Anne Francine, Roshi Handwerger, Sab Shimono, Willard Waterman, Scott Stewart, Byron Nease, John C. Becher. AL plays Mame Dennis.

Angela Lansbury first appeared onstage as an acting student in school productions. Prior to signing her MGM contract, she participated in a series of one-act plays presented at the Belasco Theater, Los Angeles. During the summer of 1952, she toured the summer theater circuit in *Affairs of State* and *Remains to be Seen*. In the spring of 1979, Lansbury and Michael Kermoyan replaced Yul Brynner and Constance Towers on Broadway for twenty-four performances in *The King and I*, at the Uris Theatre. She starred in *Mame* in San Francisco and Los Angeles in 1968. She toured in *A Taste of Honey* following its New York run; *Gypsy* prior to its New York opening; and *Sweeney Todd* after leaving the Broadway cast. She also starred in *Mame* and *Gypsy* on the summer theater circuit.

Select Bibliography

Books

Agate, James. *The Contemporary Theatre, 1924.* New Hampshire: Benjamin Blom, 1969.

Barrow, Kenneth. *Flora.* New Hampshire: Heinemann, 1981.

Baxter, John. *The Hollywood Exiles.* New York: Taplinger Publishing Company, 1976.

Billington, Michael. *Peggy Ashcroft.* Indiana: John Murray, 1988.

Blum, Daniel. *Great Stars of the American Stage.* New York: Grosset & Dunlap, 1952.

Bonanno, Margaret Wander. *Angela Lansbury: A Biography.* New York: St. Martin's Press, 1987.

Bordman, Gerald. *American Musical Theatre.* New York: Oxford University Press, 1978.

Brady, Kathleen. *Lucille: The Life of Lucille Ball.* New York: Hyperion, 1994.

Burke, Thomas. *The Streets of London Through the Centuries.* London, U.K.: B. T. Batsford Ltd., 1940.

Capra, Frank. *The Name Above the Title.* New York: MacMillan Company, 1971.

Chapman, John, ed. *The Burns Mantle Best Plays, 1948–1949.* New York: Dodd, Mead and Company, 1949.

Clarens, Carlos. *Cukor.* London, U.K.: Secker & Warburg, Ltd., 1976.

Craig, David. *On Performing.* New York: McGraw-Hill, 1987.

Curtis, Tony, and Barry Paris. *Tony Curtis: The Autobiography.* New York: William Morrow and Company, 1993.

Davidson, Bill. *Jane Fonda: An Intimate Biography.* New York: Dutton, 1990.

Denham, Reginald. *Stars in My Hair.* London, U.K.: T. Werner Laurie, 1958.

DiOrio, Al, Jr. *Little Girl Lost.* New York: Arlington House, 1973.

Dmytryk, Edward. *It's a Hell of a Life but Not a Bad Living.* New York: Times Books, 1978.

Du Maurier, Daphne. *Gerald: A Portrait.* New York: Doubleday, Doran & Company, 1935.

Ebert, Roger. *Roger Ebert's Movie Home Companion.* Montana: Andrews and McMeel, 1993.

Fehl, Fred (photographs), and William and Jane Stott (text). *On Broadway.* Texas: University of Texas Press, 1978.

Frank, Gerold. *Judy.* New York: Harper & Row, 1975.

Gielgud, John. *Early Stages.* New York: The MacMillan Company, 1939.

Gifford, Denis. *The British Film Catalogue 1895–1985.* New York: Facts on File Publications, 1986.

Goodwin, John, ed. *Peter Hall's Diaries: The Story of a Dramatic Battle.* London, U.K.: Hamish Hamilton, 1983.

Guiles, Fred Lawrence. *Joan Crawford: The Last Word.* New York: Birch Lane Press, 1995.

Head, Edith, and Paddy Calistro. *Edith Head's Hollywood.* New York: E. P. Dutton, 1983.

Hirsch, Foster. *Harold Prince and the American Musical Theater.* New York: Cambridge University Press, 1989.

Holden, Anthony. *Behind the Oscar.* New York: Simon & Schuster, 1993.

Houseman, John. *Final Dress.* New York: Simon & Schuster, 1983.

_____ . *Unfinished Business.* London, U.K.: Chatto & Windus, 1986.

Ilson, Carol. *Harold Prince: From Pajama Game to Phantom of the Opera.* Michigan: UMI Research Press, 1989.

Katz, Ephraim. *The Film Encyclopedia.* New York: HarperCollins, 1994.

Lahr, John. *Notes on a Cowardly Lion.* New York: Alfred A. Knopf, 1969.

Lambert, Gavin. *On Cukor.* New York: Capricorn Books, 1973.

Lansbury, George. *My Pilgrimage for Peace and Peace Through Economic Cooperation.* New York: Garland, 1972.

_____ . *My Quest for Peace.* M. Joseph, 1938; published in the United States by Henry Holt and Company as *My Pilgrimage for Peace,* New York.

Laufe, Abe. *Broadway's Greatest Musicals.* New Jersey: Funk & Wagnalls, 1969.

Lecesne, James. *My First Car.* New York: Crown Trade Paperbacks, 1993.

Levinson, Richard, and William Link. *Off Camera.* New York: New American Library, 1986.

Levy, Emanuel. *George Cukor: Master of Elegance.* New York: William Morrow and Company, 1994.

MacQueen-Pope, Y. *The Footlights Flickered.* London, U.K.: Herbert Jenkins Ltd., 1959.

Maltin, Leonard, ed. *Leonard Maltin's Movie Encyclopedia.* New York: Dutton, 1994.

_____ . *Movie and Video Guide.* New York: Signet, 1994.

Mantle, Burns, ed. *The Best Plays of 1941–42.* New York: Dodd, Mead and Company, 1942.

Martin, Mary. *My Heart Belongs.* New York: William Morrow and Company, 1976.

Moritz, Charles, ed. *Current Biography Yearbook.* New York: H. W. Wilson Company, 1967.

Nesbitt, Cathleen. *A Little Love & Good Company.* Maryland: Stemmer House, 1977.

O'Neil, Thomas. *The Emmys*. New York: Penguin Books, 1992.

Payn, Graham, and Sheridan Morley, eds. *The Noël Coward Diaries*. London, U.K.: Weidenfeld and Nicolson, 1982.

Phillips, Gene D. *George Cukor*. New York: Twayne Publishers, 1982.

Playfair, Nigel. *The Story of the Lyric Theatre Hammersmith*. London, U.K.: Chatto & Windus, 1925.

Pratley, Gerald. *The Cinema of John Frankenehimer*. New York: A. Zwemmer/A. S. Barnes, 1969.

Probst, Leonard. *Off Camera*. New York: Stein and Day, 1975.

Reed, Rex. *Do You Sleep in the Nude?* New York: New American Library, 1968.

Riese, Randall. *All About Bette: Her Life from A to Z*. Illinois: Contemporary Books, 1993.

Ross, Lillian, and Helen Ross. *The Player: A Profile of an Art*. New York: Simon & Schuster, 1962.

Russell, Rosalind, and Chris Chase. *Life Is a Banquet*. New York: Random House, 1977.

Scherle, Victor, and William Turner Levy. *The Films of Frank Capra*. New York: Citadel Press, 1977.

Smith, Liz. *The Mother Book*. New York: Doubleday & Company, 1978.

Spindle, Les. *Julie Andrews: A Bio-Bibliography*. Connecticut: Greenwood Press, 1989.

Stevenson, Isabelle, ed. *The Tony Award*. New York: Crown Publishing, 1984.

Stine, Whitney. *'I'd Love to Kiss You'* . . . *Conversations With Bette Davis*. New York: Simon & Schuster, 1990.

Swindell, Larry. *Spencer Tracy* . . . *A Biography*. New York: New American Library, 1969.

Taylor, John Russell. *Strangers in Paradise*. Texas: Holt, Rinehart and Winston, 1983.

Thomas, Bob. *I Got Rhythm! The Ethel Merman Story*. New York: G. P. Putnam's Sons, 1985.

Toye, Randall. *The Agatha Christie Who's Who*. London, U.K.: Frederick Muller, Ltd., 1980.

Ustinov, Peter. *Dear Me*. New Hampshire: Heinemann, 1977.

Wearing, J. P. *The London Stage 1910–1919*. New Jersey: Scarecrow Press, 1982.

———. *The London Stage 1920–1929*. New Jersey: Scarecrow Press, 1984.

———. *The London Stage 1930–1939*. New Jersey: Scarecrow Press, 1990.

———. *The London Stage 1940–1949*. New Jersey: Scarecrow Press, 1991.

Who Was Who in the Theatre. Michigan: Gale Research Company, 1978.

York, Michael. *Accidently on Purpose: An Autobiography*. New York: Simon & Schuster, 1991.

Zadan, Craig. *Sondheim & Co*. New York: Harper & Row, 1986.

In addition, articles were consulted from the following publications:
American Film; American Weekly; Boston Globe; Boston Herald; Boston Record-American; Broadcasting; Brooklyn Daily Eagle; Business Week; Chicago Sun-Times; Chicago Tribune; Christian Science Monitor; Daily Express (London); *Daily Telegraph* (London); *Daily Variety; Entertainment Weekly; Evening News* (London); *Evening Standard* (London); *Films in Review; Hollywood Reporter; Horizon; Interview; Jersey Journal; Jersey Record; Ladies' Home Journal; Life; Los Angeles Times; Mandate; Millimeter; Monthly Film Bulletin; The Nation; National Enquirer; New York; New York Daily Mirror; New York Daily News; New York Herald Tribune; New York Journal American; New York Morning Telegraph; New York Observer; New York Post; New York Telegram; New York Times; New York World-Telegram and Sun; The New Yorker; Newark Evening News; Newark Star-Ledger; News Letter; Newsday; Newsweek; The Observer* (London); *On Cable; Parade; People; Philadelphia Evening Bulletin; Philadelphia Inquirer; Photoplay; Picture Play; Plays and Players; Saturday Evening Post; Saturday Review; Screen Guide; Sight and Sound; Silver Screen; Star; Theatre; Time; The Times* (London); *TV Guide; USA Weekend; Variety; Video; Village Voice; Wall Street Journal; Washington Post; Women's Wear Daily.*

Index

About the Authors

Rob Edelman is the author of *Great Baseball Films* (Citadel Press), the first mass market book about the national pastime on-screen. He is contributing editor of *Leonard Maltin's Movie and Video Guide* and director of programming of Home Film Festival, which rents select videotapes by mail throughout the country. His work appears in several books (including *Leonard Maltin's Movie Encyclopedia* and *A Political Companion to American Film*), and he has written for dozens of periodicals (from *American Film* to the *Washington Post*).

Audrey E. Kupferberg is a film consultant, archivist, and appraiser. She is the former director of the Yale Film Study Center; assistant director of the National Center for Film and Video Preservation at The American Film Institute; and project director of The American Film Institute Catalog. She is married to Rob Edelman, and they live in Amsterdam, New York . . . a stone's throw from Cabot Cove.